FARE THEE WELL

FARE THEE WELL

The Final Chapter of the
Grateful Dead's Long, Strange Trip

Joel Selvin

with Pamela Turley

DA CAPO PRESS

Da Capo Press
Hachette Book Group
1290 Avenue of the Americas, New York, NY 10104
www.dacapopress.com
@DaCapoPress; @DaCapoPR

Printed in the United States of America
First Edition: June 2018

Published by Da Capo Press, an imprint of Perseus Books, LLC, a subsidiary of Hachette Book Group, Inc. The Da Capo Press name and logo is a trademark of the Hachette Book Group.

The Hachette Speakers Bureau provides a wide range of authors for speaking events. To find out more, go to www.hachettespeakersbureau.com or call (866) 376-6591.

The publisher is not responsible for websites (or their content) that are not owned by the publisher.

Print book interior design by Jeff Williams.

Library of Congress Cataloging-in-Publication Data

Names: Selvin, Joel, author. | Turley, Pamela, author.
Title: Fare thee well: the final chapter of the Grateful Dead's long, strange trip / Joel Selvin with Pamela Turley.
Description: First edition. | New York, NY : Da Capo Press, 2018. | Includes bibliographical references and index.
Identifiers: LCCN 2017058056 (print) | LCCN 2017058615 (ebook) | ISBN 9780306903045 (e-book) | ISBN 9780306903052 (hardcover)
Subjects: LCSH: Grateful Dead (Musical group) | Rock musicians—United States—Biography.
Classification: LCC ML421.G72 (ebook) | LCC ML421.G72 S45 2018 (print) | DDC
782.42166092/2—dc23
LC record available at https://lccn.loc.gov/2017058056
ISBNs: 978-0-306-90305-2 (hardcover); 978-0-306-90304-5 (ebook)

LSC-C

10 9 8 7 6 5 4 3

To Bobby, Phil, Mickey, and Billy...
and all the Deadheads.

Contents

1

Board Meeting

CHRIST, NOT Garcia.

Nobody expected that. True, everybody on the plane had heard him wheezing when he fell asleep on the flight home from the band's last concert at Soldier Field in Chicago, but his death in August 1995 had come as a complete and sudden shock to all his bandmates and their organization.

The Deadheads, especially the canny older guard of the band's exceptionally knowing, caring fans, were not so surprised. Many had stopped coming to shows after Garcia returned from his diabetic coma in 1987. They were heartbroken as they watched his waistline explode, his health deteriorate, and his once unparalleled skills on guitar disintegrate. As the band's performances through the nineties continued to devolve with Garcia's personal problems increasingly apparent—and their audiences almost inexplicably still growing beyond imagination—some simply stopped attending, convinced they were watching him kill himself.

Just as no other band had ever been like the Grateful Dead, Jerry Garcia had been like no other bandleader. He was the philosophical axis, the virtuoso guitar player, the father figure, the best friend. In fact, each one of the four surviving members thought that he alone had been Garcia's best friend—they held no such illusions about each other. Garcia was their true north. Since they were young men, they had set their compasses to him. His death hit them like a sledgehammer.

But in the uncertain and bewildering days after Garcia's death, it wasn't just the loss of friendship with him that they had to mourn. Their entire foundation had come loose, and they were jolted by the harsh realities that had suddenly intruded into their lives. Distraught and fearful, uncertain of the future, canceling engagements, laying off loyal crew, these men had barely seen each other since the funeral, couldn't bring themselves to. Each one had largely disappeared into his own world. Four months went by after Garcia's death before the four surviving members could muster the will to meet and decide what to do about the beast called the Grateful Dead that had ruled their lives for the better part of four decades.

After thirty years of touring, the band ached from a deep weariness that almost no one but their road crew could understand. Over the years, they had realized the Grateful Dead was bigger than all of them, had a life of its own, and created its own momentum. But could it survive without the visionary leadership of its founding father? There had been many lean years in the history of the Dead, but by the time of Garcia's death, they were playing to stadiums full of paying customers in every city in the country and it was hard not to go out and pick up the money. They had come to enjoy the charter jets, limousines, and five-star hotels. Band members, along with crew and staff, were settling down, getting married, raising families, buying expensive homes. Their employees numbered more than sixty, many of whom had been on the trip for decades.

The band's so-called career was largely an accident. The Grateful Dead never sought success. They saw themselves as musicians. They played music. The actual business of a rock-and-roll band was a mystery to them, and they couldn't be bothered with it. They didn't think in terms of wealth and fame; they hadn't sought it and didn't know how to value it. Eventually, they realized if they were going to manage their organization and continue to do what they loved, they had to come to terms with the commerce, and they made a grudging, uneasy peace with it. More than any other rock band, the Grateful Dead had enjoyed freedom from highly structured and rigid business practices. Instead of corporate bylaws, they had lived by a code vigilantly observed, which had served to create the Grateful Dead ethos. They had largely been able to approach life on their own terms, but with the level of success they had stumbled into, that carefree attitude was no longer possible.

The band members and their most trusted associates showed up Thursday morning, December 7, at the band's old Victorian in downtown San Rafael that had served as their headquarters for more than thirty years—the new Novato headquarters on Bel Marin Keys Road was not quite ready. They were there for a meeting of the board of directors of Grateful Dead Productions, the corporate arm of the famed psychedelic rock band. They were weighed down with grief and the burden of having to decide the fate of not only themselves, but of all the people who depended on the organization for their livelihood. Their long-suffering staff stood by anxiously. Drummer Billy Kreutzmann still couldn't bring himself to attend and stayed behind in Hawaii.

It would be the last board meeting at the Lincoln Street complex, held in the upstairs room in an auxiliary building across the street from the ramshackle two-story gabled house on the quiet corner. In typical Grateful Dead fashion, the band had rented the building since they first moved to Marin County and had only recently purchased the former Coca-Cola bottling plant in nearby Novato where the band's thriving merchandise enterprise had already been located under a rental agreement for several years, and where the entire Grateful Dead operation would now be centered. Just before he died, Garcia had visited the new rehearsal hall and offices and given his approval.

For the last ten years, the band had been the leading box-office attraction in rock, pulling down a hard-to-believe $370 million in gate receipts over the decade. Now that roaring river of revenue had come to a sudden and complete halt. The operation was in immediate economic free fall. They had already scrubbed an East Coast tour scheduled to start in September and laid off their thirty-person road crew. Between the office and the band's merchandise business, there were still another thirty employees.

Like many families protecting an addict in their midst, the Dead had lived in denial over Garcia's health issues. They had survived one near-death episode years before, but carried on while Garcia continued to sink deeper into the abyss. He had struggled for ten years with his heroin addiction. Only band management knew that he had secretly made plans to enter rehab at the Betty Ford Clinic after Soldier Field that July. The management team had questioned among themselves whether the September tour would happen. Garcia, chafing against the detailed routine, bolted Betty Ford after a few days, but had checked into another treatment facility in Marin County when he was found dead in the middle of the night.

With such a large organization, it would make sense that a financial plan would have been in place to cover unexpected catastrophic events such as the death of the leader. Yet nothing like a plan had ever been developed. The Grateful Dead operated like a minimum-wage worker living paycheck to paycheck, without preparation for the future, acting like things would never change. They had worked for years, but had little to show for it other than expansive lifestyles and large debts. With a number of Dead employees already gone and more layoffs looming, Garcia's death forced instant hardships on those he left behind. These were mostly people who had labored beside the band for thirty years or more. The egalitarian Dead treated them like family. They paid salaries well above the industry norm and extended all kinds of financial assistance to their people. When a fallen redwood tree crushed manager Cameron Sears's home (during a New Year's Eve show while the house was vacant), the band loaned him the money for repairs. The band routinely extended cash advances to crew and employees and then carried the debt on the books for years. Such generosity was typical of the Dead. The type of loyalty the band members showed the people who worked for them was rare in the music industry, and these layoffs cut them to the core.

Guitarist Bob Weir and bassist Phil Lesh had attended the first company meeting within two weeks of Garcia's death conducted by band attorney Hal Kant, the first round of layoffs, where anybody who had worked for the band less than ten years was let go. They hung around after the meeting to commiserate.

"This place has been a haven for the chronically unemployed," Weir told the band's computer specialist, Bob Bralove, whose relatively recent hiring meant he did not make the first cut. "You'll be all right."

The layoffs only heightened the emotional toll on this traumatized group. There was no consensus on what to do. Weir, along with drummer Mickey Hart, eager to return to performing, had committed to a summer tour to be called the Furthur Festival, which would feature a repertory-style program that included Hot Tuna (featuring Jefferson Airplane alumni Jorma Kaukonen and Jack Casady); the East Los Angeles Chicano rockers Los Lobos, who were a favorite of Garcia's; former Dead sideman Bruce Hornsby; and others. It was a hurried and unorganized effort to find employment for at least some of the crew and help cover lost income for some of the Dead's concert promoters across the country. Phil Lesh, sick of strenuous touring and father to two young sons, wanted to stay home, raise his kids, and have nothing to do with any future performances. Kreutzmann, one of two drummers in the band, who initially had dived into a bottle, went through rehab, divorced his wife, and vanished to Kauai, where he was surfing and scuba diving. He didn't even take a drum kit with him.

When Garcia died, Weir was in New Hampshire touring with his solo band RatDog. He played the show that night and returned to California the next day for the funeral, leaving his band and crew waiting in an East Coast hotel for the tour to resume the next week. The band had evolved out of a collaboration with bassist Rob Wasserman (originally called Scaring the Children) and had only recently added drummer Jay Lane. Garcia's death was announced the morning of Lane's third date with the band. After the funeral, Weir went right back on the road and stayed. He was only in town for the fateful board meeting, flying to Las Vegas for a gig that night.

Mickey Hart had been sequestered in the recording studio in his Sonoma County ranch with an ambitious solo album, a monstrously complex project that Garcia had known about and encouraged. The drummer brought in British record producer Robin Millar, best known for his ultra-sleek production with soul singer Sade, to finish the record. Millar smoothed Hart's massive percussion overdubs into silken Europop sonics highlighted by a British female vocal group, the Mint Juleps, along with some powerful songs from Dead lyricist Robert Hunter. The album brimmed with exquisite instrumental tracks and sublime vocal textures. Titled *Mystery Box*, the record became a far more polished and fully realized piece of work than any previous solo album from members of the Dead and, astonishingly enough, sounded like a record that could be a hit. Hart said later that making the album saved his life.

Such was the emotional landscape when the band members dully crowded their cars into the tiny, cramped parking spaces behind the back of the house. Grateful Dead Productions CEO and band manager Cameron Sears was to chair the meeting. The band's chief financial officer, the straitlaced former banker Nancy Mallonee, was there. Hal Kant attended, as did the head of Grateful Dead Merchandise, the band's direct mail operation, Peter McQuaid. The two remaining members of the road crew, Steve Parish and Ram Rod, came. They had already announced they would be pooling their salary and sharing it equally with their crewmate Kidd Candelario to keep him on the payroll. Keyboardist Vince Welnick, who just joined the band five years before and was given a full share from day one, was the only one wearing tie-dye. Sears's assistant Jan Simmons would take the minutes of the meeting. Even lyricist Hunter, hardly an organization man, came. Publicist Dennis McNally hovered around, in case they needed to draft a press release. The atmosphere was grim and hardly chatty.

In the boardroom, sitting in one of the dozen custom chairs, one arm draped over the signature armrests hand-carved with the stealie—the skull-and-lightning bolts trademark of the Dead—was Phil Lesh. His sock-clad feet rested on the massive twenty-foot antique oak table the band brought back from Germany on their 1972 European tour. He rolled an unlit cigar in his mouth.

The band members knew each other well. They had, quite literally, grown up together. Weir had joined the band at age sixteen; Lesh, the oldest, was almost ten years older. After almost a decade of chaos and touring in 1974, the band took a yearlong hiatus. They came back together having come to accept the role the Dead played in their lives and settled into a remarkably steady, harmonious collaboration with Garcia at the helm. There had been the typical miscellaneous arguments and shifting alliances, but no major political disputes inside the Grateful Dead.

The entire world seemed to be aware of the band's predicament. Hart and Lesh had attended a fundraising lunch for President Bill Clinton and Vice President Al Gore, and the president asked about their plans. Since shortly after Garcia's death, rumors had been flying about his replacement. David Hidalgo of Los Lobos, Neil Young, Carlos Santana, Jorma Kaukonen, and Mark Knopfler were all mentioned. The band members heard the rumors and so did the guitarists named, but there was no basis in fact. There were no plans. Nothing had been seriously discussed. The four musicians had only seen each other once since the funeral and the Golden Gate Park memorial two days later. They held a brief meeting a couple of days after, sitting around one of the front offices at the new place in Novato, vaguely tossing around some thoughts, but mostly staring at their shoes and enduring the awkward silences. Nobody thought the idea of continuing as the Grateful Dead sounded right, especially Kreutzmann, but nobody had the belly to deal with anything but the most fundamental business, certainly not facing any difficult issues at that early stage.

Four months later, this board meeting would have to address the question. It seemed almost sacrilegious to consider replacing Garcia, but there was a need among the band to come to some decision. These men were tired, bereaved, frustrated, and scared, with the enormous weight of the massive Grateful Dead organization on their shoulders and, without Garcia, no idea how they were going to hold it up. The meeting was called to order before a standing-room-only crowd.

There were many items on the agenda, but staring everybody in the face was the most basic decision that needed to be made about the band's future—how they would continue.

Discussion was relatively brief. Cameron Sears, who never met a decision he would not rather postpone, argued that no decision need be made yet. Welnick, who had been flat broke when he was hired by the band and had become greatly enamored of the Dead lifestyle, enthusiastically supported getting the band back on the road as soon as possible.

Talking from a speakerphone, Kreutzmann put the matter to rest. "I'm not going to tour anymore," he said.

With Kreutzmann's simple declarative statement, Lesh no doubt felt a sense of relief flood through him. He, too, must have been tired of the Grateful Dead hamster wheel. Maybe they weren't ready to pull the plug on their carers, but Kreutzmann's words were liberating. The overwhelming sense that they couldn't continue without Garcia took over the meeting. Nobody had the drive or interest in remodeling the band. It seemed to them that their long, strange trip had finally come to an end.

Hunter stood up to speak. More than anybody except Garcia, Hunter had been responsible for creating the Grateful Dead. While Garcia was the undisputed genius musician and bandleader, Hunter's job was to articulate the vision, to detail out the Dead world in his songs. He had risen to the occasion many times. A crusty, whimsical professorial sort not given to getting involved in band business, Hunter remained outside the day-to-day turmoil and rarely deigned to express himself. Standing to speak, he had the room's attention.

Hunter simply quoted a couplet from the end of his song, "Fire on the Mountain."

"The more that you give, why, the more it will take," he said, "to the thin line beyond which you really cannot fake."

Then he walked out.

The meeting moved on. Much business needed to be conducted, decisions that had been set aside for the past four months. The band members had held almost daily telephone conversations with the front office, but spoke with each other very little. Counselor Kant raised an issue about Garcia's will that concerned him. In the will, Garcia bequeathed the custom-made guitars he played back to the man who made them. Kant was certain that the guitars were purchased with Grateful Dead Productions funds and, consequently, belonged to the band. He wanted to take steps to make sure the guitars did not get away. Some of the musicians didn't understand that the band owned their instruments, let alone Garcia's. Garcia himself probably hadn't known.

Publicist McNally was summoned and he quickly composed a press release. A trained academician who landed his job because Garcia liked his Jack Kerouac biography, *Desolate Angel*, McNally hardly turned out typical press mill copy. It was a brief statement, tinged with poetry and regret, but it effectively closed the door on the future of the Grateful Dead:

———— FOR IMMEDIATE RELEASE ————

The wheel is turning and you can't slow down
You can't let go and you can't hold on
You can't go back and you can't stand still . . .

"The Wheel," Robert Hunter

After four months of heartfelt consideration, the remaining members of the band met yesterday and came to the conclusion that the "long, strange trip" of the uniquely wonderful beast known as the "Grateful Dead" is over. Although individually and in various combinations, they will continue to make music, whatever the future holds will be something different in name and structure.

In making this announcement, band members were especially mindful of their partners in this adventure, the Dead Heads, urging them to remember that the music, the values and the spirit of this marvelous shared journey endure.

Business operations will continue at the band's long time Marin offices.

The release would go out the next morning. Would that it could be so simple.

2

Terrapin Station

L IKE MANY Deadheads, Rick Abelson was consumed by grief over the death of Jerry Garcia. Unlike most, he was in a position to act on his bereavement. Abelson, who attended his first Dead concert in 1977 while growing up in New Jersey, was a Harvard School of Design–trained landscape architect who specialized in theme parks. He had built attractions and designed exhibits all over Asia and Latin America, remodeled American amusement parks, and consulted on projects around the world. His profession put him far outside the realm of the Grateful Dead, but Abelson was about to converge with the band in ways he could not have predicted.

Garcia's death shook him and, as he thought about what the other band members were going to do without their leader, Abelson began to develop the germ of an idea. He sketched out his thoughts for a Grateful Dead exhibition that would re-create the atmosphere of the Dead concerts without the band itself. He called it "The Grateful Dead Experience."

In October 1995, only weeks after Garcia died, Abelson sent his quickly improvised plans, some notes and a few drawings—"eye wash" in the parlance of his trade—unsolicited to the Grateful Dead office in San Rafael. His cover letter outlined a vague proposed idea detailing how the surviving members could move forward into the future without Garcia, a kind of museum/theme park. Abelson held out no special hope for the proposal. It was something he did to make himself feel better, and to offer a small contribution, perhaps, but mostly to work out his own feelings through the design process, something he had learned to do over his years in the field.

What Abelson didn't know was that the Grateful Dead had fancifully considered such an idea for years. The band, weary of the drudgery of touring, loved to talk about having a home base of sorts, often bringing up the subject among themselves in the middle of the concerts. The musicians would spin fantasies of establishing a headquarters where they could play music without having to travel and let the audience come to them. It was the kind of wishful thinking that nourished their spirit, a joking pastime the band members indulged in over the years.

As far back as the seventies, the band struggled with the whole idea of traveling from hockey rink to hockey rink, playing music in the most uncongenial environments imaginable, and enduring extraordinary hardships simply to get to the stage where they could finally play the music. Onetime manager Ron Rakow, one of the shiftiest characters in a Grateful Dead past littered with shifty characters, used to keep plans posted on his office wall above his desk for an inflatable amphitheater that would simply float from concert to concert. In case those drawings didn't adequately impress visitors, he also posted a letter from acclaimed genius of the day Buckminster Fuller agreeing to consider "certain aspects" of the project, if it ever got going. The floating arena idea never went anywhere, but the Dead always kept their eyes open for innovative alternatives to the conventional system of touring.

Abelson had no way of knowing that his package dovetailed with this long-standing fantasy of the band, more hallucination than vision, but probably only the goofy Grateful Dead would have even explored a crazy idea dropped on their desk over the transom from someone they never met. After some consideration and discussion at the San Rafael office, Cameron Sears picked up the phone and reached Abelson.

Not expecting to hear back at all, Abelson was more than surprised by Sears's phone call and that he was summoned for a meeting. He showed up at the Lincoln Street offices on December 5, one
day prior to the board meeting where the band decided to retire the
Grateful Dead. By this time, Abelson had brought aboard Economics
Research Associates (ERA), the firm founded in 1958 by Harrison
"Buzz" Price, the Stanford MBA graduate who did all the research and
planning for Disneyland. After that, the firm was a principal in virtually every major theme park development around the world. Abelson
and the two ERA associates, Steve Spickard and Jim McCarthy from
the firm's San Francisco office, knew not to wear their neckties. They
parked behind the shady Victorian in downtown San Rafael and were
greeted cheerily by Sears's assistant Jan Simmons. "You're on time,"
she said. "That's not very rock and roll."

They walked into the kitchen, where Simmons seated them at
a table for the meeting. Office manager Eileen Law met them. The
kitchen was the nerve center of the hive. The ladies who ran the
Grateful Dead office located their desks in the kitchen, where nobody
ever really cooked. A sign above one desk read, "Do you want to talk
to the man in charge or the woman who knows what's going on?"

Hal Kant, the band's rough-hewn lawyer with the business cards
reading LEGALLY DEAD, had flown in from Reno, where he had been
playing poker. He was a world-champion poker player and pursued
the activity with fierce devotion. Kant, a right-wing, old-fashioned
conservative, was an unusual associate for the hippie rock group, but
he was unswervingly loyal and vigilant in his representation of the
band. He was first hired by the band with the stipulation that they
would be his only music business client and he had stayed true to
his word. He and Cameron Sears were joined by band member Phil
Lesh, who not only enthusiastically greeted the design research team,
but immediately informed them that he had a name for what they
were planning: Terrapin Station.

Abelson outlined his vision. He exuded confidence and energy.
He saw nothing but success. He said the Dead museum project was
a "slam dunk."

"You forget who you are talking to," said Eileen Law. "The Grateful Dead."

"Yeah," said Lesh, "if anybody can screw it up, we can."

The meeting migrated upstairs to the more clubby mood of manager Sears's office. Abelson explained the concept of "charrette" to the Dead people. Originally drawn from the French word for the carts that collected final papers at the last minute from students at Paris's École des Beaux Arts in the nineteenth century, in the design community, the term had come to refer to the collaborative process of quickly collecting input from a number of people. He wanted to arrange such a workshop session with the Dead folks as soon as possible. They came to terms and the Dead agreed to underwrite the modest budget.

Three nights later, two days after laying the Grateful Dead to rest, Phil Lesh appeared on an early Internet broadcast called *Grateful Web* with Dead tape archivist Dick Latvala. Such Internet events were in such a fledgling state that the press release felt compelled to advise anybody who wanted to participate that "you need a computer with an Internet hookup and a graphic browser to read the World Wide Web." They were celebrating the thirtieth anniversary of the Dead's first appearance at the Fillmore Auditorium. Latvala's archival CD series, *Dick's Picks*, had already proved a surprisingly strong source of unexpected revenue, with orders arriving at the band's headquarters in the mail daily and experiencing a strong boost in sales following Garcia's death. Lesh and Latvala were sampling tracks from Latvala's two most recent releases, *Hundred Year Hall* and *Dick's Picks Vol. 3*. Three days after first meeting with designers, an enthusiastic Lesh was already talking about celebrating the band's legacy and culture through some kind of institution, "some kind of gathering place," Lesh said, "perhaps to be called Terrapin Station."

He envisioned a meeting place for people to continue the Grateful Dead experience without the band actually having to perform. He mentioned a performing space and virtual reality rooms, a combination of computer technology and audio science, with Grateful Dead music and videos playing continually. "San Francisco is the most logical place for it," he said, "but we are entertaining offers from elsewhere."

Lesh had no plans for the band to play. "We want to have a place where Deadheads can come and recapture as much of that experience as they can without actually having a live performance," Lesh said.

In March 1996, Rick Abelson showed up for his charrette over two days at the Wyndham Hotel near San Rafael. He immediately saw Dead roadies Ram Rod and Steve Parish wandering around like Rosencrantz and Guildenstern looking lost in the lobby. The conference room had been reserved under a fake name, so there was no sign directing guests to "Grateful Dead Museum Meeting." Instead the board in the lobby listed a family reunion under a phony name that Ram Rod and Parish didn't recognize. Abelson introduced himself and led the two rock-and-roll cowboys to the meeting.

The Grateful Dead Productions office had pulled together more than a dozen guests that included not only Phil Lesh and all the band's senior business advisors, but other key players such as lighting director Candace Brightman and audio engineer John Cutler. Long-standing office manager Eileen Law and her daughter Cassidy, who was married to band manager Cameron Sears, also attended, as did fan newsletter editor Gary Lambert and broadcaster David Gans of the widely syndicated *Grateful Dead Hour*. Also attending was a golfing buddy of Hal Kant's, a former Silicon Valley attorney named Neil Cumsky who had helped a client of Kant's acquire some oil fields in Costa Rica. Cumsky flew in from New Jersey for the meet and had everybody thinking he was some sort of gangster showing up dressed all in black. Kant had him in mind as a kind of project manager.

They sat around a table and, beginning with Abelson, introduced themselves to the group. Lesh was third. "I'm Phil Lesh," he said, "and I'm an out-of-work musician."

Abelson spent the day collecting ideas from the group. He and Spickard and McCarthy from ERA were there to hear from these people, plumb their thoughts on what this project could be, how the band's legacy could be reflected and contained inside four walls. They made notes on whiteboards. They listened as the panel considered many aspects of the idea. How big would it be? Where would it be? What components would it need to connect with the Grateful Dead experience? Abelson encouraged free-flowing dialogue, looking to get at the essence of why people would go to Grateful Dead concerts. He madly scribbled notes and recorded everything.

After the exhaustive session led into the evening and dispersed, Abelson, McCarthy, and Spickard huddled in the hotel bar. Abelson had brought a renderer from his office in Los Angeles and had dispatched the sketch artist to his room to work up some drawings based on the day's discussions. Spickard finally retreated to his room around midnight, leaving Abelson and McCarthy to close the bar.

Abelson finally made his way back to his room to supervise the final touches of the drawings his renderer was making. They cut pictures out of books. They stayed up all night putting their presentation together. At six in the morning, they took the sketches to a nearby Kinko's and made giant color enlargements of the original drawings. The man working behind the counter had read in the local paper about a secret meeting by the Grateful Dead and figured out the connection between the news report and his early morning customers, but he played it cool.

When the panel of experts returned for the second day, most of them anyway, they were greeted with the huge color sketches laid out on the conference table. The facade of the building had been drawn to look like San Francisco's Warfield Theatre, surrounded by the scaffolding fashioned to hold the Dead's historic experimental sound system called the Wall of Sound, Garcia's face at the center of a giant video screen. There was a drawing of the Dancing Bear Café, the rooftop restaurant envisioned the day before. As the meeting came to order, Abelson taped the blow-ups to the wall, but Ram Rod was so fascinated, he squatted down, inspecting the details. The sketches drew from the previous day's discussion, but now that the ideas were gloriously visualized and embellished, the project seemed even more plausible. The drawings offered a glimpse at the reality of a Grateful Dead museum, no longer just a joke for Dead insiders, but something tangible. Abelson had smashed a home run with his audience, who buzzed excitedly for the rest of the day about the prospects and possibilities. Yet they gave Abelson no direct instructions on what to do next. They figured he knew.

After a complete stop, the museum plans came as part of an unexpectedly hectic schedule, as the band sought to come out into the sunlight after agreeing to call an end to the Grateful Dead. The merchandise wing was experiencing brisk sales on the *Dick's Picks* CDs and plans to roll out a more robust release schedule were under way. Weir's RatDog and Hart's Mystery Box, the band that played on the album of the same name, had been announced even before the board meeting in December as headline attractions on the Furthur Festival summer tour. It was also announced that Lesh, Weir, Hart, and Vince Welnick would be joining the San Francisco Symphony for a new music festival in June. Lesh and Hart appeared in January at the ceremonies at New York's Waldorf-Astoria to induct their colleagues Jefferson Airplane into the Rock and Roll Hall of Fame.

Lesh was ideally suited to lead the band's exploration of the museum project. A conscientious parent of two young sons, Lesh also struggled with serious health issues. He had been dealing with the ravages of hepatitis C for years, but it wasn't getting better. He was frankly relieved to be off the road and have the Grateful Dead touring regimen off his back. He could drive his kids to school in the morning—he was taking one of the boys to summer camp when he first received word of Garcia's death—and preside over the evening family meal, prepared by his wife, Jill, and even lead the family sing-alongs after dinner. Lesh had no stomach to return to the stage. He told the band he was retiring. He intended to concentrate on projects like Terrapin Station that would keep him home.

In another project waiting for him at home in those desperate days following Garcia's death, Lesh undertook the investigation of the Dead's unfinished album project. The band had been recording a new album in starts and stops beginning with sessions November 1994 at The Site, a remote, high-end Marin County recording studio in the woods down the road from George Lucas's Skywalker Ranch. Many of the songs had been thoroughly road-tested in concert ("So Many Roads," "Days Between," "Samba in the Rain," "Liberty"), but Garcia had only laid down rudimentary guitar parts—no solos—and his indifferent vocals were little more than placeholders for the real performances that would now never come. Lesh went in the studio in January to see if there was anything that could be done with the tapes, but quickly concluded there was not enough to salvage any kind of serious album release. He was not surprised. But any disappointment he felt was ameliorated by being able to go home and sleep in his own bed every night.

His bandmate Bob Weir, on the other hand, did everything he could to stay away from home. Garcia's death came at the start of an East Coast tour by RatDog, and Weir had simply stashed his band and crew in a hotel while he returned to California for the funeral and memorial, going back to the scheduled dates the following week, almost as if nothing had happened. RatDog started as an attempt for Weir to define himself outside the Grateful Dead—the band featured no lead guitar, he was not performing Dead material and instead concentrated on blues and even occasional fifties pop standards such as "Fever" or "Twilight Time"—but it quickly became his lifeboat. In many ways, of all the Dead musicians, Weir was the one most shaken by Garcia's death, the little brother suddenly abandoned by his protector and benefactor, but he would work out his grief on the road, tirelessly grinding out a series of shows with his band for the entire month after Garcia died in August 1995 and, again, with another several weeks on tour in November and December—performances that were as much therapy sessions as concerts, for the audience as well as Weir.

He started the band with his Mill Valley neighbor Rob Wasserman, a gifted bassist and musician with whom he had occasionally played as a duo over the previous ten years. Wasserman was a formidable figure who recorded his own unique 1988 album of bass duets with vocalists such as Aaron Neville, Rickie Lee Jones, and Bobby McFerrin. He had toured with Lou Reed and played with Garcia's bluegrass buddy, mandolinist David Grisman, among many others. A serious, even dour artistic type ironically known as "Chuckles" around the stoner Grisman camp, conservatory-trained Wasserman favored the subtleties of the acoustic bass.

RatDog also included harmonica player Matt Kelly, a childhood friend of Weir's. Kelly and Weir had played together in his band

Kingfish during the seventies. Weir appeared on the first two Kingfish albums while the Dead were on hiatus in 1974. Kelly never left
Weir's orbit, guesting on occasional Dead sessions and remaining
friends until they came together again in RatDog. They added thirty-
one-year-old drummer Jay Lane just prior to Garcia's death. A former
member of quirky metal trio Primus led by bassist Les Claypool,
Lane had been part of informal composing sessions that Weir had
been holding at his house for a musical he was writing about pitcher
Satchel Paige of the Negro Baseball League.

When RatDog returned from the East Coast swing, Weir expanded
the roster to include Dead keyboardist Welnick, although he soon
grew alarmed at Welnick's mental state. Three previous keyboard players for the Dead had already died. They chose Welnick after a short
audition of five candidates largely because he could sing the high
notes. The band had no desire to drag themselves through the extensive process to find someone great. Someone good enough would
do. With the Dead, Welnick had been an agreeable bandmate and
something of an innocuous presence in the group, eager to please
and capable enough. But touring with RatDog, Welnick appeared to
be going through a personality change.

Riding on a bus on a string of dates through the West in December 1995, Weir found himself moving to the rear of the coach to get
away from Welnick, who had taken to riding for miles staring silently
ahead, a thin, eerie smile plastered on his face. Weir privately told Jay
Lane that this wasn't the same Vince that he knew from the Dead.
When he auditioned for the Grateful Dead, Welnick had been sleeping in a barn and planning to move to Mexico. He had enthusiastically embraced his leap into the major leagues and the exciting world
of touring with the band, but since Garcia's death, he had fallen
into a dark, depressive tailspin. He had been stunned by the band's
decision to retire the name and close the book, and he was hit with
instant financial problems. Deeply in debt, without the band's plush
touring income, Welnick was having problems meeting his responsibilities. His world was coming unraveled.

On the five-hour daytime ride from Santa Barbara to Santa Cruz,
Welnick retired to his bunk about forty-five minutes into the drive.

When the band arrived for the sound check at the concert, Welnick didn't show. Weir sent someone to wake him up, but the roadie returned without Welnick. "He's hard crashed," he told Weir. "I can't wake him."

Weir knew instantly what had happened. Calmly, he told the roadie to call an ambulance. The paramedics arrived and found an empty Valium bottle. Welnick had taken fifty-seven pills, the entire contents of a fresh bottle, and went to the hospital accompanied by the roadie. The band returned to the sound check and the concert. Welnick never played with RatDog again. He had violated one of the unspoken laws of the road. In the world of the Grateful Dead, it was permissible to be weird, but only so far. Suicide attempts on the band bus, no matter how lame, were over the line.

3

Johnny B. Goode

WEIR HAD determined that playing music as hard as he could was the only way to deal with Garcia's death. After finishing the RatDog tour in December (and taking an uncharacteristic month-long vacation traveling in Southeast Asia), Weir hit on a truly inspired idea for bolstering the blues bottom end of RatDog—recruiting a new pianist, one of the founding fathers of rock and roll, seventy-two-year-old Johnnie Johnson.

This little-known figure chiseled a huge mark in music history as the musical partner of Chuck Berry since the beginning of Berry's career. He helped fashion young Berry's music and provided a sturdy boogie-woogie framework to all Berry's storied fifties hits, chapters of the rock-and-roll bible like "Maybelline," "School Days," "Rock and Roll Music," "Johnny B. Goode," and "Roll over Beethoven," a collaboration that lasted for the twenty most productive years of Berry's career.

Johnson, who was never accorded the recognition (or songwriting credits) Berry enjoyed, was working as a bus driver in St. Louis when his obscurity was disturbed by his role in the 1987 film *Hail, Hail Rock and Roll*. In the movie, Keith Richards conducted a sixtieth birthday celebration concert for Berry and featured Johnson, dragging him out of Berry's shadow for the first time. Johnson subsequently enjoyed a modest late-career reprise with concert appearances and new recordings featuring him playing with an array of musicians such as Eric Clapton, John Lee Hooker, Bo Diddley, and George Thorogood.

RatDog's Matt Kelly contacted Johnson, whom he knew from blues circles, and he joined the band in rehearsals at Weir's treehouse studio in his Mill Valley home. Johnson had never heard of the Grateful Dead, but Weir and the rest of the band loved having this deep connection to the heart and soul of rock and roll playing in their band. Johnson was the master of playing a left-hand shuffle against a straight eight with the other hand, the very basis of the original rock-and-roll style. Weir was thrilled to be learning at the feet of the master.

Johnson made his RatDog debut at a raucous Mardi Gras show in February 1996 with New Orleans's Neville Brothers at the Henry J. Kaiser Auditorium in Oakland, sentimental scene of so many great Dead shows. With bluesman Taj Mahal sitting in, as well as the Nevilles joining the set-opening "Iko Iko," RatDog celebrated the band's new member by playing his tune "Tanqueray" from one of his recent solo albums and "Promised Land" from his days with Chuck Berry as the encores.

In April 1996, Weir was still the only band member doing public performances when three of the former Dead members finally took the stage together for the first time since Garcia's death to play music. Both Lesh and Weir joined Bruce Hornsby in his concert at the Fillmore. Weir strolled onstage with a guitar in the middle of "Sugaree." Three songs later, Hornsby brought out Phil Lesh for "Truckin'." The crowd cheered ecstatically when those voices blended on the opening line. They stayed for "Turn on Your Lovelight" and "Not Fade Away" before returning with an encore of the Band's "The Weight."

Unlike Weir, Mickey Hart hadn't been grieving in public. Like Weir, Hart also dealt with his grief by burying himself in work. He went into hiding, sequestering himself in the vast recording studio at his fifty-acre Sonoma County ranch, where he was finishing a massive recording project, already more than three years in the works when

Garcia died, tens of thousands of dollars over budget and ambitious beyond anything the fearless, ferocious drummer ever dared attempt.

Hart trained his intense intellectual curiosity on his bliss. The project began as an extension of his Grammy-winning 1991 *Planet Drum* album, an all-percussion collaboration by a group of percussionists drawn from different cultures that would become the biggest-selling world beat album in history. The Dead drummer had a long history with his own independent recording projects. He made his first solo album, *Rolling Thunder*, in 1972 and, over the years, did extensive recording work as an ethnomusicologist with Egyptians, Indians, and even New Guinea rain forest dwellers. He wrote best-selling books about percussion throughout world cultures. He composed and recorded portions of the soundtrack to *Apocalypse Now* for director Francis Ford Coppola. He was scheduled to lead a team of more than one hundred drummers playing his compositions at the opening ceremonies of the 1996 Olympic Games that July in Atlanta. Hart and associates Zakir Hussain, Giovanni Hidalgo, and Sikiru Adepoju began recording the *Planet Drum* follow-up in 1992. When the Dead were not on the road, he would hole up in the studio, recording extensively, almost compulsively. He logged thousands of hours.

When Dead lyricist Robert Hunter joined the project, writing songs to skeletal percussion tracks, the album began to take a different direction. Garcia had recommended the Mint Juleps, six Jamaican sisters he saw sing on a Spike Lee–directed PBS special. Now Hart moved them into the ranch and submerged them in the madness. He had them sing some songs hundreds of times, saving each version to later painstakingly assemble impossibly intricate composite vocals (what studio professionals call "gnat surgery"). He filled more than two hundred and fifty tape reels. There were more than fifteen hundred tracks recorded. Hart was awash in the music, lost in a sea of takes. He plowed ahead furiously after Garcia's death, often breaking into uncontrollable tears in the studio, once when recording an overdub with drummer Carter Beauford of the Dave Matthews Band.

Hunter showed up at the studio with a new song. Uncharacteristically, he insisted on singing the rough vocal. He refused to allow anybody to see the sheet of paper with the words written on it. The song was called "Down the Road" and it envisioned encounters with a procession of fallen heroes—Joe Hill, John F. Kennedy, John Lennon, and Martin Luther King Jr. The King verse never worked out to Hunter's satisfaction, so he had recently substituted a new final verse:

> *When the smoke and thunder cleared, enough to look around*
> *I heard a sweet guitar lick, an old familiar sound*
> *I heard a laugh I recognized come rolling from the earth*
> *I saw it rise into the skies like lightning giving birth*
> *It sounded like Garcia, but I couldn't see the face*
> *Just the beard and glasses and a smile on empty space.*

When Hunter finished his vocal, everyone in the control room was weeping. The album was growing into a magnificent animal, something far beyond any of Hart's previous works. Bruce Hornsby, who put an accordion part on "Down the Road," told Hart it sounded like soul music to him and he should contact Robin Millar, the British producer behind the Europop pseudo-soul hits by songstress Sade ("Smooth Operator"). Millar miraculously pieced together a supple final mix from the chaos and Hart prepared to take the Mystery Box band on the road after the album's June release.

Like the rest of his bandmates, Hart saw this transition as an opportunity for a clean break with the past. Like Weir, he was intent on reinventing himself. "I don't have to be Mickey Hart of the Grateful Dead," he told the *San Francisco Chronicle*. "This is a breakout, new energy, a new horizon. It's new growth, new life. It's not a retread. I'm not trying to play songs like the Grateful Dead. In fact, I went out of my way not to sound like the Grateful Dead. I want to keep the spirit, but I want it to be me. No guitars—just drums and voice.

"The audience is the Grateful Dead now," he said. "They've got the power to make it a Grateful Dead concert once the groove starts and the lights go down."

The *Mystery Box* album took on special meaning in the wake of Garcia's passing. No longer some sideline enterprise to occupy his restless creativity outside the Dead, now the album crystallized as a launching pad for a new musical life for Hart. There was a lot of optimism surrounding the record's release. It had the scent of something almost entirely foreign to the Grateful Dead world—a potential hit record. "What do I know about pop music?" he said. "We're going to find out. I'm not trying to copy any particular style. It's an experiment. If this becomes popular, then it will be pop music. If not, then it will be another one of my enthusiasms."

. . . . . .

Three days before Hart and Weir launched their respective solo bands on the Furthur Festival tour in June 1996, the first official performance by assembled members of the Grateful Dead after Garcia's death took place in San Francisco. Weir, Hart, Phil Lesh, and Vince Welnick made a bizarre cameo appearance at a new music festival with San Francisco Symphony maestro Michael Tilson Thomas, the celebrated conductor. Deadheads roamed the aisles of Davies Symphony Hall, hung around the sidewalk outside begging for spare tickets, and filled the restrooms with pot smoke. Even if the band members were only going to play a few largely indecipherable passages in the thirty-six-minute piece, eager Dead fans mingled with the blue-haired symphony regulars in an environment where they were distinctly out of place, only slightly more so than the Dead members themselves.

Lesh, of course, was the source of the infiltration. He had studied experimental classical music in college under composers Darius Milhaud and Luciano Berio and maintained an interest in avant-garde compositions. Under Lesh's influence, the Rex Foundation, the Dead's philanthropic arm, became one of the most generous supporters of new music composers in the grant world. He attended the symphony occasionally and came to know conductor Thomas through charity events involving music education. When Thomas proposed Lesh and his associates play the parts he envisioned for a rock combo in a John Cage performance at his upcoming Youth Symphony American Festival, Lesh readily agreed and corralled his colleagues.

Thomas planned to perform two pieces by Cage—"Apartment House 1776," a relatively straightforward piece commissioned to celebrate the nation's Bicentennial, and "Renga," a more free-form composition involving drawings by Henry David Thoreau with large sections of improvisation. For "Renga," Cage simply transposed stray marks and little drawings from Thoreau's notebooks on a time graph that was intended to serve as the score. It was up to the individual musician to interpret the marks. The two pieces would be played simultaneously.

The cryptic notations Cage supplied "Renga" amounted to little more than suggestions by the composer. "When you have seventy-eight people improvising together, " Thomas said to *The Chronicle*, "it requires an enormous amount of imagination. It also requires terrific restraint, to listen for the precise moment to play."

At rehearsal, the four Dead men were flanked by four vocalists who sang "Apartment House 1776," four different versions of music Cage imagined Americans would have heard in 1776, each sung independently of the orchestra and each other. Soloists stood arrayed in the balcony and Thomas presided over the full San Francisco Symphony Youth Orchestra on the stage. The first run-through was a cacophonous auditory barrage. Thomas held his finger to his lips and dropped his voice. "Have the courage to play softer," he said.

Lesh worked with the members of the Youth Orchestra for two weeks before the performance, trying to instill some of the basics of improvisation into young musicians trained only to play what they read. "Improvisation starts off with imitation," Lesh said to *The Chronicle*. "You imitate what you hear and elaborate on what it suggests to you. So you have to be listening very carefully. That's what we always did when we were collectively improvising in the band— we were always listening harder than we were playing. Any musical context, a song, for instance, is like a labyrinth. It has lots of branches, but it's closed on itself. And we were always searching for the thread that was going to allow us to find our way out of that labyrinth into open territory, or maybe even another labyrinth."

In the carefully calculated thirty-six minutes, scrupulously counted down by television monitors onstage, the Dead musicians may have played a total of two minutes—a couple of squawks on keyboard, some screechs on guitar, a few flamadiddles on the drums—and could barely be detected above the orchestral din that surrounded them. After the unsatisfying performance, Bob Weir stopped on his way home to jam at the tiny Mill Valley nightclub Sweetwater and played the rest of the night in front of a dozen drunks.

A day later, Weir and Hart left town for the summer tour. After short, hurried rehearsals in Georgia, the Furthur tour opened June 20 in Atlanta. The show was a seven-hour ordeal featuring at least eight acts, and a grueling thirty-one-city march across the country. Instead of the deluxe travel arrangements and accommodations of the Dead tours, the pack moved like a traveling circus in fifteen buses and vans, stopping, when they did, at motels and an occasional Marriott. The duration of the show meant crews and musicians spent all day and most of the night at the concert site. Hot Tuna, who opened the shows in broad daylight often before a scant few hundred fans, stayed to participate in the show-closing jam session at the end of the night like bit actors in *Macbeth* called to play parts in the first and fifth acts.

While Bob Weir and Mickey Hart may have set out to reinvent themselves, the producers of the Furthur Festival, John Scher and Cameron Sears, sought to surround their new incarnations with as much of the conventional trappings of a Dead concert as they could muster. If this tour was about new life for the Dead musicians and crew, for the Deadheads it was about the passing of Garcia and a combination celebration of life and grief-counseling session. Quickly, the audience's attention migrated from the Dead solo acts to the half-hour jam tacked onto the end of the RatDog set that closed the show.

Backstage didn't look much like a Dead show. It was all business, no party, not even much pot in evidence. No dancing was allowed in the wings and there was a lot of pressure to adhere to a strict schedule. New regulations in the parking lot led to grumbling on the part of many long-standing vendors, accustomed to a more freewheeling scene before the shows. Intermission acts singer-songwriter John Wesley Harding, bluesman Alvin Youngblood Hart, and juggling troupe the Flying Karamazov Brothers shared dressing rooms and buses. Weir and Hart had buses of their own, but they routinely ate with the crew. Only a part of the old Dead crew was on this trip; the well-oiled way of doing things on Dead tours had been replaced by a disciplined, professional hierarchy that featured a lot of new faces.

With Garcia's death, New York–based producer John Scher, who had worked with the band since the early seventies and acted often as a quasi-manager, faced losing as much as 40 percent of his business. Deeply worried, he had moved quickly behind the scenes that fall to put together something to pass through the amphitheaters the next summer, even before December when the band dropped their name. Grateful Dead Productions declined to finance the venture, so Scher and Cameron Sears pooled resources and went into business together as the tour producers. Some GDP board members would later grumble over Sears's participation as tour producer, claiming it would be overstepping his duties as the band's manager.

As the shows settled into their groove, interplay between the acts grew to be part of the daylong event—John Wesley Harding singing with Hot Tuna, Hart and Weir sitting in with Hornsby, Weir and Hornsby joining Hart's set, everybody piling on at the end of RatDog, often with Hornsby vocalist Debra Henry leading the ensemble in a spirited version of "White Rabbit." Everybody quickly learned to build Grateful Dead material into their acts. Los Lobos closed their sets with "Bertha," a rollicking version the band first recorded for a Dead tribute album. Hornsby invariably trotted out "Going Down the Road Feeling Bad" to great response and sometimes brought Weir to do "Jack Straw." Even the juggling Karamazov Brothers got into the act, bringing out folkie Wes Harding to sing "Uncle John's Band."

The only two acts not trading on the Dead songbook, ironically, were the ones featuring the former Dead members. Hart's Mystery Box was a radical departure from the Dead world with the Europop dance beat, no guitar, and supple polyrhythmic undercurrents. Hart stuck to performing material from his new album, ending his set with a sort of rapping vocal on "Fire on the Mountain," the only song from his Dead days he played, often with Weir joining for the number. RatDog only knew two Dead songs—"Cassidy" and "Throwin' Stones"—although the band sometimes performed old blues associated with the Dead such as "I Know You Rider" sung by Matt Kelly, not Weir. Like Hart, Weir also consciously avoided having a lead guitar in his band. To Weir, RatDog was kind of the anti-Dead, but that concept was largely lost on the audience.

There were tense hours backstage at the Gorge Amphitheatre in Washington State when the news of the bombing at the Atlanta Olympic Games hit. The explosion happened directly beneath the sound tower operated by the Grateful Dead's old sound company and many of the road crew and production staff were in Atlanta working the Olympics. Several anxious hours passed before all hands were reported safe. Warren Zevon joined the bill for a few dates, which meant adding "Werewolves of London" to the closing ensemble jam session. Every so often, guitarist David Hidalgo of Los Lobos would slip his fiery version of Hendrix's "Little Wing" into the encores.

At Shoreline Amphitheatre in Mountain View, forty minutes south of San Francisco, in what passed for the hometown stop on the tour, Hart brought out a couple of surprise guests during his set; his "retired" bandmate Phil Lesh and Hart's new best friend, Sammy Hagar. Only a month before, flying to Hawaii on a rare family vacation, Hart met Hagar in the first-class cabin. At first, he thought the shaggy rock star was only another friendly Deadhead, but Hagar was headed to his Hawaiian home after just having been fired from Van Halen. Hart showed up at his house every day he was on the islands to cheer his new pal. The Shoreline faithful may not have been particularly surprised to see Lesh join the band for "Fire on the Mountain," but there was no way they were expecting Sammy Hagar. He was nonetheless welcomed back at the end of the RatDog set to join Weir, Hart, Lesh, Hornsby, and Hot Tuna's Jorma Kaukonen for "Truckin'" and "The Other One" jams.

At the end of the day, the Deadheads went home slightly confounded. They could cling to the half-hour repertory close to the concert as a slender slice of Dead musical anarchy and take some comfort in having been able to come together once again around, at least, the spirit of the Grateful Dead. But Hart's Mystery Box proved controversial with fans—some loved it, others hated it—and Weir's RatDog, with his devotion to blues and ballads, a kind of Bob Weir lounge act with Rob Wasserman's chamber music bass playing, was frustrating to all the Deadheads. Not only did he refuse to have a lead guitar in his band, he wouldn't even play rock music, let alone Dead songs. Weir was determined to do what he wanted and refused to adapt to audience expectations despite pleas from tour producers. Weir was doing this to save his life, not theirs.

. . . . . .

In June, Rick Abelson submitted his "red book" version of the Terrapin Station business plan, a forty-four-page, oversized spiral-bound handbook stuffed full of photographs and drawings of the proposed project, now outlined in detail. Plans called for two theaters, six themed rooms, a café, and merchandise store. The cost including real estate was estimated at $40–45 million and the opening date was targeted for spring 1999.

Along with ERA analysts, Abelson and the team looked at the Rock and Roll Hall of Fame in Cleveland; Graceland, Elvis Presley's home in Memphis; and the Country Music Hall of Fame in Nashville for comparisons and projected more than a million visitors the first year for Terrapin Station that would stabilize down to 875,000 a year. The plan forecast an operating budget around $5 million a year and net income of more than $11 million a year, which would pay off the entire investment in four to five years.

Abelson's Deadland vision as outlined in the document called for visitors to enter through a lobby dominated by a replica of the Wall of Sound, the historic gargantuan sound system the band used briefly in the seventies, leading to a dimly lit re-creation of backstage with the show about to begin. The adjacent Jerry Garcia Theater would be the location for a multimedia orientation and a second theater, The Wheel, would feature holographic imagery of the band playing in a 360-degree setting.

The experience would revolve around six specific rooms. Eyes of the World would be a room devoted to the visual arts—concert posters and artwork from fans. The Music Never Stopped room would house the band's concert recordings, more than three thousand performances, otherwise known as the Vault. The Rhythm Devils room would contain an interactive percussion display to include "The Beast," the massive contraption built for Dead drummers Hart and Kreutzmann, and the "Thunder Machine" from the Merry Pranksters. Space and Place would be dedicated to the venues the band had played around the world. The Truckin' room would feature a timeline of the band's career illustrated with memorabilia such as Pigpen's organ or Garcia's Uncle Sam hat. The Other One, the final themed room, would reflect the colorful parking lot scene of Dead concerts.

Plans called for a building with fifty thousand square feet, the size of a large supermarket, and the average visitor experience was reckoned to last three hours.

> Imagine giving young music fans, as well as long-time Deadheads, the opportunity to "touch the Grateful Dead," to pass through the rich history of the music and its tangents by presenting a fascinating and incisive panorama of the Grateful Dead with the use of authentic memorabilia and state-of-the-art media.
>
> It will be a mystical place to invigorate the senses. Something to capture the tried and true, as well as the curious imagination. Terrapin Station will be the most unique educational and spiritual music attraction ever assemble [*sic*] in America.

Abelson made the prospect look possible, even relatively routine, and eminently doable. He estimated planning and construction could be completed in under thirty-six months. There was talk of a reunion concert at the place on New Year's Eve 1999.

4

Widows

THE FESTERING war between the widows first broke out into the open on the pier of Schoonmaker Marina in Sausalito. It was a blustery gray April day with high seas and rain. Garcia had requested that his ashes be scattered under the Golden Gate Bridge, and now everyone, including Garcia's ex-wife, Carolyn Adams Garcia—known as Mountain Girl or MG—were on the dock waiting to get on the boat, the *Argosy Venture*, owned by Dead music business associate Bill Belmont. But the widow, Deborah Koons Garcia, was in control and was having none of Mountain Girl. The widow ordered that Mountain Girl not be allowed on the boat. Six-foot swells tossed the large, expensive yacht like a toy against the pier as Koons Garcia crouched down in the bridge of the boat and Mountain Girl screamed on the dock to be let on board.

"Can we get out of here?" Koons Garcia said to Belmont.

"Deborah," yelled Mountain Girl. "This is family."

Garcia and Mountain Girl's three daughters were already on the boat, stricken that their mother was not allowed to participate in this last tribute to their father. Belmont tried to talk Koons Garcia into changing her mind, without success.

The women had been at war for many years, since Mountain Girl first confronted the young Koons over her affair with MG's then-husband in 1973. At that time, she presented the twenty-three-year-old Koons, who had met Garcia at a New York concert, with a one-way plane ticket home. A chance encounter in a Marin health food store more than twenty years later, long after his marriage to MG, renewed Koons's romance with the Dead guitarist. They had only been married eighteen months when Garcia died, but widow Koons Garcia quickly took charge. Mountain Girl had already infuriated her at the wake when she snapped a Polaroid of herself with Garcia in his coffin, and she had decided then that MG would not be allowed at the funeral. But this latest screaming match was being played out in full view of her daughters and his horrified closest friends, who had all known Mountain Girl a lot longer than the widow.

In the middle of this tense scene, the perennially tardy Bob Weir and his girlfriend Natascha Muenter finally sauntered down the pier. Belmont and his two-man crew prepared to shove off. As Weir started to climb aboard, MG got his attention.

"Bobby, they won't let me come," she screamed over the weather.

One leg on the dock, one leg on the rising boat, a surprised Weir was literally trapped in the middle and immediately indignant on MG's behalf while the deck heaved precariously beneath him. He paused, but was pulled on board and Phil Lesh prevailed on Weir to settle down. They had spoken to Mickey Hart on the phone, who was still at home in Sebastopol, an hour away, under the impression the boat trip would be postponed due to bad weather. They also gave up on Robert Hunter, who didn't like boats. They pulled away and motored out over the choppy swells, leaving Mountain Girl behind standing alone on the dock, sobbing hysterically.

Things had already started to go weird two weeks before when Bob Weir and Koons Garcia took a portion of Garcia's ashes to India and scattered them on the Ganges River. No one understood the mysterious action at the time, least of all Garcia's daughters, who were not informed beforehand. It was only much later that it was revealed this had been one of Weir's strange ideas, which had come to him in a dream. Although he sought and received the approval of his bandmates, he neglected to inform any of Garcia's daughters or their mother about his plans. They read about it in the newspaper. "There was no reason on Earth to take Jerry's ashes to India," an outraged Mountain Girl told the *San Francisco Chronicle*, "a country he'd never been to, and dump them into the most polluted river on the face of the Earth."

Weir had wakened from a dream with a vision. While sitting in Garcia's onstage tent during concerts, he and Garcia used to talk of going down to the river with the geese. Weir felt it was a sort of shared sanctuary of the imagination, mostly Garcia's, which would take him to a place of peace during a show. They would return to the image over and over and Weir never knew if the river was real or mythical. The image came to him in a dream after his friend's death and it was finally revealed to him—the river was real and it was the Ganges.

Weir, believing in the power of dreams and that his old friend had contacted him with instructions, presented his idea to the other bandmates and he received their straight-faced unanimous approval. It only remained to convince the widow that it was a good idea, since she was the keeper of the cremains. He knew this would not be easy, as Koons Garcia had been contentious since Garcia died and showed no signs of being anything else. Summoning all the requisite diplomacy, deftly allowing the widow to take a certain proprietary interest in the idea, he hoped she might feel as if she thought of it herself. The plan worked and Weir convinced her to take the trip.

On March 25, 1996, they waded into the peaceful, crystalline span of the Ganges, a rare pristine place in the river where the waters roared out of the mountains into calm, scenic national forest outside Rishikesh, India. As a pair of filmmakers hired by Deborah to record the event followed them, Weir and the widow rolled up their pants and splashed into midstream where they tossed handfuls of Jerry's ashes and a few flowers. Like a fresh breeze blowing through his mind, Weir felt overcome with a serene elation, a deep sense of duty fulfilled, a moment of true peace he traveled halfway around the world to find. He felt Garcia approved.

Of course, that was short-lived. He returned home to newspaper headlines and angry quotes from Jerry's daughters and their mother.

The scattering of the remainder of Garcia's ashes in the San Francisco Bay with his family was quickly scheduled. Mountain Girl showed up at the Sausalito marina that gray day with flowers and a box of Bozo noses and Groucho glasses, which she managed to sneak on board before the widow showed up. As different as these women were—the raucous, voluble hippie earth mother and the grim and proper East Coast trust funder—they were both formidable. Mountain Girl could scream and kick all she wanted, but Koons Garcia was not going to let her get on that boat.

The mood was subdued as they rode the bumpy waves out toward the edge of the Pacific Ocean under the Golden Gate Bridge. Although the rain had let up while the boat was docked, the squalls picked up again as they headed out. Steve Parish, Garcia's loyal Sancho Panza, withheld the package of Garcia's ashes under his jacket and gruffly ordered everyone to get along. Koons Garcia sat in the salon with Belmont, while Garcia's daughters, his brother Tiff, bandmates Lesh and Weir, and the few others left her alone. Nobody knew what to do and nobody stepped forward to take charge. They simply bounced on the foaming sea, waiting. With the vast, angry open ocean growing ever closer ahead at Point Bonita, Belmont's wife Janice, who was at the helm, shouted that they needed to start spreading those ashes or she was heading out to Hawaii.

They reached into the Ziploc bag and leaned over the gunwale with their handfuls, only to have the gusting wind blast the ashes back wet against the side of the boat while the dust went everywhere in the storm. If he weren't already dead, Jerry would have died laughing. His windblown remains could not be contained. He belonged to the breezes now. They threw some gardenias in after, but the flowers were anticlimactic. Everybody wanted to be done. This had been some miserable business. Janice Belmont struggled at the wheel to keep the boat moving, while her husband hovered over the party on deck to make sure nobody went overboard. Weir was concerned about the unceremonious send-off. "You've got to get it all in the water," he said.

As one of Belmont's crew held his belt, Weir leaned far over the rail in the heavy seas, wielding a hose, and washed his friend's remains off the boat. The ride back was quiet, but once they docked at Schoonmaker, Parish broke out a bottle of Wild Turkey and some food was served. Mountain Girl was long gone. Koons Garcia didn't stay and Lesh and his wife left quickly, but the rest hung around downing the booze and eating the food in the rain.

That Deborah Koons Garcia had so immediately taken total control of Garcia's estate after her husband's death set off alarms throughout the Dead world. Not only was she a relatively recent addition to the extended family, but women in Dead circles tended to be kept in the background. Girlfriends and wives were not allowed to cause problems. Mountain Girl had earned her unique status through many long, difficult years. As soon as Garcia died, Deborah started making people uncomfortable with her demands. She closely scrutinized the plans and the guest list for the funeral and, days later, stopped paying everybody.

It was probably true that people in the band around Garcia may not have treated her with what she considered adequate regard while her husband was alive. She was an outsider amidst an especially clannish bunch. She not only failed to develop any close personal alliances in the group, she saw no reason to trust management and crew now that Garcia was dead. She could be imperious and haughty and didn't bother to make anything easy for the organization. Indeed, it appeared that Koons Garcia went out of her way to make everything more difficult, but she was effectively limited in her sphere of influence from the start.

Although she was in firm control of the Garcia estate, Hal Kant had long before crafted a "Last Man Standing" clause to the band's partnership agreement, which allowed the surviving members to buy the partnership percentage back from any deceased member for an advantageous "book" value (Garcia was the fourth member of the band to die). With this clause, Koons Garcia was quickly paid off and eliminated from any Grateful Dead business dealings.

But she took full charge of the estate. The widow immediately stopped the monthly payments of $20,000-plus Garcia had been making to Mountain Girl under the terms of a $5 million divorce agreement. She also cut out monthly child support payments of

$8,000 to Manasha Matheson, the mother of Garcia's nine-year-old daughter, Keelin. She also stopped paying another $3,000 monthly to yet another ex-girlfriend, Barbara Meier of Taos, New Mexico, to whom Garcia proposed marriage in December 1992, before changing his mind three months later. She even stopped making payments on a car owned by twenty-one-year-old Theresa (Trixie) Garcia, a high school graduation present from her father.

In all, the estate was hit with more than $35 million worth of claims in the first ninety days. The most pressing—and personal— single demand came from Mountain Girl, who wanted the rest of her $5 million settlement. The widow hired additional legal help from attorney Robert Gordon, who also handled the Janis Joplin estate.

"This is not my favorite case, to say the least," Gordon told the Marin County probate judge he was appearing before. "It has made my life miserable from time to time, being involved in this estate."

Everybody in the Dead camp felt the same way. They wished it would go away quietly, but, of course, it would not. One of the prime principles of the band had been to never publicly air private beefs. It was written in the code of the Dead. Mountain Girl squaring off in court with Deborah Koons Garcia in an unseemly battle over filthy lucre violated every aspect of that long-held code. It was a classic Grateful Dead catastrophe. This kind of public exposure added more trauma to an already severely injured group.

To make matters more ridiculous, the entire proceedings were selected for daily broadcast by the surging cable TV outlet Court TV, one year after splashing the O. J. Simpson trial across cable TV franchises over the country—a nightmare for the Dead. The Simpson media circus was a pivotal event in the culture, and the Court TV broadcast had established the new channel as a certified phenomenon of cable television, treating actual trials like sports events complete with play-by-play announcers, color commentators, and halftime interviews. Court TV decided *Garcia vs. Garcia* would be perfect fare for their audience.

On December 11, 1996, at the Frank Lloyd Wright–designed Marin County Courthouse, the show got under way. Mountain Girl, who didn't know the proceedings were going to be broadcast until she walked into court that first morning, sat next to her lawyers directly opposite the camera, which was positioned above the defense table. Deborah sat beneath the camera and rarely appeared in the shot. She invariably looked composed in black pantsuit and a single strand of pearls. Gray-haired, wearing no makeup, MG sat glumly and stiffly in the camera's glare, never fully comfortable. On the stand, she cried reading a love letter from Jerry, only to have that emotional moment undermined later, when, under cross-examination, she was forced to admit the letter was written many years before she had indicated.

Garcia had met Mountain Girl when she was the nineteen-year-old mother of Ken Kesey's daughter Sunshine (Kesey, the best-selling author and LSD evangelist, had other children with his wife Faye—it was the sixties). She moved in with Garcia at the band's Haight-Ashbury headquarters in 1966. She and Garcia lived together on and off through the seventies and had two daughters of their own, Annabelle and Trixie. By the time they were married by a Buddhist minister between sets backstage at a Dead concert on New Year's Eve in 1981, they were living apart. The marriage served to formalize their family relationship. In 1986, when Garcia awoke from a diabetic coma that nearly killed him, MG was by his bedside, and he moved back in with her and the girls for his yearlong convalescence. Despite the unconventional nature of their relationship and his many other women, nobody in Dead circles doubted the central role Mountain Girl played in his life.

At issue was a homemade, thirteen-line divorce settlement agreement Garcia signed in 1993 that promised to pay Mountain Girl the sum of $5 million over the course of twenty years. He had made eighteen monthly payments before he died and the widow stopped the checks.

The defense position was that the marriage was a scam to avoid taxes, not a real marriage, and the divorce agreement was not even a proper contract. Attorneys for the estate painted Garcia as drug-addled and nonconfrontational by nature, an easy target for manipulation by Mountain Girl and her lawyer. In her turn on the stand, Koons Garcia admitted that not only did she and Garcia maintain separate residences during their marriage, but, after first insisting she took no money from her husband, she also eventually acknowledged she extracted a monthly payment from him marginally larger than the one he paid his ex-wife.

Such tawdry personal details of the lives of the Grateful Dead had never been aired in public before. The Dead always saw themselves as an outlaw bunch. They identified with motorcycle gangs, Native American tribes, cowboys riding the range in the Wild West. Living in the spirit of sixties communalism, the Dead managed to stand by the creed of the counterculture long after that phase had passed from most of the rest of society.

While other members of the Woodstock Nation had quickly been transformed by the so-called Me Decade of the seventies into responsible, taxpaying, semi-upright citizens, the Dead had negotiated their own terms to a surprising degree. They continued to live the hippie dream, and even though band members now earned millions of dollars, owned their own homes, and were raising families, they stayed true to their original code. They distrusted businessmen. Most of their managers had been either visionaries or con men and most of their money had disappeared in the process. They met Cameron Sears, who had handled their affairs as much as anyone since 1987, when he was their guide on a white-water river boating expedition. They weren't looking for expertise, they were looking for heart. As long as they could sell out football stadiums and baseball parks, there was enough cash flow to support the illusion.

The economic impact of Garcia's death had already been made abundantly obvious to the band members, but now the strain on the philosophic underpinnings of the Dead would also begin to show, many years after the exigencies of real life had imposed similar compromises with reality on San Francisco hippie-rock compatriots such as Jefferson Airplane, Quicksilver Messenger Service, and Big Brother and the Holding Company. Those bubbles had burst long ago.

The defense went right after the Dead's code of silence, beginning with Phil Lesh, who took the witness stand wearing sneakers, jeans, a canvas jacket, and a smirk. Lesh played it like the cocky kid in the principal's office. A reluctant witness—from his choice of dress to his cavalier attitude on the stand to his wry answers to questioning—he

was still adhering to the Grateful Dead playbook. He gave the proceedings the absolute minimum amount of seriousness required.

Lesh said that he didn't remember seeing Mountain Girl on tour
with the band during the eighties, despite her testimony to the con-
trary ("I went as much as I could," she had said). He also allowed his
memory might not be the best. "Those were hazy years," he said. He
was asked about Jerry Garcia.

"He was a cool dude," Lesh said with a grin.

Asked to elaborate, Lesh said, "How much time do you have?"

He testified that Garcia failed to mention getting married to MG.
"Jerry and I never really talked about his private life," Lesh said. "It
was none of my business."

The attorney asked if Lesh considered Mountain Girl to be a
bully. "I am familiar with that component of her personality," he
said. "None of Jerry's women had exactly been shrinking violets."

Under cross-examination, when Lesh was questioned again about
his recollections from the eighties, he repeated that his memory
wasn't clear. "From this period?" asked the attorney.

"Any period," said Lesh. "The last thirty years are one smoky
haze." The courtroom broke into laughter.

In contrast, Steve Parish took his role seriously as Falstaff to the
Grateful Dead. Parish showed up in protest, dressed in a dark blue
blazer, charcoal gray slacks, and tie. He was openly antagonistic at
the prospect of testifying. Nobody believed in the code more than
Parish. He had been plucked off the sidewalk outside the Fillmore
West and added to the band's road crew in 1969. He stood guard at
Garcia's dressing room door for thirty years. His fierce loyalty went
unquestioned. The large, genial ex–New Yorker was as hard driving
a rock-and-roll cowboy as the West ever saw. He knew the Grateful
Dead had their own rules and he lived by them. He looked ill at ease,
but he was not slyly sarcastic like Lesh. Parish was openly combative.

He had gone to Koons Garcia personally and begged her not to
have him testify. He had never so much as given an interview, never
helped anyone writing a book. He had not once violated the sanctity
of his unspoken oath. The defense had taken Parish's deposition,
but they were not prepared for his testimony in court. "I told you to

leave me alone—I want nothing to do with this unseemly affair," he snapped at the defense attorney. "Is that so difficult to understand?"

"Did you say if I put you on the stand you would hurt my case?" the estate attorney asked. The judge cut off this line of questioning before Parish could reply and stipulated that Parish was "a reluctant witness."

The attorney next asked Parish whom he had discussed the case with. "My wife," said Parish. "A girl named Linda . . . A guy named Billy, a guy named Dick. This is big. Everyone in the Grateful Dead is talking about this."

Agitated, Parish tried to explain the unconventional nature of Garcia's relationship with Mountain Girl. He understood they weren't Ozzie and Harriet. "We didn't play by the marriage game," Parish said. "At that time, it wasn't a priority for us. We were pretty much an artistic bunch. We weren't living by normal rules."

Another one of the key points of the estate's case—that Garcia's lawyer was more Mountain Girl's lawyer than his—Parish swatted down like a fly. When the defense attorney contended that Parish had said that, Parish exploded. "Why would I say that?" Parish said. "Sir, I would never say that. It's absurd."

Then Parish undermined the defense's entire case by recalling under direct examination a conversation with Garcia the night he married Mountain Girl.

"I asked him what he had been doing backstage and he told me he was getting married," Parish said. "I asked him why would he want to do something like that. He said 'I love Mountain Girl and I've got to square up my taxes,'" Parish told the court.

On cross-examination, Parish threw further wrenches in the Koons Garcia case by testifying he wouldn't be surprised if Phil Lesh never saw Carolyn Garcia at concerts because Lesh always came late and didn't mingle with the guests. Parish shifted awkwardly in his seat, no more comfortable under cross-examination than he was under direct, but the damage had been done.

After a fourteen-day trial, the judge returned his decision January 14, 1997, on behalf of Carolyn Adams Garcia, ordering the Garcia estate, managed by his widow, to pay her the rest of the five million as well as her legal fees and court costs. She eventually settled for $1.2 million. It was a victory for Mountain Girl and her daughters, but in many important ways, the verdict was beside the point. The caustic side effects of such a public airing of laundry were both immediate and long-term. The painful trial caused Trixie Garcia, one of the guitarist's four daughters, to vow never to marry a rock star. "It's better to play it safe, and low key, and have a good quality of life, than to amass a large fortune and a lot of fame," she said.

But the real fallout from the trial was to the code the Grateful Dead had lived by for thirty years. The one tenet they all knew and followed, like musketeers, all for one and one for all, turned out to be one of the first things to go. In a fit of ancient resentments and greed, in one major fell swoop, it had been destroyed.

5

Furthur II

RATDOG CONSUMED Bob Weir. After more than fifty shows with Johnnie Johnson on piano, Weir began to chafe at the restrictions. Johnson was strictly a blues and boogie player—one of the greats—but he couldn't get his head around the more exotic chordings in some of the Dead material. In December 1996, Weir brought on board a second keyboard player named Mookie Siegel, while finally starting to sprinkle RatDog sets with old Dead staples. He added "Sugar Magnolia" and a couple of other judicious entries to the RatDog songbook, but not without trepidation and careful consideration. In December, feeling the need of an additional soloist, he brought twenty-nine-year-old saxophonist Dave Ellis into the band. A lead guitarist was still out of the question.

Weir and Wasserman first heard Ellis play when they went to watch RatDog drummer Jay Lane perform with the Charlie Hunter Trio, a group of strictly jazz musicians twenty years younger. Guitarist Hunter had been discovered and recorded by Les Claypool, the electric bassist and bandleader of Primus, the iconoclastic funk/punk/metal hybrid rock trio with whom Jay Lane had been working prior to joining RatDog. Claypool released the Hunter Trio's debut recording on his own Prawn Song label in 1993. Hunter was an immediate sensation on the progressive jazz scene, using his custom-made eight-string guitar, simultaneously playing bass lines and guitar parts. Weir and Wasserman were taken with both Ellis and Hunter.

Ellis was a different kind of musician for the Dead crowd. Not only did he graduate from Berklee School of Music in Boston, but Ellis was also a product of the same multiracial Berkeley High School jazz department that had produced upstart jazz red-hots such as Joshua Redman, Benny Green, and Peter Apfelbaum. In high school, Ellis held a jazz snob's contempt for the music of the Grateful Dead and knew nothing about it. His entire career had been acted out in the relatively provincial world of the Bay Area jazz scene and, once he hit the road as a member of RatDog, he felt like a rookie at the Super Bowl.

With RatDog about to mark the band's hundredth show in less than two years and despite his initial reluctance, Weir was consciously evolving his relationship with the audience, clearly trying to make the music more appealing to the Deadheads. He enthused about expanding the repertoire on a freewheeling radio interview with broadcaster David Gans on his KPFA show, *Dead to the World,* in May 1997.

"There are a number of those tunes that I am not altogether prepared to live the rest of my life without playing," he said. "There'll be a few more of 'em; in fact, there'll be a bunch more of 'em. Also there'll be a bunch of new material as well."

Weir made the radio appearance in part to promote an upcoming May 28 benefit at the Warfield Theatre in San Francisco, where he planned to be joined by slide guitarist Bonnie Raitt and harmonica ace Charlie Musselwhite. The show would be the final appearance by seventy-three-year-old Johnson, who would be departing for at least the duration of the summer tour. His bad back was not going to hold up for sixty days on a bus. The benefit would also be the first appearance in the Dead world by a keyboardist who would replace Mookie Siegel and find an enduring role for himself in the Dead's music, another young jazz musician recommended by Dave Ellis named Jeff Chimenti.

Also for the first time, Weir brought a lead guitarist—a forty-four-year-old black man with dreads from Berkeley named Stan Franks.

Franks first turned up at Weir's house with saxophonist David Murray, who had been recruited to work on Weir's Satchel Paige project several years before. Weir had put a lot of time and money in the enterprise, and the American Musical Theater Festival in Philadelphia had commissioned *Satchel*, the planned musical about the outrageous star baseball pitcher of the Negro Leagues in the thirties, and expected the debut to take place next year.

The whole thing started on a Mexican vacation a few years before when Weir fell into a conversation in a bar with a screenwriter. Weir had just read a newspaper article about Paige, a legendary black baseball player and showman who spent the most productive years of his fabled career playing in the segregated leagues before Jackie Robinson. The screenwriter convinced Weir to write about Paige and he returned home to start working with Marin County music business associate Michael Nash on a song titled "The Ballad of Satchel Paige." Weir soon decided Paige was more than a song and began to envision the project as a stage musical. He dispatched Nash across the country to videotape interviews with surviving Negro League veterans and assemble a research library on the topic. He brought in bluesman Taj Mahal to work on the songs in sessions at Weir's home studio.

It was Taj who brought along jazzman David Murray, another Berkeley jazz prodigy who had gone on to become a founding member of the World Saxophone Quartet and a mainstay of the downtown avant-garde New York jazz scene in the eighties, playing with far-out musicians such as Anthony Braxton, James "Blood" Ulmer, and Henry Threadgill. Weir brought Murray onstage to play a set with the Dead at Madison Square Garden in 1993 and, the following year, the band's philanthropic arm, the Rex Foundation, gave Murray their $10,000 annual Ralph J. Gleason Award. Weir made a guest appearance on Murray's 1996 album of Grateful Dead material, *Dark Star*, and both Lesh and Weir joined Murray on the title track of his album when his band played the Fillmore Auditorium in March 1997. Murray had known Stan Franks since he brought down the house in fifth grade playing guitar at the school assembly and took him over to Weir's to play on some of the *Satchel* songs. Weir thought Franks was fun to play with.

That summer's second Furthur Festival, while not exactly a disaster, could have hardly been encouraging. With RatDog and Mickey Hart's Planet Drum—the Mystery Box band minus the singing sisters from Jamaica, the Mint Juleps—returning, the Deadcentric program would be preserved, along with their sometime bandmate Bruce Hornsby. The Airplane's Jorma Kaukonen was back from the previous summer, this time without bassist Jack Casady and their Hot Tuna unit. A representative of the new generation of jam bands emerging on the scene called moe. and a young black female fiddler named Sherry Jackson opened the seven-hour shows. Arlo Guthrie of "Alice's Restaurant" acted as a kind of host in between acts and did a set of his own.

RatDog did a regulation rock band set and Weir and Wasserman took the stage for a nightly acoustic jam. The Black Crowes, a Southern jam band that may have been more influenced by the Rolling Stones than the Grateful Dead, were the titular headliners, a bewildering selection that made even less sense as the tour wore on. Even with the Otis Redding song "Hard to Handle" in both bands' repertoires, the Crowes were musically, chemically, and spiritually remote from the Dead scene. Their willingness to jam seemed to be the major common ground. As with the previous Furthur Festival, members of all the bands made guest appearances on each other's sets throughout the program and came back together at the end of the Crowes' anticlimactic set for a half-hour jam.

These shows were not greeted with the same enthusiasm as the previous summer. Deadheads were still grumbling about RatDog's un-Dead set from the first tour, and nobody cared about seeing the Black Crowes. Some of the early dates on the East Coast were especially lightly attended, but sales picked up as word spread. The Deadheads who did show up were still grieving, at loose ends. There was an awkward atmosphere, a slightly forced sense of these people wanting to come together, wanting to continue the annual migration, but not sure entirely how to proceed. The musicians and crew were also still in something of a state of shock, rolling in a fog through their grueling concert schedule, modest circumstances, and uncertain futures. Although word had yet to filter out through the jungle tom-toms, Weir was now playing almost entire sets of material from the Dead with RatDog, and he and Wasserman were further exploring the catalog during their half-hour acoustic performance, where they were invariably joined by other cast members. Still, amphitheaters more than half full were rare.

Tensions spread from the front office to backstage. At the Raleigh, North Carolina, stop the first week, Mickey Hart told manager Cameron Sears he didn't want to see Weir on his bus that night. In the middle of Hart's spaghetti dinner, however, Weir climbed aboard Hart's bus and started making his way down the aisle. "Don't you RatDog this band," shouted Hart.

Weir unceremoniously dumped Hart's plate of spaghetti on his lap. Judo black-belt Hart leaped out of his seat, slapped a quick move on his erstwhile bandmate, threw him down to the floor—"You understand that I love you," he told Weir—and escorted him off the bus. Nobody said a word.

The next night was an off night in Virginia Beach, and Hart sent a room service spaghetti dinner to Weir and his girlfriend, Natascha. "I love you more than spaghetti," read the note. When he joined them for the dinner, they sat down talking like nothing had ever happened the night before. Brothers will fight.

The Crowes came with bad habits of their own. Dropping by the band's trailer with his girlfriend to discuss that evening's jam session, Weir found himself in the middle of a *Pulp Fiction* revival of an overdose victim. It didn't take long for Weir to commence to revisit his own bad habits from the past.

Robert Hunter joined the troupe for a few dates on the West Coast. At Shoreline Amphitheatre in Mountain View—as close to San Francisco as the tour would get—Hunter rattled off a pitchy but heartfelt half-dozen songs, accompanying his off-key vocals on acoustic guitar. Backstage after, he was enraged with himself for not hitting the notes, while Hart chuckled at Hunter's frustration. Later that afternoon, Bruce Hornsby coaxed all the extant Dead on site onto the stage during his set—Weir, Hart, and Phil Lesh. With Bonnie Raitt on bottleneck guitar, they ripped through an inspired version of the Dead staple "Jack Straw" that left all involved ecstatic. "Ooh-wee," exulted Raitt as she left the stage having blasted molten steel into her guitar solo on the song. "I was in the Dead."

Phil Lesh watched all this with benign amusement. Joining the Furthur scene at Shoreline and playing "Dark Star" at the Fillmore with David Murray were the only times Lesh had played music in public all year. He had long since given up on producing a new Grateful Dead record, although he did spend some time combing the archives to assemble a release on Grateful Dead Records, which had turned into a gold mine after Garcia's death. He contemplated a long-held project—a symphonic piece based on instrumental themes drawn from Grateful Dead music to be called "Keys to the Rain."

For so long, he had been the bitter, drunken, and neglected member of the band until he met his wife Jillspeth Johnson in 1981, a waitress at his morning breakfast restaurant, the Station Café, in San Rafael, where the whole band liked to eat. She sobered him up, brushed him off, and polished him up. They lived the hippie rock-star dream in the exclusive Marin County enclave of Ross, raising their two sons, Grahame and Brian, ages nine and six when Garcia died. Since 1990, after being diagnosed with the incurable hepatitis C, Lesh had cut out drinking and become a vegetarian. Still, his health was precarious. Touring had become tough. He was glad to be off that merry-go-round, but he couldn't really find purchase in his new life as a stay-at-home dad and house husband.

During the band's lifetime, the members of the Grateful Dead had mixed feelings and a decidedly complicated relationship with their fans. While the Deadheads often presumed that the band members were just like they were, the musicians had no such idea. Despite their devotion, the view from the Dead and their crew ranged from bemused confusion to thinly veiled contempt for the unwashed hippies who followed them from town to town. They simply didn't understand them. "Stay away from the kelp dancers," Mountain Girl always warned her children at the concerts.

As a result, they paid little attention to the parking lot scene and the sprawling Deadhead culture in their wake and had no idea how pervasive it had truly become. Off the road for the first time in his adult life, Lesh watched with growing fascination the determined Deadhead response to Garcia's death. They would not let this community they so identified with perish. He slowly began to glimpse the full breadth of the band's impact on its following and began to think about ways he could find a place for himself there.

In September, Lesh accepted an invitation from David Gans of radio's *Grateful Dead Hour* to join him and his band, the Broken Angels, at a little Deadhead scene Gans had been developing in a small club called the Ashkenaz, a uniquely Berkeley multicultural establishment that featured folk dancing and fruit juice. Lesh had been casually jamming privately with Gans for some time, feeling the need to get back up to speed on the bass and missing that connection between musicians. For the past year, Gans and his revolving cast of guest musicians had been practicing what Gans liked to call the musical vocabulary of the Grateful Dead every week, drawing an enthusiastic audience glad to pull together their community again, even on this modest scale.

It was not an altogether new idea. The Zen Tricksters, one of the first of the tribute bands, had been playing Dead covers since 1979 around Long Island and had only recently broken out in metropolitan New York through appearances at the Tribeca nightclub called Wetlands that was catering to the Deadhead crowd. The Dark Star Orchestra was a Chicago-based outfit that caught on quickly, performing entire shows from the Dead archives song by song with a remarkable Garcia imitator named John Kadlecik in 1997. Cubensis, another tribute band, started in Los Angeles the same year.

Lesh, whose wife was out of town, only let Gans know he would be attending that morning, arriving by himself. Lesh and Gans stood in the back watching the first set. It was Lesh's first time hearing Grateful Dead music from the audience. He was stunned. He stared as the audience danced and Gans narrated the scene. The Grateful Dead is a language that many people speak, he told Lesh. There was a recognizable style that could be isolated, distilled, repurposed. It was a brief conversation, but for Lesh it was nothing short of a revelation. "This is really something," he said.

In front of this casual, small audience with Gans and his semi-professional musicians, Lesh felt comfortable enough to sit in with the band and jam on a few songs. The place went crazy. Lesh not only strapped on his bass and joined the band for most of the rest of the first set, he agreed to appear with Gans's band again and to allow it to be advertised. With that inducement, Gans was able to move to the two-thousand-capacity Maritime Hall in San Francisco, an upstairs former union hall that drew such a resolute hippie crowd that the smell of marijuana and body odor filled the hallways outside. In November, a packed house danced to Dead songs by an augmented edition of Broken Angels including their distinguished guest bassist, who played two complete sets with the band before retiring from the third. Lesh phoned Gans the following morning to compliment the musicians. He was captivated.

Lesh went back to the Maritime Hall with another idea. He had been thinking about this Deadhead community spirit and wanted to try to figure a way to harness it. With Christmas coming up, he booked the hall in December 1997 for what he called "Philharmonia" as a kickoff benefit for the new philanthropic charity he and his wife were launching, the Unbroken Chain Foundation. Jill Lesh had tried to join the board of the Grateful Dead's charity, the Rex Foundation, while Garcia was still alive, but was turned down. Lesh was furious and wrote to the other band members, "If you don't love my wife, you don't love me." Much had happened since then, but the Leshes never forgot the snub. In a further step away from the band, the Leshes were now starting their own foundation.

Lesh's novel idea was to gather a group of his musician friends onstage, hand out lyric sheets to the audience, and hold a Christmas carol community sing-along. With Bob Weir, Mickey Hart, Bruce Hornsby, Graham Nash, Edie Brickell, even Michael Tilson Thomas from the San Francisco Symphony in the choir, the show was an instant sellout with scalpers asking $100 for tickets outside in the pouring rain. "People like to see us just standing together," Mickey Hart told the *San Francisco Chronicle*. "We don't even have to play music."

With sponsorship from the Hilton Hotel arranged by a close friend of Jill Lesh's who worked there as an executive, the after-party moved to the Hilton, where the Broken Angels took the bandstand with Lesh, Weir, Hornsby, and others. Weir and Hart, emboldened by the congeniality of the evening, suggested to Lesh he join them on tour next summer. "I'd love to go out with you guys," Lesh told the astonished pair, "but instead of some forty-five-minute jam at the end of seven hours, why don't we make a real band of it?"

6

Phil and Friends

Phil and Friends

P HIL AND Friends made their debut February 27, 1998, at the Fillmore Auditorium, site of so many epochal evenings for the Grateful Dead. For the occasion, Lesh simply borrowed RatDog—Weir and all—and added a lead guitarist, Weir's friend Stan Franks. It was a calculated return to performing by Lesh, who, assuming the role of bandleader, had never been a bandleader before in his career.

Lesh only picked up the bass in the first place to join the Grateful Dead at the suggestion of Jerry Garcia. He had not even been in a rock band before. He was a classical music nerd who played violin in the Youth Symphony before switching to trumpet.

In the Dead, he was never a major songwriter or much of a lead vocalist. His wheezy, pitchy vocals were always an issue with the band. But as an instrumentalist, he made a considerable contribution to the band's sound. Jack Casady of the Airplane, who arrived in San Francisco having played Fender bass in rhythm and blues bands around the tri-city area of Baltimore, Philadelphia, and Washington, DC, for years, watched Lesh impressively learn the instrument on bandstands they shared and was astonished at what he saw.

Classically-trained Lesh pioneered a personal style on the instrument that employed a lot of the contrapuntal underpinnings he learned from Bach. Rather than concentrating on rounding off the bottom end, Lesh was constantly orchestrating the band from the lower ranges. But he never acted as the front man or took center stage. Although not without personal charm, Lesh was not a natural entertainer or a charismatic personality.

Now encountering Grateful Dead music through the Broken Angels, Lesh was like a fresh convert. He had finally and irrevocably discovered the power of their music, the language, as Gans described it. Pumped, he had played two more exploratory shows a month apart with Gans's sprawling, revolving repertory company.

In January at the Fillmore, Gans had brought a raucous cross-section of local musicians to a feverish capacity crowd. Jazz vocalist Kitty Margolis sang "Friend of the Devil." Steel guitarist Joe Gold-mark added the twang. Vince Welnick joined the fray. As he routinely did, Gans videotaped the show. He did not realize the rules had changed, the taper code was no longer in effect, and now he was required to ask permission of the Leshes before making decisions. When the Leshes discovered the videotape, they cut off Gans without a word. He never heard from Lesh again.

Lesh was beginning to see the light. He quickly understood the Dead in new terms. Unlike Weir, Lesh was not a musician seeking to express himself in some meaningful personal way. Lesh was responding to his discovery of the demand for Grateful Dead music. But it wasn't simply the songbook; it was a community built around the music. People didn't want to give it up just because Garcia was gone. Lesh had seen what he needed to see.

Also unlike Weir, he was not conflicted about the legacy. He could play the psychedelic classics even the Dead hadn't touched for years. He could use the songbook for even longer improvisations. The idea of using a rotating cast meant each performance was a unique event, adding another level of improvisation to the enterprise.

Lesh knew he needed a lead guitarist and he wasn't hung up about it. He had played with Stan Franks and Weir when they sat in with saxophonist David Murray and did "Dark Star" at the Fillmore the previous March. At that strange gig, Murray and his three jazz horn players were set up on one side of the stage, with Lesh, Weir, and Franks arrayed on the other side. To Lesh, it sounded like two different bands playing the same song at the same time, entirely different approaches that never blended, a dizzying cacophony that didn't resolve. But both Lesh and Weir had been blown away by Franks that night.

David Murray grew up down the street in Berkeley from Franks, who was the first talented musician Murray ever knew. When they formed their first band in junior high, the Notations of Soul, Stan had already recorded a folk version of "When the Saints Go Marchin' In" for a local hootenanny album when he was twelve years old. He went to Berkeley High School before the jazz program was established that produced Dave Ellis and so many other young jazz musicians, but later he played frequently with Berkeley High classmate Peter Apfelbaum and the Hieroglyphics Ensemble, a landmark maverick jazz unit.

He tended toward the challenging and exotic, never restricting himself to one kind of music. Playing behind a local Filipino group called Maharika, he opened for the Jackson Five at the Oakland Coliseum. He played reggae with the Caribbean All-Stars, an East Bay band, and was one of the first Americans to appear at Jamaica's Reggae Sunsplash, where he backed vocal group the Mighty Diamonds. He dipped into the rising hipster jazz scene around San Francisco's Up & Down Club, where Dave Ellis and Jeff Chimenti also played. He played on the platinum debut album by his friend, rapper Tupac Shakur, and taught heavy metal guitar at Cazadero Music Camp. He didn't appear on Murray's record of Grateful Dead compositions, but he played in the band touring behind the release.

Franks, who grew up poor, rejected the starving artist life. A quintessential Berkeley proletariat artist, Franks was married—his wife worked as a photographer—and they were raising a family. He managed a modest stock portfolio, loved to cook, and was a skilled organic gardener. He owned a small apartment building that he bought with hard-earned money he scrupulously saved and, in addition to playing music, always worked steadily at home maintenance and car repair. Franks was an extremely self-reliant, well-liked, grounded man who had spent years improvising on guitar in a variety of contexts. He certainly was anything but just another rock guitarslinger.

Franks proved inspiring in rehearsals and convincing both musically and personally. He was easy to be around, a forthright, loose guy who could interpret the Garcia parts, not mimic them. That would be too creepy for the band—they wanted a fresh, live musician who could make his own voice work in their music. The presence of Jerry Garcia was so powerfully embedded in the music there would be no way to make him disappear. They needed another interpretation of Garcia, a virtuoso with his own voice, someone not afraid to be his own man, yet who could understand and respect the legacy. Franks appeared to be exactly that guy.

In February at the Fillmore for the first Phil and Friends show, the music bubbled up out of the dark from a gaggle of squawks and squeaks and an unlikely belch of Coltrane from Dave Ellis on saxophone, as the band tumbled into "Hell in a Bucket" with Weir on vocals, Franks fumbling around in the background with some wah-wah effects. The second song, "Sugaree," with Lesh taking the lead vocal, found Franks loosening up, starting to unpack his sound, zigzagging across the loping beat. With every song, he grew stronger, more confident.

And what a set list. Lesh dragged out songs fans thought they would never hear again, like "The Other One" or "Dark Star," with Franks trying out some of his avant-garde jazz moves where the Dead would have resorted to space-rock noise. He began to assert himself on the material. By the time the concert was two and a half hours in, Franks was coaxing rolling waves of electric flames out of his guitar, crashing down on the finale "Not Fade Away."

Back behind the amp, Garcia's roadie Steve Parish felt the hairs on his arms standing on end. "We found another one," he thought. The audience showered applause on Franks when Lesh introduced him and the band retreated to the dressing room, collapsing in a happy, sweaty, triumphant celebration.

Three days later, the next summer Furthur tour was announced. Instead of a repertory company this year, however, the bill would be topped by a band called the Other Ones featuring three of the four of the living Dead men. Taking the Garcia guitar chair would be the unknown Stan Franks, along with Dave Ellis, Jeff Chimenti, and Bruce Hornsby drummer John Molo (Kreutzmann would be sitting out this tour). The six-week, twenty-five-city tour would start in June. The musicians were coming to terms with the Dead's music. "I put it away," Mickey Hart told *The Chronicle*. "When it was over, it was over—for everybody, I think. Nobody was thinking about Grateful Dead music."

Weir praised Franks, acknowledging he would be taking on a hot seat. "He's a wonderful guitar player, " said Weir. "He's also nothing like Jerry, which is, I think, the exact right place to look. The only way he is reminiscent of Jerry is that he's wide open. He is willing to and capable of exploring any direction."

They showed up at Bel Marin Keys in Novato and rehearsed daily. All this was new to Franks—the facility, the staff, the equipment. As Franks struggled to learn the massive amount of material, especially the country-and-western-oriented pieces, and the starting date of the tour loomed closer, he began to falter. Just coming up to speed on the vast, diverse repertoire, which, on any given night, could touch on blues, jazz, country, folk, and rock, was a Herculean task. Also, the Grateful Dead was no nursery school; Franks would not be coddled. But he made friends easily.

He converted the usually suspicious Parish to a strong ally and friend. Weir thought they had made the right choice and Lesh had agreed. But with a fragile power balance among the surviving members and so much at stake, Franks was pretty much on his own. If circumstances had been even slightly different, if Franks had had the chance to learn the catalog without the immense pressure of looming deadlines and pervasive grief, if he had had the luxury of organically incorporating his style into the milieu of the band, the casting of this jazz musician might have been the most inspired decision the band made since Garcia died. They wanted Stan to be Stan and Franks wouldn't have had it any other way, but he was trying to replace the irreplaceable Jerry Garcia. Perhaps he was bound to fail.

The next Phil and Friends show in March featured Lesh, Franks, and a completely different lineup. In April, on his third Phil and

Friends show, Franks joined Lesh, Weir, Hornsby, and drummer Molo (with saxophonist Branford Marsalis) at the Warfield less than six weeks before they were scheduled to go out on the road as the Other Ones. By then, Franks was struggling with the repertoire and not getting the support from his bandmates that he needed. He was a nervous wreck at rehearsals. He froze, frustrating the band.

When Franks wasn't there, Lesh was wondering aloud if they had made the right choice. Every day frustration grew. Everybody knew what was happening, but it wasn't until Mickey Hart returned to town from the Planet Drum tour and joined the Other Ones rehearsals that Franks's fate became clear to everyone. Hart, who may have been somewhat distracted by having Molo in the drum chair since the beginning of the Other Ones rehearsals, did not seem to jive with the new guitarist. He tersely suggested to Franks he play more like Garcia.

"I'm not going to play like no dead guy," said Franks.

On May 15, Franks backed up Weir with Wasserman and Hart at Wavy Gravy's annual SEVA benefit at the Berkeley Community Theater (Lesh joined David Crosby for a few numbers at the same show), but it was clear he wasn't working out. Stan Franks was a genius local musician and a gentleman who was suddenly drafted into the big leagues, but the band didn't have the time or inclination to break him in. When he couldn't duplicate his first night's performance on cue, the end was near and his downfall abrupt. It wasn't long after that Weir called Franks with the bad news. Weir was upset, but Lesh no longer supported Franks and Hart was also against him. Franks was disappointed, but not devastated. He had seen it coming in the final days. He went back to work on his apartments the next day.

With less than a month now before the first concert, the band hurriedly held auditions for the guitar job.

The last time the Grateful Dead auditioned for a new member was after Brent Mydland's death in 1990, when they hired Vince Welnick. The position paid big money. The Dead gave the new keyboard player full participation in revenue. They could have scouted the entire world of rock for the highest levels of talent, but that is not how the Dead do things. They checked their phone books and called the five piano players around Marin County they knew (having played in the same band for so long, the members of the Dead didn't know a lot of other musicians) and tried them out over the course of two days.

Similarly, when Garcia died, the names of a lot of famous guitarists were floated as possible replacements—Carlos Santana, Neil Young, Jorma Kaukonen, David Hidalgo, Mark Knopfler. When the surviving members finally got around to hiring a new guitarist more than two and a half years later, none of the four guitarists who tried out had anything like a national reputation. Tony Gilkyson was the closest to qualify; he belonged to the highly regarded, modestly successful Los Angeles country-rock group Lone Justice and worked for ten years with a latter-era version of the Los Angeles punk rock band X.

Oddly, the most obvious choice was Steve Kimock, little known outside Dead circles around Northern California as lead guitarist for Zero, a band that always counted many Deadheads in their crowds. He could play so much like Garcia, without exactly imitating him, it could be spooky. It is not that they sounded alike; they were guitarists who thought alike. Zero was a psychedelic instrumental band Kimock cofounded that worked around the Bay Area during the eighties featuring Quicksilver Messenger Service guitarist John Cippolina, one of Garcia's peers from the dancehall days of the San Francisco scene.

A quote from Garcia during an interview with a guitar magazine calling Kimock one of his favorite unknown guitarists would dog Kimock for years, as if Garcia had somehow anointed him. Yet, although they had many friends and musical associates in common— Martin Fierro, Merl Saunders—Kimock didn't really know any of the Dead members personally besides Garcia. The audition would be the first time he ever played with them. Kimock came the second day after all the other candidates had come and gone. He thought he blew the audition. He didn't know the material. He made no attempt to have anything prepared. He thought he sounded like shit and left thinking he couldn't have been more lame. The Dead don't like front-runners anyway.

The least likely candidate was Lauren Ellis. Remembering the version of "Jack Straw" the band had played with Bonnie Raitt at Shoreline, John Molo suggested they try this female blues slide player from an all-girl r&b band, the Scarletts, that he knew from the Los

Angeles nightclub scene. Ironically, the forty-two-year-old Ellis grew up in Marin County and dropped acid as a teenager at Grateful Dead concerts only to be certain Jerry was spending the entire evening playing just to her. She had moved to Los Angeles with her boyfriend, ex-Monkee Peter Tork, and was working on her own music when Molo called and told her the band was thinking about going in a different direction. She was astonished by the call, eager to take the shot.

Ellis didn't even spend the night. She caught a flight from Burbank to Oakland in the morning, rented a car, and drove across the bay to the Novato headquarters for her four-hour session. They played "Sugar Magnolia." They did "Friend of the Devil." She sang a little with them. Ellis found it challenging to make the slide guitar sing in the Dead sound, but she gave it her best.

When Ellis left, waiting outside for the next session was another little-known player from Los Angeles the band brought up, Mark Karan. Although Karan also grew up in Marin and dropped acid at Dead shows at Winterland, he had been living since 1990 in Los Angeles doing utility guitar work where he could. He was currently playing dates with Dave Mason. While he had been living in the Bay Area, he had bounced around various nowhere bands without brushing up against even the middle time. He had never met any of the guys from the Dead before, let alone played with them.

They did "Sugar Magnolia," "The Other One," "Friend of the Devil," songs Karan knew from his days following the band. He felt quite comfortable with the music, but couldn't read the reception. Phil Lesh seemed especially cool, but it was Lesh who sought Karan out after the session when he had gone out into the front office to talk business with Cameron Sears. "I just wanted to thank you," Lesh told Karan. "We weren't sure this could still be fun and you just reminded us."

After Karan was offered the job, Lesh went home and told his wife Jill, who said that she and her Deadhead girlfriends all wanted Kimock to get the nod. Lesh grew concerned about creating discontent in Deadhead circles and decided Kimock needed to be included, but Weir remained adamant about not using someone who sounded so much like Garcia. The first day Karan arrived for rehearsal, Lesh was not there. He had left word that he would not be coming until Kimock was included. Kimock was summoned.

The rehearsals were not without tension. The next day, Karan, Kimock, Chimenti, Dave Ellis, and Molo, the hired hands, sat in the studio while the partners quarreled in the control booth. As these band meetings became more frequent, the sidemen took to passing the time by holding little jam sessions, which Hornsby would frequently sneak out and join. Hart intimidated Ellis, telling him about his hatred of the saxophone that went back to his days in marching bands. The two new guitarists eyed each other uneasily. Lesh was tired, his health poor. He didn't say much and would have to lie down from time to time. There was a huge amount of material to go through in a short time. Hart could be either a cheerleader or critic with equal intensity. He cut Karan short rehearsing "St. Stephen," after Karan protested that he had tried to play the part like Garcia.

"Yeah, well, Jerry isn't here now, is he?" Hart said.

Without a designated bandleader to direct traffic, rehearsals tended to revolve around the lead vocalist of the song being practiced. Lesh was a generally encouraging presence, but it was Weir, who could be extraordinarily spacey and unmoored in his personal life, who always seemed to know where he was in the music. He was not a dogmatic conductor or bandleader, but he often knew the territory when those around him were lost. Even then, he didn't necessarily try to keep his hands on the wheel. The subject of what to do with "Playing in the Band" came up.

Hart: Hey, Bob, I thought we were starting in the zone.

Weir: No. Here's the plan. I've had this straight all along, but I haven't been able to get it across to anyone.

Lesh: We were doing it the other way the other day.

Weir: No, no, Phil. We started at the end because we figured let's do "Playing in the Band" because we haven't done that yet, but the fact is, in actuality, we will have done it, you see?

Hart: I see. But I don't see.

Weir: Here's the deal. For maximum impact, to give all those screaming hippies out there something to love, what we're going to do is we're going to do "Playing in the Band" and in the minor part of the jam, we're going to go into "Baba Jingo."

Hart: Bob, may I? The first time we started this, we started it there . . . in an atmosphere, what Bruce calls "world music." Then we went into some things and then you brought "Playing in the Band" out. Then we went from "Playing in the Band" into the solo section and then into the minor section.

Weir: OK, fine.

Hart: That's the way we did it the other day and it seemed to work.

Weir: OK, fine.

Hart: You mind doing it that way, Bob?

Weir: No, that's actually a better way to do it.

Two nights later, June 4, ready or not, the Other Ones took it out of the rehearsal hall to a high-priced benefit for rain forest relief before a capacity crowd of excited but wary Deadheads at the Warfield Theatre in San Francisco. A little more than three hours later, the verdict was in: the good times were back. The Other Ones were attempting to emerge from the Grateful Dead with some identity of their own. They brought new material, Rob Wasserman's "Easy Answers" and "Banyan Tree," from Weir and Hart with lyrics by Hunter. They did Hornsby's songs. Hornsby ably handled Garcia's vocals. They resurrected "Mountains of the Moon" after a forty-year absence from the repertoire. For the first time in Dead history, there was a jazz component in the band, although Ellis and Hornsby could quote Coltrane's "A Love Supreme" and nobody else on the bandstand would know what was going on. Instead of opening shows as the Dead did with regulation-length songs, the Other Ones stretched everything they played out to the ten-minute mark and beyond. The "St. Stephen/ The Other One/Lovelight" suite lasted almost thirty minutes by itself.

The third official Furthur Festival tour opened three weeks later in front of a half-capacity crowd at Lakewood Amphitheater in Atlanta with Rusted Root and Hot Tuna on the bill. The band sounded great and the next night they played the hell out of "St. Stephen," a fan favorite seldom featured in the Dead's concert repertoire. Word went out on the Deadhead grapevine. The next show at Nissan Pavilion in

Bristow, Virginia, was sold out with ecstatic Deadheads. For the first time since Garcia died, shows went clean throughout the tour and, with expenses down and ticket prices up, the band members made some serious money, which they all needed.

The band was enthusiastically received by the Deadheads, even if the three-guitar lineup often made for traffic jams onstage and a lot of the fans shared Mickey Hart's distaste for saxophone. Karan, perhaps understandably nervous on the bandstand, may have been somewhat less inspirational on lead guitar by Grateful Dead standards, but he was a diligent craftsman. Kimock was a crew nut who liked to hang out with the roadies. He rode on their bus with them, went to the shows early to watch them build the stage, and always set up his own gear. During the shows, he sat on a stool, often barefoot, and largely ignored the audience, but his playing could spark imaginative turns in the jams. With the in-ear monitor system allowing for individual mixes, Kimock thought most of the musicians were turning themselves up in the headsets and not listening to each other. There may have been some truth in that; Hart said he always heard Garcia in his deaf left ear when they played. Although Lesh's ill health dogged him, ashen-faced and looking cadaverous at thirty pounds underweight, he played great. The tour proved more taxing than he imagined, and he and Jill Lesh kept largely to themselves.

The Other Ones rolled into Shoreline Amphitheatre in Mountain View July 24–25 for the final two dates of the triumphant tour. A drunken Billy Kreutzmann showed up for the first night. Hart handed him an African hand drum and he tottered onstage during the first few numbers of the opening set, returning in the middle of the show to take over Molo's drum kit for "Iko Iko." He was surly and disheveled, fresh off the islands. It wasn't some joyful, jolly reunion. Kreutzmann sulked around backstage feeling like a stranger who didn't belong. They didn't even put his hand drumming in the mix.

Never one of the most sensitive of men, Kreutzmann had come largely unwound in the wake of Garcia's death. In his case, his father died only a few weeks after Garcia. They had become close and his father had moved to Mendocino to be near Billy. In the next few months, Kreutzmann would divorce his wife, enter rehab, and move to Kauai without so much as a drum kit, all before the first Grateful Dead Productions board meeting after Garcia's death. Kreutzmann smothered his pain surfing, scuba diving, fishing, and growing pineapples on the north shore on Hawaii's most tropical island. He consciously avoided contact with his old bandmates.

Before the end of the year, however, he was playing small gigs around the island with a couple of local musicians, jamming on Dead songs and calling themselves Backbone, enjoying his local celebrity in dive bars around the islands. But Kreutzmann was still a mess. In December 1997, he had been arrested and jailed in Kauai on a domestic violence beef. He was not going through a happy period. Hanging out backstage at Shoreline didn't make him sentimental.

The next night, a couple of hours before the final show, tour coproducer John Scher was summoned to the Leshes' trailer backstage. He listened in utter disbelief as Lesh and his wife laid down a set of demands that must be met if the other members ever wanted Phil to play with them again. They had been furious about Cameron Sears participating as both a tour producer and band manager of the first Furthur tour—accused him of essentially double-dipping the band— even though Lesh was not even playing on that tour and presumably they didn't have a dog in that race. At Shoreline, they told Scher that they wanted to renegotiate the division of tour proceeds, which, of course, had been agreed to before the tour began. The Leshes insisted that Bruce Hornsby be paid as a sideman not a partner. They wanted Cameron paid wages like a Grateful Dead Productions employee, not a partnership in tour revenues he was due as coproducer. They further demanded that Scher tell the others of their demands before they went onstage that night.

Scher was astonished. He did not see this coming. Lesh had been largely isolated with his wife during the tour, but they had been an uncomplaining, agreeable presence. Having worked with the Dead for thirty years, Scher had known Lesh since they were both young men. He could see that the tour was wearing Lesh down. He figured Lesh and his wife were largely keeping to themselves because of Lesh's health issues and didn't realize there was any quarrel between them and the rest of the band. This came as an unwelcome surprise.

With a sour feeling in his stomach, Scher assembled the rest of the band in another nearby trailer and laid out the Leshes' demands. Their reactions were predictable. Hornsby dismissed it as bullshit. Hart was more forceful. He called it crazy and said so bluntly. Weir was incredulous. There had been no preamble, no hint of dissatisfaction, no discussion between the long-standing bandmates. With only one show left, the tour had been a huge success from every viewpoint—musically, financially, consumer satisfaction—which may have caught the Leshes by surprise. They may have anticipated a more tepid response and modest earnings along the lines of the previous two summer tours. But the Other Ones had worked out much better than anyone expected. It had likely begun to occur to Phil and Jill Lesh that the only difference was Lesh himself. Phil Lesh, who had always felt underappreciated in the Grateful Dead, now had proof of his value. Without him, the amphitheaters had been half-full. He could now claim his due.

But, much like a baseball team that argues in the locker room and hits the field united against their opponent, the four men took the stage with their band that night and, for two hours, put aside their feelings and played music. Hot Tuna guitarist Jorma Kaukonen joined the band on the set-closing "Lovelight" for a little Fillmore homecoming and Weir brought everything to a close in a rare encore: "Playing in the Band" into "Touch of Gray," the exclamatory chorus "I will survive" ringing almost dolefully in the chilly night air at Shoreline as the concert—and the tour—came to an end.

The phone lines buzzed continually the next week. Lesh called Sears repeatedly, who could clearly hear Jill Lesh piping up in the background. Nobody saw any reason to concede to any of the Leshes' demands and didn't particularly take his threats seriously. All appeared well enough when Lesh resumed his monthly Phil and Friends shows August 7–8, two weeks after the tour ended, in two sold-out shows at the Fillmore with a band that was essentially a streamlined version of the Other Ones—Weir, Kimock, Chimenti, and Ellis with drummer Prairie Prince from Todd Rundgren's band.

Everything took a sudden, drastic turn on September 8, when Lesh was having dinner with his two children. Jill Lesh was at a meeting. Lesh became suddenly, violently ill at the dinner table, vomiting blood and falling off his chair. As his vision turned gray and his hearing dimmed, he glimpsed the horrified faces of his two young sons looking down on him and flashed on five-year-old Jerry Garcia watching his father drown. He was rushed to Marin General Hospital, where Garcia had been taken when he went into a coma in 1986. In a haunting echo, band members and their families gathered around his bedside. Everybody was stricken, anxious, deeply concerned. Bob Weir, usually unsentimental about death, looked at Lesh's gaunt, gray face and thought another one was gone.

Lesh had experienced a massive blocking of the vein in his liver and had, indeed, almost died. His hepatitis C had brought him to this—he now had end-stage liver disease and needed a transplant to live.

For the next three months, he worked his way up the waiting list for a liver at Stanford Medical Center and stayed close to home. It did not look promising. He was surrounded with support from the Dead family. Sears's assistant Jan Simmons closed her office door and cried after she heard the news of his diagnosis. In a hospital room at Stanford University, Steve Parish sat with Lesh and watched the old black-and-white Preston Sturges movie *The Great McGinty*. Peter McQuaid, whose star inside the Dead world was rising alongside the gross revenues at Grateful Dead Merchandise, accompanied the Leshes to tests at UCLA.

Lesh was strong enough to take his family to go see Bruce Hornsby play an Oakland jazz club called Yoshi's in November and he returned to the club over the weekend with Kimock to play with Hornsby. They did a few Dead tunes and a couple of Hornsby numbers. Lesh had a date on hold for December at the Fillmore for his next Phil and Friends show, but he was notified of a liver donor before he could do the show.

Weir, realizing the gravity of the situation and looking at the possibility of losing another band member, had sprung into action. His pregnant fiancée Natascha's father, Dr. Manfred Muenter, was chief of neurology at the Mayo Clinic in Arizona. Weir called his future father-in-law and explained Lesh's situation. Dr. Muenter expedited Lesh's admission at the clinic's Florida location, and, in December, a liver was found, saving his life. Weir was never sure if Lesh even knew he had made that call.

As if that wasn't enough, about the same time Jill Lesh was diagnosed with thyroid cancer. Since her condition was less urgent, her surgery was postponed until they dealt with Phil's crisis. These were desperate times for the seriously ill parents of two young children. They clung together all the more tightly.

The weekend before he and his family left for Florida, Deadheads organized "Five Minutes for Phil" over the Internet, the rapidly emerging communications tool that was becoming widely adopted by Dead fans. These fans planned a nationwide, coordinated prayer circle for Lesh—a gathering of the vibes. At the appointed time, Lesh and his wife went out and sat down on their front porch only to be, as Lesh later described, almost physically knocked over by the wave of psychic energy that swept over them. Four days later, December 17, surgeons at the Mayo Clinic in Jacksonville, Florida, performed a liver transplant on Lesh, giving him an organ from a teenager named Cody from Arizona killed in a car crash.

Three days after his surgery, his wife Jill wheeled him out the hospital front door to see the sunset. Lesh broke down at the sight. After months of secretly thinking he would not see many more sunsets, he was flooded with gratitude. The ordeal was over. He would live to see his children grown. He wept in thanks and relief that his life had been spared to witness such simple but profound beauty. Back from the brink of death, he determined he would live the rest of his life in the moment, without concern for the past or the future, on his own terms.

7

Grateful Dead Merchandise

W HEN REAL estate investor Neil Cumsky went looking for
venture capital money for Terrapin Station, it was not
surprising that he would find his way to hippie tech investor Roger
McNamee of Silver Lake Partners. Not only was McNamee playing
one of the hottest hands in Silicon Valley, but he led a part-time rock
band called the Flying Other Brothers, a psychedelic rock group that
grew out of late-night jam sessions at tech conventions.

At age forty-three, long-haired McNamee was already a figure of
considerable repute in the tech investment world. In the late eighties,
as a tech analyst at T. Rowe Price in Baltimore, McNamee managed
the top-performing tech fund in the country and led daring but immensely successful venture investments in Electronic Arts and Sybase.
He relocated to California in 1991 and immediately established himself as an outspoken Valley visionary, founding three groundbreaking
tech funds, Integral Capital Partners, Silver Lake Partners, and Elevation Partners.

What Cumsky didn't know was that McNamee was also a fiercely
dedicated front-of-the-house Deadhead with two hundred shows under his belt. He had never met any members of the band or even set

foot backstage, but he had played music his entire life and followed the Dead since he was a kid in upstate New York.

In fall 1998, McNamee cautiously received Cumsky's business plan and asked to speak to someone directly affiliated with the band; Cumsky introduced McNamee to Peter McQuaid of Grateful Dead Productions, who extended an invitation to meet with the band and their advisors at the Novato headquarters. Phil Lesh, awaiting his transplant, was receptive to McNamee, enthusiastic even, but the rest were more skeptical. After meeting with the band, McNamee and Bob Weir held another session on a couple of stools before the entire staff and crew and underwent a thorough grilling. After McNamee was able to establish his Deadhead bona fides, the skeptics in the crowd calmed, but when Ram Rod and Parish showed up at his band's next gig to help with the load-in, McNamee knew he had been accepted on an important if unspoken level.

McNamee's standing in the financial or tech world didn't impress them and this bunch didn't care for outsiders. Essentially all the band wanted to know was why they should trust him. McNamee told them he knew nothing about real estate, but the Internet was something he did understand and the Dead's little www.dead.net was already a huge success—the largest platform for direct-to-fan commerce in the world—even though its underlying technology was created not by a software engineer but by a member of the crew, who had operated it for a 10 percent commission. That may have seemed like nothing when he started but had mushroomed into serious money.

The Internet was about four years into mainstream acceptance at this point. Amazon had established the concept of cyber-retail, although the widespread advent of downloading audio on mp3 files was still off in the near future. Since the very beginning of the World Wide Web, Deadheads have been at the center. The Well, the Internet's first practicing bulletin board and social network, was essentially the realm of Deadheads. The Internet Underground Music Archive (IUMA) was an outgrowth of the tape-trading culture fostered by the band's most avid fans since the seventies and the first site to host a vast music library on the Net containing thousands of recordings of Dead concerts. Dead lyricist John Perry Barlow founded the Electronic Freedom Foundation, the first digital rights group, in 1990 after being visited by an FBI agent in regard to some hacking issue and realizing the agent knew far less than he did about the technology. The first news post on Yahoo was the death of Garcia, which happened the same day as the IPO for Netscape, the first popular Web browser.

Since Garcia's death, business at Grateful Dead Merchandise had gone through the roof. In the fall of 1995, GDM operators handled more than twenty-two thousand calls in one day amidst the flood of orders. The next year the band made $50 million without touring. There were displays of Dead merchandise in Best Buy stores and Deadhead basketball star Bill Walton could be seen hawking Dead wares on cable television.

Peter McQuaid, a former Merchant Marine whose previous relevant experience was working for his brother who ran fan clubs for rock groups like Journey and others, had come aboard to head Grateful Dead Merchandise in 1992. The company had released two CD packages from their archive. The first, *One from the Vault*, had sold more than 150,000 copies and the second release had done nearly as well, but finicky Phil Lesh had declared those two the only recordings of high enough quality for release. McQuaid had to bring a box of substandard bootlegs to convince the audio-conscious band that the recordings already circulating were far inferior to the tapes in the Vault before they would dig back into their vast collection of live recordings, warts and all, to give the fans what they wanted.

In a small windowless, climate-controlled, heavily alarmed room behind the control booth in the band's rehearsal hall, industrial shelves held rows and rows of tape recordings collected over the years by Dead sound men and women, beginning with Augustus Owsley Stanley III, the LSD king and early audio pioneer with the Dead.

The importance of Stanley—known universally in Dead circles as Bear—to the Dead cannot be overstated. Not only was he the first private party to synthesize LSD and produced the first perhaps million doses circulated to the public, he also provided the material for the acid tests, financed the band with his LSD revenue during the earliest days, and was a prime contributor to the whole concept of the Grateful Dead.

As the band's original audio expert, Owsley instituted the unheard-of practice of recording the Dead's live performances early in the band's career. Almost all the 2,314 shows in the band's history were routinely recorded, and the archive had been adroitly indexed and curated by Dead tape archivist Dick Latvala since the mid-eighties. The Grateful Dead archives, known to one and all as the Vault, was a literal King Solomon's Mine in rock-and-roll tape collections.

In 1992, the first in the CD series *Dick's Picks*, named after archivist Latvala, who was producing the releases, sold like crazy, available only through mail order from the band. They had released a second set by the time Garcia died, but after that, Grateful Dead Merchandise accelerated the release schedule, pumping out three new Vault releases a year, and they were all selling. *Dick's Picks* sold a million records in the first three years after Garcia died and that was direct to fans by mail order, no middleman, all proceeds to the band. The warehouse at Novato frequently shipped more than a thousand packages a day. In a music industry about to undergo a radical transformation in the marketplace, this direct-to-fan merchandising was revolutionary.

With touring income gone, this unexpected gold mine turned into a welcome bonanza. The merchandise wing published a quarterly catalog that included $190 silk tour jackets, $120 sunglasses, "Workingman's" briefcases, even sets of skis painted with the skull and roses. Liquid Blue, a T-shirt manufacturer the band plucked out of the parking lots at their concerts selling bootlegs in the late eighties, was putting $4 million worth of T-shirts and such into retail outlets every year without the Dead touring.

Bewildered band members would look at proposed designs of dancing bears on clothing and other merchandise and wonder why anyone would buy something so silly, much less wear it. They may not have understood it, but they allowed McQuaid to turn bootleggers into partners, a brilliant subversion of the gray market around Dead shows. The band only went into the T-shirt business on their own after being convinced they were giving up $250,000 every show in missed revenue (the last year the band toured, they made $50 million in ticket sales and $35 million in merchandise). Now Grateful Dead Merchandise had become the tail that wagged the dog. While gross revenues may have gone down, the net income grew. This was a miracle nobody saw coming that could save the organization. The two business entities—Grateful Dead Productions, the touring/band management arm, and the merchandise operation—were merged, and McQuaid replaced Cameron Sears as CEO of GDP, although Sears remained as manager of Weir and RatDog.

The nonstop wildfire of merchandise sales was one of the key factors encouraging the development of the Terrapin Station museum project. In January 1998, the band unveiled the plans in lengthy articles in the *New York Times* and *San Francisco Chronicle*. They hired one of the city's top architects, Cathy Simon of the firm Simon Martin-Vegue Winklestein Moris, and her firm completed an exciting, attractive preliminary design. Simon was responsible for the extraordinary transformation of San Francisco's grand but largely abandoned Ferry Building into a thriving open market and community center, one of the city's leading tourist attractions from the day it opened. Rick Abelson continued to direct the Terrapin Station project, although he had little experience with constructing a building. Weir and Lesh would attend meetings at the architect's downtown San Francisco office. Weir, who would often lean against windowsills throughout the meetings, demanded a *feng shui* consultant for the project. He liked the idea of having a roller coaster on the roof. Naturally, everything the band especially liked about the project cost a lot of money and produced little revenue. Cumsky pushed to add some income-producing condominiums to the plan (to be called "Mars Hotel"— they even trademarked the term).

The project organizers had been seeking a real estate developer partner and taken a big-shot magnate down to Shoreline Amphitheatre to see the Other Ones. He brought along his son but regretted it immediately. The man was horrified at the rampant, open drug use and declined the opportunity. They went looking for investors elsewhere. The representatives for the band held meetings with city officials and were looking at two properties seriously, while still exploring other possibilities. At this stage, the venture had been easily financed with the band's own funds through sales of one limited-edition CD set from the Vault.

McNamee spent many hours meeting with band members, equivalent to more than a day a week for six months. In the early days, most of the interaction was with Phil Lesh, whose thoughtful and business-like approach to the Terrapin Station project was appealing. McNamee concluded that he did not have the skills to help the band succeed with a massive real estate project, but he was in a great position to help the band grow its technology-driven mail-order business. The technology underlying Dead.net needed a massive upgrade, and the band needed to decide if it wanted to finance that investment or work with outsiders. Either way, McNamee thought the best strategy was to make the Dead.net platform available to other bands for a fee.

The Dead were so far ahead of the pack in the emerging field of e-commerce that getting partners would be relatively straightforward. If the band were willing to go for the brass ring, it could take in outside capital, federate its platform to other bands, and create a uniquely valuable Web commerce platform that might one day lead to a public offering of stock. This kind of business strategy McNamee was uniquely qualified to lead.

He finally addressed a board meeting with his proposal. He would come to work with the band one day a week pro bono—and, in 1999, with the Internet and tech investments going through the roof, McNamee's time couldn't have been more valuable—on two conditions: (1) the Vault must never be sold and (2) no fighting among band members. McNamee, a tie-dyed-in-the-wool Deadhead, saw the Vault as a national treasure. The band had envisioned some kind of access to the tapes for fans at Terrapin Station in a room devoted to listening stations, but at this point, the mining of the collection by *Dick's Picks* was tremendously successful, with no sign of slowing down. There proved to be such a large percentage of Deadheads who wanted to acquire everything the band released, it didn't seem to matter how widely circulated a tape of a concert had been; fans wanted to buy the band's official version of even the most common Dead tapes.

McNamee went to work developing the Dead's Internet strategy, driving an hour or more up Highway 101 one day a week to work out of the Novato headquarters. He understood that the Dead had already created a superior model for direct relations with their fans. Phone orders were answered by operators saying "Grateful Dead," giving the fans the assurance they were dealing directly with the band. Also aware of the powerful new attribute of the Internet to facilitate community, McNamee realized the unique opportunity the Dead had to create an even more cohesive network of followers.

Almost since the beginning of the band's history, the Dead have sought autonomy in their business dealings, the exact kind of independence and freedom the Internet offered. They started Grateful Dead Records in 1973. They sent newsletters and demo discs of new releases to members of the Deadhead fan club. They built their own sound company, guitar shop, even travel agency. They pioneered their own ticket sales. They created their own merchandizing business and their own Web commerce platform. With his experience in all things tech and with a unique understanding of its role in society, McNamee was the ideal ambassador for keeping the Grateful Dead relevant in the digital domain.

Creating a wide-ranging role for the band on the rapidly emerging Internet with a state-of-the-art platform, McNamee wanted to streamline ticket and merchandise sales and expand the band's direct connection with the fans. He also wanted to enlist other bands into a super site for rock bands. McNamee called the project Bandwagon, a comprehensive site for many bands, led by the innovative Grateful Dead. Between this inside link with Silicon Valley and the visionary museum project, the Dead appeared to be harnessing the future as the century ended.

. . . . . .

In April 1999, just over six months after he collapsed on his dining room floor near death, and four months after a liver transplant, Phil Lesh, the formerly retired bass player, went back on the stage with another new Phil and Friends in San Francisco. For such a momentous comeback after this huge turning point in his life, Lesh needed to make a statement. Early in his recuperation, he called Steve Kimock, Lesh's choice for lead guitar in the Other Ones, and Kimock came over and played music with him, helping Lesh find the groove again. Kimock was a guitar monk who didn't have a car or even an apartment of his own. Joining the Other Ones meant he had to come in from the cold with the IRS as a tax outlaw because he had never made enough money before to file taxes and the government had taken most of what he earned that summer. Kimock didn't care; he was there for the music. Lesh could use Kimock as his pocket Garcia, but his reentry had to be grand, had to serve notice. He had been lying back, studying Deadhead culture, taking notes and making plans. To complete this auspicious inaugural version of Phil and Friends he invited the two princes of jam-band America—guitarist Trey Anastasio and keyboardist Page McConnell of Phish.

Emerging from the rock underground, Phish was, at that moment, reaching a kind of critical mass in the culture. When Garcia died, the Vermont-based rock quartet had already been selling out concerts at Madison Square Garden and other East Coast basketball arenas, but after Garcia's death, the band shifted into another jet stream. In the absence of the Grateful Dead, Phish became a fevered obsession across a large demographic of college-aged fans. They even got their own Ben and Jerry's ice cream flavor, Phish Food, following in the illustrious footsteps of Cherry Garcia, anointing them in the popular culture.

Phish's popular breakthrough represented the emergence of this new generation of jam bands that had been stirring in the underground beneath the shadow of the Dead for some time at little preserves like the Wetlands in New York City. Quietly, without many who didn't belong to the scene noticing, this pocket of the music world had been scraping along for years, slowly building a solid yet loyal constituency whose tastes ran the gamut from world beat Afropop to guitar-heavy Southern blues-rock.

Even while the Dead were still active, a younger generation of jam bands had begun to define this scene on their own. Banding together for a summer 1992 amphitheater trek called the H.O.R.D.E. tour (Horizons of Rock Developing Everywhere), Phish was part of

a daylong program that included contemporaries such as Blues Traveler, Spin Doctors, Widespread Panic, and Col. Bruce Hampton and
the Aquarium Rescue Unit. These were a new raft of jam bands with
one thing in common—a fundamental admiration of the Grateful
Dead and dedication to their spirit of improvisation.

Phish, determined to create their own identity in the jam-band
scene, had long been wary of specific Dead associations and consciously steered away from any connection to the band. They had begun life as something of a Dead cover band, but in 1986, deliberately
decided to no longer play Dead songs. In August 1998, on the third
anniversary of Garcia's death, the band did play the Dead's "Terrapin
Station" during an encore, and in the weeks before coming to California to rehearse with Lesh and play the Warfield Theatre shows,
Anastasio tried out an acoustic version of "Row Jimmy" with his solo
band in a small club in Vermont. Tapped by Lesh to accompany
him on his return to performing, the two Phish men, Anastasio and
McConnell, were thrilled. Lesh's invitation was a kind of ultimate ac-
knowledgment of their own trajectory, being invited to participate in
what would be a jam-band summit meeting and certainly a keystone
performance in the career of the original Grateful Dead bassist.

At the Warfield, Lesh and Kimock came out in front of the curtain to open the show, trailed by Lesh's sons, Grahame, thirteen, and
Brian, ten, whom their father introduced to the crowd as "my best
friends." They added little choirboy harmonies to Lesh singing the
sentimental Eric Clapton song "Hello Old Friend," which Lesh plural-
ized to "Friends" for the occasion. Bringing out his kids was the exact
sort of show business stunt the Dead always assiduously avoided.

Turning on a dime, Lesh parted the curtain and cranked up the
electric rock band portion of the program flat-out with a thirty-plus-
minute version of "Viola Lee Blues," a song the Dead had not performed in the past thirty years. More interesting is that Lesh had
transformed the cornerstone track from the band's 1967 debut album
into a sleek, reconfigured platform for an entirely different kind of
jam than usually associated with the number, allowing Kimock to
lead the piece into spacey, atonal sonic pastures and omitting the
classic dramatic return to the final chorus that used to blow minds

at the Fillmore and Winterland. Phil and Phriends—as it was spelled on the marquee—took it straight into the zone right out of the gate. It was a sensational show that mingled some Phish material amidst reimagined Dead classics, such as an epic Afrobeat-propelled "Uncle John's Band," a walloping "Going Down the Road Feeling Bad," and an ecstatic "Not Fade Away."

The next night, Lesh dusted off "Alligator" for the first time since Pigpen died and dedicated Pink Floyd's "Wish You Were Here" to Garcia. They opened the third night with a monumental mashup of "Dark Star" and "Days Between." Vocalist Donna Jean Godchaux McKay, who belonged to the Dead during the seventies glory years, joined the band each night. It was during this run that Lesh introduced what came to be called the "Donor Rap," where he appealed to audience members at the end of every show to become organ donors. This speech would become a feature of every subsequent show by the ever-earnest Lesh, grateful not to be dead.

These were wonderful, glorious nights. Phish bassist Mike Gordon cheered his bandmates along from the audience. Deadheads were in heaven with Phil and Phriends. The small theater reverberated with the fans' joy. Not only did the band make the Dead songs come alive again in new and powerful ways, but the entire enterprise shined a light pointing forward. It was joy, but it was also hope. A jazzed-up Lesh spoke afterwards about releasing "every note" of the three nights on a ten-CD set, although that never happened.

Two weeks later, Lesh joined his Other Ones bandmates Bob Weir and Mickey Hart, along with Hart's pal Sammy Hagar, slide guitarist Roy Rogers, and a raft of others, at a benefit that had been organized by Hart's environmental activist wife, Caryl Orbach Hart, in Santa Rosa to save some nearby redwood trees. Nobody knew it at the time, but it would be years before these three would play together again.

Returned to strength, with the vigor of a man with the liver of a teenager, Lesh went on a tear. In May, he took Phil and Friends featuring guitarist Warren Haynes to the Mountain Aire Festival in the Sierra Nevada gold country, another familiar Grateful Dead hunting ground. Haynes, a longtime associate of the Allman Brothers, would prove to be one of the most enduring and crucial of Lesh's musical collaborators. In June, Lesh returned to the Warfield with yet another lineup featuring Jefferson Airplane guitarist Jorma Kaukonen with Kimock and, again, in July with the David Nelson Band—longtime Dead associate from the New Riders of the Purple Sage—with guest Bill Kreutzmann on drums.

Lesh kept Kimock on guitar and Molo on drums, but he was swapping around bands like he was trying on different suits of clothes, drawing from different camps of the jam world—Allman Brothers, Hot Tuna, New Riders. He was testing out the material in different contexts.

In August, he was offered his first real out-of-town Phil and Friends opportunities, eight Western amphitheater dates as part of a repertory company called "Summer Sessions 99" featuring jam bands Gov't Mule, String Cheese Incident, moe., and Galactic. Jonathan Levine, a booking agent for Monterey Peninsula Artists, the agency that also represented Phish, heard about the Phil and Phriends shows at the Warfield and made a cold call to the Lesh household. Since they had no manager or agent, he made the arrangements with Lesh's wife, Jill. Lesh took Kimock and drummer Molo and pulled his other Friends for the occasions from the different bands on the bill.

"I discovered this massive pool of musicians out there who love the Dead's material and get off playing it whenever they can," Lesh told the *Denver Post* in advance of the show at Red Rocks Amphitheatre. "I'm trying to tap into that concept of treating it as repertoire material, and finding new doors, as it were, from these guys and myself."

While they still used Cameron Sears at the office to make and take calls on their behalf, the business strategy behind Phil Lesh's career began to emanate more and more directly from his wife, who finally underwent her thyroid cancer surgery in June. With Lesh absent from his official duties and the office more frequently, McQuaid would often volunteer to take copies of minutes or other documents over to his house. Explaining his absence from the office and meetings, Lesh complained about the stress, so McQuaid would show up, only to find his wife acting as a surrogate. Interestingly, Jan Simmons had run into Jill at the baby shower for Natascha Muenter (Weir's future wife) in late 1997 before Lesh's transplant. Simmons had left the

Dead office to go to work with Deborah Santana, the wife of the lead guitarist, who had started managing her husband's affairs. During the conversation, Simmons couldn't help but notice that when Jill realized that Carlos Santana's wife was officially acting as his manager, her eyes lit up.

Shortly after Garcia died, Lesh expressed an interest in serving as chairman of GDP and was given the post. He was closely overseeing the Dead's reissue program, deeply involved in Terrapin Station, and initially supportive of the Bandwagon project at the time, not playing music with Phil and Friends. The band's business advisors had difficulties with his obsessive reluctance to sign documents; however, he did chair board meetings and took an active role until his veto power was overruled.

For years, the Dead had operated under unanimous rule. Only policies universally approved by band members would be adopted. In that way, at their eighties peak, Lesh had been able to keep the band from making new studio albums for more than six years, declaring the recording studio too clinical a place to make music, and at a time when the band was playing before stadiums full of fans and demand for their records had never been greater. The other band members finally settled the argument by renting Marin Veterans' Memorial Auditorium, bringing in recording equipment, and recording an album there without an audience. At this, Lesh relented, and the band cut *In the Dark*, the Dead's first million-selling album, in 1987.

After Garcia's passing, the political climate in the GDP boardroom was not so harmonious. In the ongoing debate over Bandwagon, which Lesh had inexplicably started to back away from, the other members finally had enough of Lesh's uncompromising positions. They reluctantly passed a motion placing the board under majority rule, essentially stripping Lesh of his cherished veto power. It only served to strengthen Lesh's resolve. Lesh broke with the other band members openly after the vote. He abruptly stopped attending board meetings. He spoke only infrequently to the other band members, which left him ill-informed on details of projects.

No one, not even other band members, knew the scope of Lesh's alienation since his transplant. The other members had waited for

Lesh's recovery from surgery to plan a summer tour with the Other Ones. Lesh held back, giving excuses for not making a commitment only to decide instead to test-drive Phil and Friends out of town with the eight dates on "Summer Sessions 99." By the time he informed his bandmates of his plans, it was too late for them to mount tours of their own, leaving them without a tour or income for the summer.

Lesh posted a statement on the Dead's Web page: "I enjoyed playing with each and every musician in the Other Ones last year, but the tour was extremely stressful due to business and creative differences. I honored my commitment and made no promises for future shows. After my surgery, I was approached about doing another tour, but it became clear that the same unresolved issues were still haunting us."

At least, that was true for him. The other members were caught off-guard by Lesh's announcement of the divorce. He was asserting his dominance and abandoning even the pretext of all-for-one. He drew a line in the sand. "Everyone was more interested in doing their own thing," Lesh told the *Denver Post*, "so we decided to give it a rest." And he did.

Undaunted, when plans for any Other Ones tour evaporated, Mickey Hart moved ahead. His latest version of his solo group Planet Drum was built around the talented Latin musician Rebeca Mauleón, and everything was splashed in Caribbean and African flavors and rhythms. Mark Karan played guitar. Hart released a new Planet Drum album, *Spirit into Sound*. A book of quotations about rhythm and percussion with the same title was about to be published (his third book as an author). Hart had also been named that May to the board of trustees of the Library of Congress's American Folklife Center. Hart liked to stay busy. He took his new large band on a brief August tour that included a not-so-sentimental stop at Woodstock '99, where Hart and John Entwistle of the Who were the only two veterans of the historic 1969 festival.

As Phil and Friends played their monthly concerts and built up steam in Deadhead circles, Weir, for the first time since Garcia's death three years earlier, retreated from constant touring to the relative obscurity of the recording studio. All year, Weir had been largely buried in the studio with RatDog, playing just a handful of dates and many of those with only bassist Wasserman and drummer Lane. The recording sessions for the debut RatDog album dragged endlessly, as the band and engineers struggled to learn digital recording, moving from pre-production in Weir's home studio to Bel Marin Keys. Mark Karan joined the band after the Other Ones tour, so RatDog finally had a lead guitar. Both Weir's Dead collaborator (and childhood friend) John Perry Barlow and Robert Hunter contributed lyrics, and Weir spent countless hours fiddling with the recordings. He was also drinking heavily again.

Weir felt challenged by Lesh, whose Phil and Friends had abandoned Weir after he had played every show with Lesh's band the first year of its existence. Lost, at first, a competitive spirit soon stirred in his head. He needed to develop a program of his own. Weir thought he could take the advantage by producing a new album of original songs, forging ahead with fresh creative ideas, extending his band's identity, and making a serious effort at establishing RatDog as a recording act. While the Internet was only months away from punching a hole in the record business's bucket, devoting the time to make a credible RatDog album made a certain strategic sense.

And, of all things, he was starting a family. On July 15, he and Natascha were married by a Buddhist minister in the street in front of their house. The fifty-one-year-old groom wore a Scottish kilt and the bride, twenty years younger, was dressed in an antique white gown. She held their year-old daughter, Monet, in her arms through most of the ceremony. John Perry Barlow acted as best man. Bandmates Hart and Lesh were among the forty or so guests. "Three words we thought we'd never hear," said Lesh. "Bob Weir wedding." The party repaired to the Mill Valley Outdoors Art Club—the newlyweds arrived by horse-drawn carriage—to dance to the music of the Dave Ellis Quartet led by the RatDog saxophonist, who managed a jazzy version of "Terrapin Station" for the occasion. Ellis was now well beyond his youthful jazz snobbery.

8

Phylan

STEVE PARISH wasn't sure about going back on the road. When he tried to beg off going out with Phil and Friends, Lesh would have nothing of it. "This is your life," he told Parish. "This is what you do. You'll be fine."

It wasn't that he didn't like Lesh—Parish liked Lesh plenty—but Parish secretly sensed he was still traumatized from the sudden end of the Dead. No roadie in rock had ever been more loyal than Parish was to Garcia. He was like a soldier with shell shock being sent back to the front, although Parish, he-man that he was, banished any doubts and pressed forward.

Lesh was on a roll. Three weeks before setting sail on his band's first serious out-of-town tour opening for Bob Dylan, Lesh wanted to warm up with some October shows by Phil and Friends at the Warfield. For these, Lesh brought out a pair of musicians from a Grateful Dead tribute band that operated largely in and around New York City called the Zen Tricksters—guitarist Jeff Mattson and keyboardist Rob Barraco. The Tricksters had been playing Dead covers since starting out around Long Island in 1978 and, since Garcia's death, had become a hugely popular attraction in Deadhead circles. Lesh didn't know any of this when the two Tricksters showed up in Marin County to rehearse.

In his studies of Deadhead culture, Lesh had been made aware of the tribute bands for the first time and they bothered him. "They're making a living off our music," he often said. Around that time, one of his associates slipped him a CD of the Tricksters doing their own original material. Lesh was impressed with how well they jammed in the studio although he was unaware of their basic premise. They sounded strangely familiar to Lesh's ears. He invited the two soloists to play with him at the Warfield without knowing that the Tricksters were actually one of the best and longest-running Dead tribute bands. During the first rehearsal, Lesh was surprised at how well the two musicians knew the material.

Lesh opened the first of those Warfield shows with a twenty-two-minute version of Van Halen's "Jump." This didn't come as a complete surprise to Barraco and Mattson, who were driving around that week in an extra car of Lesh's and saw the Van Halen cassette lying on the seat, figuring it was something his young boys liked. Lesh was in a highly experimental mood that weekend. He opened the next night with Miles Davis's "Milestones," not exactly a staple of Deadhead repertoire, and did a fifteen-minute version of John Coltrane's "My Favorite Things" during the second set opening night. Lesh was trying to expand the horizons.

Kimock played on all the shows. Since the transplant, he had become Lesh's most trusted musical intimate. Kimock was both an easygoing, genial presence backstage and a valuable, inventive player, a highly original guitarist who could effortlessly evoke a wide range of diverse styles—from Jerry Garcia to John Abercrombie. He could play pristine, almost miniaturist arabesques or go boldly, noisily into the zone. He practiced guitar eight to ten hours a day. He could be commonly seen strolling around backstage, guitar slung over his shoulder, running scales. He had played every Phil and Friends show since Lesh came back.

Growing up in western Pennsylvania, Kimock had never been especially keen on the Dead—he was more of an Allman Brothers fan—but the other guys in his band at the time were such Deadheads, they decided to move to Marin County and Kimock went with them. Almost from his first days in California, he was compared to Garcia, especially after he hooked up with former Dead members Keith and Donna Godchaux and began playing in their Heart of Gold Band in 1980.

After Garcia gave the guitar magazine that quote about Kimock being his favorite unknown guitar player, Kimock knew it was a compliment, but he also felt it was something like a piece of gum stuck to the sole of his shoe. He deliberately began to avoid comparisons, changing equipment, not playing certain songs, finding other voices for his solos, but the association never went away. He was well-known in Dead circles, if nowhere else. He played briefly with Missing Man Formation, keyboardist Vince Welnick's band after Welnick's departure from RatDog.

Phil and Friends were headed out for a month in October, beginning with a three-show weekend at the Denver Fillmore, before hitting the road as opening act on seventeen dates with Dylan through the Midwest and East Coast. To round out his little rhythm section of Molo and Kimock and himself, Lesh invited guitarist Paul Barrere and keyboardist Billy Payne from the fabled Los Angeles rock band Little Feat. Even with extensive rehearsals in Marin, there was too much material for the Little Feat fellows to learn, which meant they were taking music stands onstage and reading sheet music while they played for the first time in their lives.

The weekend in Denver was stressful for Steve Parish and his partner Ram Rod. They hadn't been out on the road in the recent past and neither cared to make excuses for how the strain affected them. Parish was snapping at other crew members, surly to one and all including the Leshes. Jill Lesh was now officially acting as manager and she had opinions on a wide range of production issues, going so far as to include how the equipment should be stowed and unloaded. Parish and Ram Rod looked at Jill Lesh and didn't see a manager. They saw a former waitress who once served them breakfast, but married their boss and now lorded over them, making what they considered uninformed decisions about key touring issues from routing to what was acceptable attire onstage. She banished headbands and other forms of hippie-wear. Parish fumed that Garcia never wore anything for anyone else's pleasure. He didn't bother to control his temper. At the end of the three-night run at Denver, the Leshes presented both with airplane tickets home.

Kimock spotted the pair lingering backstage with the tickets in their hands. He had spent most of his time with the crew, where he felt more at home. Parish was humiliated because he knew he had brought this on himself, but he was also angry. He wanted to cause some trouble. "Are you still making five hundred dollars a week?" he asked Kimock. "Jerry would have paid you five thousand. Go in there and ask what's up with the money."

Kimock had been growing increasingly uncomfortable with the atmosphere surrounding the enterprise. He felt himself being subjected to loyalty tests and subtle inquisitions, and Kimock had no taste for politics. He was there for the music. He had been questioning Jill Lesh making more and more decisions that weren't necessarily hers to make, stepping outside of established protocols, but sending Parish and Ram Rod home seemed like a last straw to the guitar monk. He decided to address his issues with the Leshes and, egged on by Parish, went to their dressing room.

It did not go well. Jill Lesh went into a tirade. After listening to her rant about his lack of respect and loyalty, he left their dressing room. Lesh, who was watching TV, closed the door behind him. Minutes later, Jill Lesh charged into the crew food buffet, still yelling at Kimock, who was standing in the stairwell. She confronted him, enraged, and threw crumpled dollar bills in his shocked face. "You want money?" she said.

Kimock took his gear off the truck, slept with it locked in his room, got up the next day, rented a truck, and drove back to California. A few days later, he left a cryptic post on his Web site:

> *Dear Friends & Family:*
> *We regret to announce that Steve Kimock has chosen to flee the Bob Dylan / Phil Lesh Tour.*
> *We apologize for any inconvenience, pray for your forgiveness, and look forward to your continued support.*

"I ain't gonna work on Maggie's Farm no more . . ."
Signed,
      running & shooting behind him as fast as he can . . .
—Steve Kimock

While most had little difficulty understanding the reference to the Dylan song ("He hands you a nickel, he hands you a dime, he asks if you're having a good time . . ."), the "running & shooting" line was more obscure. When he first contemplated going to work with the guys in the Other Ones, he had consulted Robert Hunter, longtime lyricist for the Grateful Dead who knew Kimock from his songwriting for Kimock's band Zero. "Run," Hunter had told Kimock, "and keep running and keep shooting behind you as fast as you can."

When Parish and Ram Rod returned to Bel Marin Keys, they held a festive barbecue to celebrate their firing. A sign on one of the vans in the lot read "Welcome Home." They fired up the Weber outside the eyesore production trailer that served as their office in the parking lot and entertained the crew and staff. Mickey Hart, who was working in the studio, joined the celebration. Peter McQuaid couldn't help but notice the encroaching rivalry, a fierce divide emerging. There was an us-against-them mentality breaking out beyond the boardroom, he thought.

On the road, the Leshes scrambled to get guitarist Derek Trucks to fly in and join the tour, although he missed the next three dates and Lesh, Molo, and the two Little Feat guys with their music stands had to fend for themselves. Trucks was the twenty-year-old nephew of the Allman Brothers drummer who played a lot of hot Duane Allman licks. The next night, the revolving cast again rotated. The Little Feat guys were gone—replaced by guitarist Warren Haynes and keyboardist Rob Barraco of the Zen Tricksters and the October Warfield run. Jefferson Airplane lead guitarist Jorma Kaukonen also joined the band for the final few dates.

Dylan was a remote presence on the tour. His band would do the sound check without him. His RV would arrive backstage shortly before showtime. He would emerge, walk straight to the stage, play his show, and leave without any further interaction. Dylan was no

stranger to borrowing the Dead's audience. In 1987, when he was at a
low ebb creatively and commercially, he joined forces with the Dead
as his backup band to make a triumphant summer tour of packed
football stadiums he could have never even half-filled on his own.
Dylan was extremely fond of Jerry Garcia and attended the funeral.
He had genuine respect for the Grateful Dead. On the road with the
untried Phil and Friends, from the first night it was clear that the audience was packed with Deadheads; the opening act was pulling its
weight at the box office. By the end of the tour, Dylan was calling out
Lesh to play bass on a Dead tune like "Alabama Getaway." That was
as much jamming as Dylan was going to do.

The same day Lesh started the Dylan tour, RatDog hit the road
until December, a killer thirty-date tour headlining largely three-
thousand-seat theaters and adding more Dead songs to the set almost
every night. The battle of the bands was under way on the road.

Back home behind the scenes, the antagonism between the
band members was boiling up to a horrifying peak, as Lesh chose to
publicly break with the other three over the Bandwagon project, one
of the most promising possibilities the Dead ever contemplated.
McNamee was getting ready to poise the Dead at the forefront of
the Internet explosion. Plans called for participation to be spread
throughout the Dead organization, which would have meant more
than saving jobs; it would have been an investment they all shared.
As venture capitalists met with the band to investigate ways of financing the ambitious undertaking, Lesh got cold feet. He completely ignored, or chose to forget, McNamee's stated insistence
on not putting the Vault on the table. He lashed out at McNamee
and his bandmates in a carefully prepared statement released to
the press in December 1999: "The Grateful Dead have never accepted corporate sponsorship or venture capital money, and I remain unalterably opposed to any deal that would lease, license or
otherwise collateralize the music in the vault," Lesh wrote. "The
Grateful Dead have a history of mismanagement and bad business
decisions, and I fear that this current plan will become the crown
jewel in that collection."

Openly breaking with his band members raised their conflict to a new level of hostility and violated their brotherhood in a new and particularly traumatic way. Lesh had always strictly observed the band's code of silence, even when called to testify in the widows' lawsuit, and for him to take his internal disagreements into the open was evidence of how the principles at the core of the Dead's life for all these years, the basic agreement by which the members lived and worked, had broken down. "This situation is very sad for me on many levels," his statement concluded. "It has brought me to the realization that the Grateful Dead is now only a corporation, with whose directors I no longer share a common vision."

It was the opening public salvo in a simmering feud that had been going on undercover for more than a year. Lesh's outburst caused such a stir among the fans that the other three members felt obligated to post a statement "To the Deadheads" on the band's Web site signed by Weir, Hart, and Kreutzmann: "There has never been— nor will there ever be—any discussion of selling our Vault, our music, our name, our legacy. Not to Microsoft. Not to anyone. The Vault is part of our heart and soul . . . and yours. We're taking steps to preserve it for all time. . . . We have an opportunity to take the lead as music and the Internet converge. Opportunities like this come along very, very rarely."

But the full depth of the acrimony behind the scenes only broke into public view when Mickey Hart gave an unfiltered interview shortly thereafter. "Nobody's at war with Phil," Hart said. "He's just out of the loop. He just hasn't paid attention for years. He's just in the Phil zone, God save him. Nobody pays much attention to him. He's sort of on the outside. He's of no consequence really.

"The Grateful Dead has always worked as a democracy," Hart continued. "Phil's the odd man out. So he took his marbles and split, like a little boy would. That's his prerogative; God bless him, I wish him well. But believe me, we don't miss him. We're having a great time without him. It couldn't be better. If someone doesn't want to play with you, you don't play with them. We have no fight with him; he's sort of at odds with himself. I think that liver transplant didn't go so well. He might have gotten the liver of a jerk."

Hart quickly apologized. Apart from the politically incorrect remark about the organ donor, his comments may have been cold, but they accurately reflected the sentiments of Lesh's bandmates at the time. They were all but entirely alienated. Lesh had concentrated exclusively on his Phil and Friends rehearsals and shows and was entirely absent from company meetings; now he was even out of social contact with the other members. The Terrapin Station project he had once championed had stalled. Cumsky had located an Orange County–based real estate development firm ready to partner. A piece of property had been purchased in mid-1998 in downtown San Francisco, and the architects made some minor adjustments to their existing plans, but Cumsky couldn't get the band to budge. They seemed distracted with their infighting. Frustrated, he gave up trying to get their attention.

Phil and Friends was consuming a tremendous amount of Lesh's time. At the end of the Dylan tour, Lesh had played forty-three shows with thirty-six different musicians. Few of them were that well acquainted with Dead music, which can be complex and challenging and comes with a giant songbook. After spending his life playing the same music with people who all knew the music intimately, Lesh found himself devoting endless hours rehearsing other musicians. After running through five guitarists on the Dylan tour, his next guitarist was yet another unlikely but inspired choice, blues guitarist Robben Ford.

Ford grew up in remote Ukiah, California. As a teenager, he started a blues band with his brothers and backed harmonica ace Charlie Musselwhite. At twenty-three, Ford joined the band behind George Harrison on his 1974 US tour led by saxophonist Tom Scott. He worked with Joni Mitchell and Miles Davis over the course of his long career and made a series of outstanding blues and R&B solo albums. But Lesh had never heard of him when drummer Molo brought up his name. Ford flew up to Marin from his home in Southern California and spent three days jamming with the band. He knew nothing about Grateful Dead music and the job didn't seem to call on his expertise in blues. He knew it wasn't a jazz gig, but he could jam. He loved playing with Molo and found the guitar-oriented music set him free in ways he couldn't have imagined. Ford was astonished at how much fun he had. He told Lesh he was down with whatever he had in mind.

What Lesh had in mind was matching Ford as the surprise guitarist with the two Little Feat guys at his sixtieth-birthday Phil and Friends benefit concert for his Unbroken Chain Foundation in March 2000 at the Henry J. Kaiser Auditorium in Oakland, a particularly sentimental site for Deadheads. Next to Lake Merritt in downtown Oakland, the parking lot and adjacent park were filled once again with the camp followers and itinerant hippies who thronged the place on many grand New Year's Eves past when the Grateful Dead played. It had always been one of the favorites settings for Dead shows, one of the original parking lots. The funky old hall was the scene of some indelible Dead moments, like the year the band rang in the new one with Etta James and the Tower of Power horn section singing "In the Midnight Hour."

In the year since his return to action, Lesh had clearly established the Phil and Friends concept with the Deadheads and grabbed the banner with his fan-friendly repertoire, heavy emphasis on jamming and a rotating cast of guest musicians. Rumors had been flying among the Dead circles, where rumors fly easily, about what guests Phil and Friends would include on this auspicious occasion, his return to Oakland and the first show of the new century—Bob Dylan? Bob Weir? Trey Anastasio? They knew Lesh always kept the Phil and Friends lineups secret until the curtain went up. The Deadheads went along with the game. The parking lot filled up days before the show. The circus was back in town.

At age sixty, every man takes stock of his life. It cannot be avoided. It is a milestone of indisputable proportions; the gateway to old age and the end of youth. One year from a drastic, lifesaving surgery, at the absolute peak of his professional career, for the first time in his life leading his own band that, in less than two years, had grown in popularity to the point where he could now attract crowds that rivaled those drawn by the Dead themselves during the late seventies and early eighties, Phil Lesh had good reason to feel immense pride and deep satisfaction.

At the Kaiser, he was returning to celebrate at the scene of greater glories. He had psychedelic poster artist Stanley Mouse, co-creator of the skull-and-roses logo and so much more Dead emblemology, make a brilliant poster for the concert showing Lesh playing bass astride a giant dragon. He took the stage playing guitar with Mike Gordon of Phish on bass for the first two numbers, before settling into his customary role on the bass. Guitarists Ford and Barrere lit the place on fire, pianist Payne feeding the flames with his piercing, flickering solos, making for what was undoubtedly the most raucous—and least Grateful Dead–like—Phil and Friends yet.

After the concert, for an additional $150, VIPs could attend a reception in the auditorium's upstairs ballroom, where they nibbled expensive desserts and listened to a string quartet play while a bluegrass fiddler sat atop a large wrapped gift box and sang "Box of Rain." Wavy Gravy, the clown prince of Woodstock, dressed as Ludwig van Beethoven, sang "Happy Birthday" to the birthday boy, who was accepting his well-wishers while seated on a king's throne on the stage, as regal as a king without actually wearing a crown.

"Don't eat the brown strudel," warned Gravy.

9

Soul Battle

WHILE THEIR adoring public imagined only a golden circle of love inside the band, it was, in reality, a bitter civil war. They had been able to orbit somewhat peacefully around Garcia, but they always knew peace was tenuous among a group of such dedicated contrarians. After a press conference backstage at UC Berkeley's Greek Theater, where the Dead were celebrating the band's twentieth anniversary in 1985, Phil Lesh was buttonholed by a reporter and asked what he thought was the main reason the band lasted so long. Lesh assumed a mock contemplative pose, hand on chin. "I think we're all waiting for a chance to get even," he said.

He wasn't entirely joking.

Since Garcia died, the dynamics among the guys had changed so many times that nobody knew what to expect any longer. Without Garcia, nobody could find a lasting equilibrium under which the survivors could operate. In those dark days, out of grief and confusion the band let their basic product lapse. They almost deliberately dismantled the brand, making some precipitous, dubious business decisions that would hamper them for years. Retiring the name alone was a completely unnecessary shot-in-the-foot that left the band limping. There was other self-sabotage as well. In the midst of their

own indecision and separate directions, they confused the public, undermined their connection with the most loyal fan base of any rock
band, and did everything they could to destroy their standing in the
marketplace. Even when the surviving members could finally agree
to play music together again three years after Garcia's death, they still
couldn't face using the band's name and came up with the Other
Ones dodge. Nor could they solve the guitar issue.

Without Garcia around to mediate, the four had little in common
other than their fates as members of the Grateful Dead. Even Hart and
Kreutzmann, the drum brothers, could be contemptuous of each other,
as close as they were from all the years of sharing rhythm, psychedelics, and everything else. College graduate Lesh likely looked down
on all three as his intellectual inferiors. Weir could be extraordinarily
instinctual or unbelievably goofy, but he was never entirely grounded.
Plus he had a tendency to drink, sometimes mixing booze with pharmaceuticals, which could make communication difficult. Cast adrift
together, it had become difficult for them to find common purpose,
unified direction, or even a consistently congenial relationship.

Lesh had a long list of beefs with his bandmates, extending back
to rejecting his wife for the Rex Foundation board. Most recently, he
had taken up arms against Bandwagon with a fury. He raged against
McNamee and the suits in Silicon Valley, accused McQuaid of taking bribes from bankers, and told interviewers the other band members wanted to sell the Vault, which was never under consideration.
A serious financing proposal was in negotiation and McNamee was
reaching out to other acts, from the Dave Matthews Band to Pearl
Jam to U2, about joining forces with the Dead on the Internet, but
Lesh's early enthusiasm for the project had turned to an outright
antagonism that no one understood, especially given he was no longer keeping abreast of developments or attending any meetings since
recovering from the liver transplant.

As Lesh's understanding of the Dead culture grew from his experiences in Phil and Friends both with other musicians and the audience, he took bold, definite steps to capture the banner that the
others left where it fell when Garcia died. With RatDog, Weir had

gone looking to find himself. Mickey Hart was really an activist mu-
sicologist whose work was more conceptual art than anything else.
With Phil and Friends, Lesh waved the flag and rallied the troops.
He was willing to super-serve his core audience and they responded
wildly. Hungry for the Dead-like experience Phil and Friends provided, an eager minority of Deadheads embraced the band—and
Lesh's repertory concept, which (kind of) solved the guitar problem—
with breathtaking speed.

Following the smashing success on the Dylan tour, Phil and
Friends were booked into multiple nights in April 2000 at big-city
East Coast theaters where Lesh sold out six shows at New York City's
Beacon Theatre, four nights at Boston's Orpheum Theatre, and three
nights at the Tower Theater in Philadelphia. He was suddenly a cer-
tified attraction.

However close they had been before, since the transplant, Phil
and Jill Lesh were welded together into one. To others who knew
her as the scrupulous, caring mother and calmly supportive wife on
Dead tours, her transformation into fierce music business adminis-
trator and Phil Lesh guard dog came as a surprise. Her steely drive
and cold ambition were a rarity in Dead circles, where such values
were never considered cool. The life-or-death ordeal of Lesh's liver
transplant (not to mention Jill's thyroid cancer surgery) undoubtedly fused their intimacy. Indeed, nobody doubted that the Leshes
spoke as one person. Lesh had frequently sulked in the background
during his time with the Grateful Dead and for years had quietly
nurtured his resentments against his bandmates. He did not want
to suffer fools any longer. After his transplant, he would not. In
the collapse of the long-standing leadership in the Dead world that
followed Garcia's death, Lesh had finally navigated himself into a
position of power. His days of standing in the corner were over. He
clearly decided to take over as master of the legacy, and his wife was
determined for him to have it.

Lesh no doubt thought: who else could it be? He could well
have determined that it couldn't be benighted Bobby Weir, drunken,
dysfunctional, dreamy, and fumbling. Or hardheaded Mickey Hart,
the pseudo-intellectual drummer who was losing his hearing and

couldn't keep time. Brutish Billy Kretuzmann, who was busy picking pineapples and dropping acid in Hawaii? No, Lesh alone was suited to take the lead. Only he could restore the soul of the Grateful Dead.

Lesh had largely cut off his contact with the other band members when he called a meeting at his house. It was a summons, really. Weir and Hart left after a business meeting at Bel Marin Keys with Peter McQuaid. Phil and Jill sat together on their couch, holding hands, fingers entwined. While Phil stayed largely quiet, Jill explained the new world order to her astonished guests.

She began by telling them it was clear that she and Phil now were the protectors of the spirit of the Grateful Dead. The Leshes had become the true champions of the band's legacy. There was no longer any need on their part for further association with the rest of the band. Phil would carry the banner. They would take it from here. Caught up in her fervor, she summarized with a stunning pronouncement. She told the other lifelong members of the original band: "You don't know anything about the Grateful Dead."

Bob Weir exploded off the piano stool, where he had been sitting. He stood up and shouted. "Wait a minute," he said. "How many Grateful Dead shows have you played?"

Usually easygoing and slow-talking, Weir was furious. He had been holding back his anger and resentments toward Lesh for some time. Years actually. Lesh had always been a stumbling block, a sarcastic older brother figure who had not been averse to slapping around teenage Weir in the band's earliest days. If the emergence of Phil and Friends had sparked some competitive impulses with Weir—prodding him into adding a lead guitarist and more Dead songs to RatDog—he had been able to largely ignore Lesh's complaints or at least write them off as the understandable irritability of somebody going through a major health crisis. But this pronouncement from Jill Lesh was something he could no longer ignore.

This was a battle for the soul of the Grateful Dead. Band members' wives did not dictate band policy. Jill had not even come along until the band had been through two of the most tumultuous, creative, and momentous decades of their career. The Dead have long memories. Keyboardist Brent Mydland played in the band for more than ten years and was still "the new guy." For Jill Lesh, the waitress his bandmate married, to lay claim to the mantle of all that Weir had struggled to achieve, the tens of thousands of miles he traveled; the thousands of gigs he played; the blood, sweat, and tears spilled over many long years, was simply not acceptable. He wrote many of the Dead's greatest songs and sang even more. Lesh wrote exactly one of the band's great songs and if Weir had sung it instead of Lesh, "Box of Rain" would be one of the best-remembered Dead songs ever. Listening to Jill's crazy rant made him sick to his stomach. Even more unacceptable was his bandmate sitting beside this upstart, nodding his tacit approval. The meeting ended quickly and badly.

A torrent of mean and angry emails followed, Weir blasting the Leshes in long, passionate letters, even going so far as to blame Jill's thyroid medication for creating a personality disorder. War had broken out into the open.

In June, Lesh headed out on a second Phil and Friends tour with Bob Dylan, this time as co-headliner. The plan called for each act to alternate closing, but after watching Lesh close the first show in Portland to an audience teeming with Deadheads, Dylan decided he would rather take the opening slot. The Deadheads turned out in droves to see Phil and Friends and Dylan didn't mind being the opening act. He could get back to the hotel earlier.

On the April tour of East Coast theaters, Lesh had taken guitarists Jimmy Herring of Dead cover band Jazz Is Dead and Jeff Pevar, whom he met sitting in with David Crosby. For the summer tour, he brought back bluesslinger Robben Ford and the Little Feat guys, guitarist Paul Barrere and keyboardist Billy Payne, who showed up exhausted coming off eight straight weeks on the road with the Feat.

Bill Kreutzmann had moved back to Marin County. He had married again and his new wife, his fourth, was tired of living in Hawaii. He bought a house in Ross, a few miles west of San Rafael. Even from a long distance, Kreutzmann had been dismissive of Lesh's complaints and supportive of Weir and Hart's perspective. He had made a show-of-strength appearance at the 1999 New Year's Eve show by RatDog and the Mickey Hart Band at the Warfield Theatre (and the GDP Christmas party the night before at the Fillmore) before moving back to town. He sat in with both bands, all three bandmates playing together at midnight at the Warfield, while Phil and Friends sat idle that New Year's.

It was summer 2000, after he had bought the house in Ross, that Kreutzmann found himself at the Bel Marin Keys rehearsal hall. The latest edition of the Other Ones had assembled to begin rehearsals and start seeking a second drummer to play a summer tour, since Molo would be going out with Phil and Friends. Kreutzmann took the empty drum chair next to Hart on a lark for one song. Instead of Lesh, the band had drafted Alphonso Johnson of jazz-fusion greats Weather Report, although more importantly, since 1998, bassist with Jazz Is Dead.

Jazz Is Dead was a high-concept instrumental act put together by a booking agent around Dixie Dregs keyboardist T Lavitz and Miles Davis drummer Billy Cobham. Jimmy Herring was the band's original guitarist. The band played jazz-inclined interpretations from the Grateful Dead songbook, yet another example of how musicians were approaching the Dead as repertoire. Alphonso Johnson knew how to walk the thin line between playing the root at the bottom end and keeping the flexibility for improvisation. Also, unlike Lesh, he did not mind coming down on the one. The drummers loved him, if only for that. Sometimes Hart thought Lesh would be buzzing like a bee around the bottom, never sure where to land. Sometimes, if Lesh was in a particularly foul mood, he might fool with the drummers purposefully, coming down on the sixteenth note after the beat just to throw off the groove.

One song was all it took Kreutzmann to decide whatever these guys were doing, he wanted in. He said so. "The original drummer?" said Johnson. "Oh yeah, let's take him."

Hart was juiced anyway. He had just returned from the Democratic National Convention, where he had pounded tom-toms onstage while his friend Al Gore was nominated for president. Hart and Weir had played a few big-ticket fundraisers in Silicon Valley for the campaign backed by Roger McNamee's band, the Flying Other Brothers, but Hart had come to know the vice president and his wife, Tipper, over the course of the Clinton administration. Tipper was not only a drummer, but a big Deadhead. She sat in on congas with the band at venture capitalist billionaire John Doerr's home. Al Gore and Hart had spent considerable personal time together, and offstage and at ease, Gore was an entirely different person than the stiff public face. They became friends. Hart's frenetic energy could be contagious to many; he was a late-life sailing partner of television newsman Walter Cronkite.

The federal government was filled with Deadheads. President Clinton had been seen wearing Jerry Garcia ties. Senator Patrick Leahy of Vermont had been a fan for years. But Wall Street firms were also stacked with Deadheads. This was not as surprising as it may seem. Not all Deadheads were hippies. During the eighties, East Coast prep schools were a hotbed of Dead tape traders, and the culture incubated among the nascent upper class. Like they say, politics makes strange bedfellows. Hart came back from the Los Angeles convention having hobnobbed with pol pals like Senator Harry Reid, the Mormon lawmaker from Nevada whom Hart came to know through his work with the Library of Congress.

Mickey Hart parlayed his political enthusiasms into a board seat of the Library of Congress's American Folklife Center, where he was deeply involved in sound preservation. Rooting around the archives, Hart found a 1938 recording by fiddler Al Gore Sr., the vice president's father, and presented Gore Jr. with a copy. He and Weir appeared in April at a Library of Congress bicentennial concert also featuring Pete Seeger, Tito Puente, and others. He also joined the board of the Institute for Music and Neurologic Function to further pursue his studies of the seat of music in the brain. His wife, Caryl Hart, was appointed to the state Parks and Recreation Commission in March after having been recommended for the job by Vice President Gore.

Hart spent all May on tour with his new Mickey Hart Band featuring former Dead keyboardist Vince Welnick, whose Missing Man Formation had fallen apart and who was glad to have the opportunity to be back in the fold. He showed up with fresh vigor for the Other Ones, pumped to be reunited with Kreutzmann, his partner in rhythm since 1967. With Johnson replacing Lesh on bass, the bottom end was contoured to a more conventional approach, but Kreutzmann and Hart combined for a signature drum sound that instantly spelled Grateful Dead. Saxophonist Dave Ellis was gone—he left RatDog the previous December, a victim of clinical depression and too much road. They worked up a couple more of Hornsby's numbers ("The Way It Is," "The Valley Road") and kept the new Robert Hunter songs from the previous tour. Rehearsals were mainly devoted to tightening up the new rhythm section on the existing repertoire. "It's basically a new band, but I have the benefit of knowing the songs," said Kreutzmann.

The debate about how much rehearsal is good before it robs the band of spontaneity has been going on as long as there has been a Grateful Dead. During the band's 1975 hiatus, they never rehearsed and the few gigs they did play were highly satisfactory to band and audience alike, evidence invariably cited in almost all future arguments against too much rehearsal. Hart picked up the refrain with Hornsby, explaining he didn't want the songs too tight.

"No," Hornsby said, "we want to get them as tight as possible and take off from there."

"I just don't want all those guitar players tripping over each other," said Hart.

"101 Strings," said Hornsby, laughing.

"My worst nightmare," said Hart. "At least there's no saxophone."

That August, this time, the tour was greeted with enthusiasm from the start by the Deadheads, who thronged the sheds the band played. They occasionally brought out opening act Ziggy Marley, Bob's son, to sing one of his father's songs like "Stir It Up" or "I Shot the Sheriff." Hart added an electric kalimba to his arsenal during the nightly drum solos. If the response to the shows lacked the surprise element that the previous Other Ones tour supplied, the shows sold out and the band was greeted like conquering heroes.

For his fall tour, Lesh brought together a Phil and Friends configuration that would prove more enduring than other editions. Bringing back Molo on drums and Barraco on keys, he added guitarists Jimmy Herring, who had been playing with the Allman Brothers since his East Coast tour with Phil and Friends ended in April, and Warren Haynes, another Allman Brothers guitarist who had been playing on and off with Phil and Friends since early 1999. This lineup, which fans would come to call The Q—for quintet—started life with an October sweep through multiple nights in East Coast theaters that included a stunning seven sold-out shows at New York's Beacon Theatre, home turf in New York for the Allmans since 1989.

By comparison, the RatDog fall tour started in the West and moved through clubs and single nights in theaters. RatDog came through Chicago to play one night at the Riviera Theatre in November two weeks after Phil and Friends did four sold-out shows in the hall.

After receiving word from the Lesh camp that he would be spending New Year's Eve in Florida, the Other Ones announced an ambitious New Year's Eve concert at the 16,000-seat Oakland Coliseum Arena, only to have the rug pulled out from under them when Lesh suddenly switched plans and booked a Phil and Friends show for New Year's Eve down the freeway a few exits at the Henry J. Kaiser Auditorium in Oakland, a sentimental favorite with Deadheads. This was an open act of warfare. He cut down the audience for the Other Ones by half, while Phil and Friends sold out the eight-thousand-seat HJK.

It was a mean, deliberate power play by Lesh. By planting his flag a mere five miles from his erstwhile bandmates the same night, he was making a statement. He was also taking the backstage battle into the public arena, making their fans take sides on the Deadheads' special night. With the Phil people packed into the Kaiser and the Other Ones crowd rambling around the half-empty, antiseptic basketball arena, the victory was all Lesh's, even if he made the Deadheads choose, like children of a divorced couple, whether to spend the holiday with Mom or Dad.

10

Garcia's Guitars

DOUG LONG became an attorney somewhat late in life. After he started his practice in the remote Central Valley town of Visalia, he phoned his ex-wife, a lifelong attorney, in Sonoma to tell her he had joined her ranks. A few days later, she called back. "Your old friend Doug Irwin is in trouble and I don't have time for this," she said. "Since you are just starting out, maybe you do."

When Long lived in Sonoma, he came to know Irwin, a luthier (guitar maker) with a shop in downtown Sonoma. Long was in public relations at the time but played in bands and commissioned Irwin to build a guitar for him around the same time Irwin was building a guitar for Jerry Garcia that would be called Tiger. Some leftover pieces of wood from Tiger found their way onto Long's Irwin guitar.

Jerry Garcia had walked into Doug Irwin's studio one day in 1972. He paid $750 for a guitar Irwin had in the window and asked Irwin to build him a second guitar. Garcia and Mountain Girl returned with a pile of cash and Irwin and his assistant went to work on a guitar they called in the shop "The Garcia." When he delivered the instrument in May 1973, it was named Wolf. Garcia was so pleased with the guitar, Irwin went to work on another guitar for him.

The next guitar, Tiger, took six years for Irwin to make. Altogether, Irwin would build five guitars for Garcia.

Long found Irwin in jail on an assault charge. In 1997, Irwin had suffered severe brain damage when he was struck by a hit-and-run driver while riding his bicycle. The brain damage imposed severe personality changes on Irwin, made him subject to sudden, irrational mood shifts and angry outbursts. He had been arrested after a confrontation with another motorist while on his bike had gotten out of hand. Long went and got him out of jail.

Irwin, he soon discovered, was not doing well. He was living under a bridge. His shop had been closed and his tools were in storage. Irwin was mentally ill and only marginally able to care for himself. He was no longer capable of running his own business. Then he told Long the story about how the Grateful Dead wouldn't let him have the guitars Jerry Garcia left him in his will.

This was no hallucination. When Irwin consulted the will, sure enough, there it was. Not only was it the first bequest in the will, above the gifts to family members, but it was the only such mention in the entire document of anyone outside Garcia's family. Long called the Dead office and reached Cameron Sears, who told Irwin he was the sixth or seventh lawyer to be heard from. "But I'm the lawyer who is going to sue you," Long said.

GDP counsel Hal Kant had long cautioned the GDP management about the guitars in Garcia's will. Kant was certain the guitars had been paid for with corporate funds and, consequently, belonged to the company. The band members feared that Irwin was going to turn around and sell the guitars to the highest bidder and that their bandmate's precious instruments would disappear from public view. They knew he couldn't resist the money. Of course, Terrapin Station, officially on hold, was still in their minds, but they realized they needed to take action to counter looming public relations problems.

In February, mindful of Irwin's new legal representative and the gathering storm, GDP contacted the Rock and Roll Hall of Fame in Cleveland and offered to loan them five of Garcia's guitars (they did not offer Wolf because they were no longer certain the band held title to that guitar and turned it over to the Garcia estate). The Dead made one Dead-like proviso: the guitars must be displayed where people do not have to pay an admission price to see them. In a minute, the guitars were whisked to Cleveland and placed on display in the lobby.

In March 2001, attorney Long filed Irwin's suit against Grateful Dead Productions in Marin County Superior Court.

On March 27, Weir, Hart, and Kreutzmann—with Lesh notable by his absence—signed a defensive thirteen-hundred-word post on the band's Web site stating in detail the band's case and refuting some of the public statements by Irwin and his attorney.

"During the time that GDP was a partnership," the statement read in part, "and then later when it became a corporation, we as a group always bought and maintained the instruments used by the band on stage and in recording. We did this purposely. Because all of the stage instruments were bought and maintained in the same way, we thought we had avoided any arguments over who owned what. We all owned it all. All for one and one for all."

The "Letter to the Dead Heads" acknowledged the fans' stake in the debate. Only the members of the Grateful Dead would feel compelled to make such a detailed public explanation of pending litigation. In conclusion, the band invoked Lesh's name, at the same time, responding to his comments to the press that the Dead had simply become "just another corporation." The statement concluded:

Finally, there is a theme in some circles that GDP is becoming just like other corporations, and that it is now run by faceless executives who do not understand the Grateful Dead journey. The corporation is now, and always has been, a democracy made up exclusively of members of the band. At present, the directors and sole owners are Bob, Phil, Billy, and Mickey. No one makes decisions for us and no one is leading us down any garden path. We respect your right to disagree with what we think is best, but understand that the same people who have always made the decisions still make them. Regrettably, this matter will apparently be decided in the courts. We believe we will prevail and we also believe that we have dealt with Doug in good faith and that he and his lawyers have not dealt with us in the same way. No one detests litigation more than we do. We did not start this. But we must finish it.

(Signed) Bobby Weir, Mickey Hart, and Bill Kreutzmann
for Grateful Dead Productions

In April, Long took the depositions of both Weir and Lesh. Lesh destroyed the defense case by stating that the collective ownership of instruments was nothing more than a tax dodge. Lesh also gave interviews to the press harshly critical of his bandmates over this issue.

"I don't agree that justice has been done to Garcia's wishes," Lesh told *Rolling Stone*. "For him to do something that specific in the will means that he wanted that to happen."

Lesh told the magazine he wanted Irwin to have the guitars, but "since Jerry died, consensus has degenerated into democracy, and I was outvoted. . . . Now that Jerry's not here to play them, I don't care if they go into someone's vault."

Reading Lesh's comments while riding his bus, Bob Weir almost punched out the screen to his laptop. He well remembered Lesh's express desire to retain the instruments as centerpiece exhibits at the planned Terrapin Station. He also knew Lesh had instructed Steve Parish to stage a midnight raid on the band's rehearsal hall to grab Lesh's basses "to be photographed." They were never returned. Lesh's presumed moral superiority infuriated Weir, especially knowing his fierce initial resistance to giving up the guitars.

The guitars were only the latest reversal in Lesh's positions. He had initially thought Bandwagon was a great idea, but he had since turned on the project with a vengeance. The idea had attracted a $17 million first-round financing offer from Silicon Valley venture capitalists, but that came off the table after the dotcom crash of summer 2000. Roger McNamee was putting together a formidable coalition of rock bands ready to join the Web enterprise. When Bandwagon began, selling merchandise through mail order was the business model, but as technology rapidly expanded other possibilities emerged. With the advent of mp3.com and Napster, the feasibility of sharing audio files across the Internet suddenly became reality and the prospect of being able to put the entire Vault online dramatically altered the potential of Bandwagon.

McNamee envisioned a superstore Web site that would combine advance ticket sales, merchandise, fan clubs, and, now, audio downloads. Bandwagon would put every band directly in touch with their fans. He was holding fruitful talks with many major acts. Meeting with U2 management, McNamee found the Irish rock band was well aware of the unique community of fans that surrounded the Grateful Dead and openly envied the band's close relationship with their fans. The Dave Matthews Band, one of the first acts to engage on Bandwagon, was managed by Coran Capshaw, who modeled a lot of his business strategy on the Dead. Pearl Jam loved the idea. Dylan's people were interested.

Meanwhile, as one of the "four amigos" running Silver Lake Partners, he launched the first private equity fund focused on technology. Silver Lake, created to prosper during a bear market, was one of the top tech investment firms in red-hot Silicon Valley, with a $2.3 billion fund that McNamee started about the same time he began working on Bandwagon (while still managing to play occasional gigs with his Flying Other Brothers).

In April, as he was closing the deal with U2 to sign up with Bandwagon, he found himself—in the space of one week—flying from San Francisco to Dublin, back to San Francisco, then New York, Dublin again, back to New York, and home to San Francisco. At the end of his trip, McNamee was struck down by not one, but two strokes at age forty-five. He was forced to retreat into months of painstaking rehabilitation at this crucial stage in the project, and Bandwagon suddenly stalled.

· · · · · ·

The Sweetwater was a tiny bar a block off the town square in sleepy downtown Mill Valley with live music seven nights a week. A sold-out house was eighty people, jammed together at little tables and arrayed down the bar and along the wall. A postage stamp–size stage stood in the corner. While most nights featured little-known local musicians, the club over the years became a kind of unofficial private club of the Marin County rock scene. Bill Graham would stop by for a drink on his way home. Sammy Hagar would rent it out for his Halloween parties. One night in 1989, Jerry Garcia jammed with Elvis Costello and James Burton, guitarist for the other Elvis. Dan Hicks did an annual Christmas show. You weren't anybody in Mill Valley until Maria Muldaur had danced in the aisles at your Sweetwater show.

One Sunday night in June 2001, a group called the Crusader Rabbit Stealth Band was the announced attraction. Crusader Rabbit was a black-and-white cartoon character on fifties television that young Phil Lesh knew from growing up in Berkeley. The Crusader Rabbit Stealth Band was a pseudonym for Phil and Friends with one very important addition. For the first time in more than two years, Phil Lesh would be joined onstage by his estranged bandmate Bobby Weir. Not since Lesh, Weir, and Hart joined by Sammy Hagar played Caryl Hart's save-the-redwoods benefit in Santa Rosa had they appeared together.

The place was packed to the doorway and overflowed onto the sidewalk outside, where gawkers strained for a glimpse through the doors. A light-footed jam started to emerge from the random noises onstage and, after reaching a critical mass on their instruments, Lesh and Weir stepped to the mikes and joined their voices on "Truckin'." The little room erupted.

Lesh had not played the Sweetwater before. Sneaking his popular band into the beloved cozy bar dropped him into the bosom of the hip Marin music scene, an instant event made all the more so by publicly burying the hatchet with Weir. Nothing was said. Weir, who had stopped by the Sweetwater on his way home and wound up playing all night many, many nights before, was perfectly at ease, singing the Dead songs and playing with the latest edition of Phil and Friends, drummer Molo, keyboardist Barraco, and guitarist Herring. When Warren Haynes joined the band for the encores, it was The Q with Bob Weir as guest. It was Lesh's world. Weir was only living in it.

A month later, RatDog was opening shows on a handful of Phil and Friends amphitheater dates in the Midwest and East Coast. Weir would join Phil and Friends for a couple of the early numbers in the first set, but Weir had accepted his secondary role in the kingdom.

As furious as he had been with Lesh, he never lost touch with the brotherly love he felt in his heart for the man. Weir had been absorbed in the battle and lost perspective. Angered and aggravated, Weir had responded like an enraged animal without considering the bigger picture. Like all of them, he had no expectations of life after the Dead and had been basically bouncing along from one seemingly good idea to another without any apparent strategy or overview. Battling Lesh had been nothing but destructive. He had also come to understand that more things would be possible through unity than adversity. And he could read the writing on the wall. He knew how intractable Lesh could be. He surrendered. Weir was not the full extent of Lesh's rapprochement. In July at Jones Beach Amphitheater on Long Island, a couple of nights after the run of seven dates with RatDog, Lesh welcomed Mickey Hart onstage to join Phil and Friends. Hart had never been to any Phil and Friends shows. He sat in for the first several numbers of the opening set. As eighteen thousand fans showered them with applause, Lesh planted a kiss on Hart's forehead. "The good times are back," he said.

Lesh let Weir know he would consider playing together again, but only under certain conditions. He wanted things his way now. With sales finally dwindling at Grateful Dead Merchandise, money was thinning out. McQuaid managed to keep appealing material in the pipeline like the twelve-disc boxed set of the Dead's albums for Warner Brothers that he arranged with reissue specialists Rhino Records. But since Garcia died, they had released twenty multidisc *Dick's Picks* sets and, as they flooded the market with three or four new releases a year, demand slowed predictably. Only Lesh was making any money on the road on his own. The prospect of a lucrative onetime reunion looked attractive.

Lesh was in a position to dictate. Newly sensitive to the hue and cry among Deadheads, he wanted the Irwin suit settled. Although he originally strongly backed their case in private, now he turned on the band in public. As much as the others felt that their legal case was sound and that they had been abandoned by Lesh, they also knew the entire episode had been a public relations nightmare. There was no way they could effectively communicate their position to their fans. The Deadheads couldn't get past the idea that the band was not acting in accordance with Jerry's wishes. The fine-point detail of collective ownership was lost on the fans. The Terrapin Station project was growing colder and more remote all the time, so the guitars' significance had shifted. Work had almost entirely ceased on the museum since the acquisition of the downtown San Francisco real estate intended for the site in June 1998. Lesh was pushing to settle.

Easier said than done. With his volatile moods and often deranged thinking, Irwin could reverse himself in midsentence during negotiations. Long interrupted one session to lead Irwin out of the room, returning to continue without him. "He's staying in the car," Long said. The Dead team at one point offered Irwin an annuity of fifty thousand dollars a year to settle the suit and let them keep the guitars. They thought an annual stipend was the most humane, reasonable way of dealing with the mentally handicapped Irwin, but he remained convinced the guitars were worth millions of dollars.

In October, attorneys hashed out a deal. The Dead agreed to give Irwin the two key guitars—Wolf (retrieved from the Garcia estate) and Tiger—on condition that the band be allowed to match any possible sale price when the guitars went on the market and that Irwin agree to a mutual press release and promise to keep his mouth closed about the matter henceforth. Irwin went ballistic, sent out his own press release saying he was being deprived of his free speech rights. The agreement went south, but the Dead had capitulated. Lesh had his veto power back.

In October, Roger McNamee, weak and still recovering from his strokes, met with the GDP board to discuss Bandwagon. Lesh did not attend, but all three of the others were there. The project would require an initial $2 million investment, which McNamee said could be raised either by the band themselves or taking on one or two outside investors who would certainly be glad to invest in GDP. Kreutzmann, who did not want to take on outside investors or reduce his own revenue by investing the band's money, asked if there was any way to borrow the money. McNamee pointed out that would require putting up the Vault as collateral, one of the conditions he made on accepting his role as consultant. With Lesh counting himself out and Kreutzmann unwilling to accept either of the two options that McNamee laid out, Bandwagon was dead. Coran Capshaw, who started his own mega-band Web site, Musictoday, picked up for a song what remained of Grateful Dead Merchandise, and whatever program the band had once envisioned about building back employment for their former associates was officially abandoned.

Lesh sought to systematically strip his business involvements with his old bandmates, almost as if he wanted to financially cripple his former partners by disrupting GDP. He wanted all the real estate sold (Lesh had already declined to join the partners in purchasing a second tract of land on Bel Marin Keys). Instead of preserving employment, he demanded the businesses close, the office shut down, the staff be laid off, all long-term obligations be ended. His final condition was that Peter McQuaid be fired and Cameron Sears be brought back to oversee Grateful Dead Productions. Lesh was taking the opportunity to use his advantage to put himself in charge and get free of any future entanglements with the Dead, a coup of sorts.

Sears had left the company in May 2000 after having been reduced to strictly manager of RatDog to join Jerry Harrison of the Talking Heads in a Silicon Valley start-up called garageband.com. He was surprised when Phil and Jill Lesh phoned him in September 2001 to discuss the possibility of his returning to work with the Dead. Weir and Kreutzmann took McQuaid to lunch.

McQuaid had just delivered the most profitable year yet in his time at GDP, six years after Garcia's death. He had managed to make the merchandise sales grow significantly, made some smart licensing deals, and did what he could to advance the brand amidst the past two years of intense infighting between the partners. For his reward, he would walk the plank. "We hate to say this," they told McQuaid, "but Phil wants to let you go."

With McQuaid gone and Sears on his way back, Lesh's coup was complete by the time Phil and Friends took the stage New Year's Eve at Oakland's Henry J. Kaiser Auditorium. After The Q delivered a sterling opening set and the hall darkened in anticipation of midnight, strains of "The Sorcerer's Apprentice" boomed out of the sound system as a float carrying four Harry Potter–style magicians made its way slowly through the crowd. At the stroke of midnight, as the four sorcerers doffed their caps and took their places onstage, the audience exploded in cheers, applause, whistles, foot stomping. Standing onstage together were Phil Lesh, Bobby Weir, Mickey Hart, and Billy Kreutzmann—the Crusader Rabbit Stealth Band. With the crowd still screaming and cheering madly, the band slammed into a propulsive "Not Fade Away" and carried everybody into the new year.

After a rollicking ride through a half-dozen Dead standards, played end to end Phil and Friends style, the four departed the stage to make way for the final Phil and Friends set. Lesh returned for the encore without his Dead associates to deliver the obligatory "donor rap."

"If the harmony and love manifested in the room tonight continues throughout the year and even further, I think we're going to have a damn good year. Bless you all. . . . I want to thank everybody in our crew for making a great New Year's Eve celebration tonight. I especially want to thank Bob Weir, Mickey Hart, and Billy Kreutzmann for joining us. Unity is possible."

11

Alpine Valley

THEY WELL remembered the Grateful Dead in Walworth County, Wisconsin. The last time the band passed through town in 1989, more than seventy-five thousand fans overwhelmed the tiny East Troy hamlet—almost half of the crowd outside the venue without tickets—and the band was permanently barred from returning to the nearby Alpine Valley Music Theater. Built in 1977, the thirty-seven-thousand-capacity open-air amphitheater with the wood roof has hosted summertime music events ever since. The Dead played there twenty times before the final, cataclysmic appearance. In June 2002, one month after the instantly sold-out two-day return to Alpine Valley by what was being called "Terrapin Station: The Grateful Dead Family Reunion" was announced, the Walworth County Highway Commission denied permission for the band to hold their concerts there.

The corporate concert promoters, Clear Channel, who had failed to take out adequate permits prior to announcing the show, were required to guarantee as much as $200,000 for police overtime, forty tow trucks to enforce parking violations, and a $100,000 bond against property damage claims that might arise. Clear Channel had originally hoped to stage the event in Chicago's Grant Park, but city fathers there turned them down cold. In July, after Clear Channel had taken the suggested precautions and satisfied the Highway Commission, the Walworth County board unanimously reversed the previous month's ruling and the show was back on for August 3 and 4 at Alpine Valley.

The Deadhead world exulted at the news. All four of them—the core four—would play together for the first time since Garcia died as the Other Ones. Having met Lesh's behind-the-scenes conditions, the band eagerly looked forward to what was planned as a onetime reunion. Also appearing over the weekend would be Phil and Friends, RatDog, Bembe Orisha—Mickey Hart's new multi-kulti world beat outfit—and the Tri-Chromes, the band Bill Kreutzmann had started since he moved back to the Bay Area. Robert Hunter would also play. Other bands would perform on a second stage. The Other Ones would headline both nights. Bruce Hornsby didn't come, turning down a million-dollar bonus to join the tour, opting instead to tour on his own in support of a new album and work on the soundtrack to the Spike Lee documentary about basketball star Kobe Bryant. He was tired of the strife in the band anyway.

The band started rehearsals in May at Novato with both Jeff Chimenti of RatDog and Rob Barraco of The Q on keyboards and Jimmy Herring on guitar. The summer would be busy, beginning with the release in May of *There and Back Again*, the first studio album by Phil and Friends—The Q—under a big-money deal with Sony Music (not Grateful Dead Records). Recorded at The Plant Studios in Sausalito where Fleetwood Mac made *Rumours*, the Phil and Friends record revolved around a handful of new Lesh-Hunter songs (most notably "Night of a Thousand Stars," cowritten with Warren Haynes), a Garcia-Hunter leftover from Dead days ("Liberty"), and a few songs from the other guys in the band. Despite the quality of the record and the rising popularity of Phil and Friends, the record would ultimately sell fewer than 50,000 copies, the Internet having already cratered the CD market.

The good vibes were now prevailing and Lesh included all his bandmates' bands—RatDog, Bembe Orisha, and the Tri-Chromes—as opening acts on dates in his busy summer, which began with a prestige headline appearance by Phil and Friends with guest Bob Weir at the first Bonnaroo Festival on a seven-hundred-acre farm outside

Manchester, Tennessee. Lesh also did a series of co-headline shows in July with the Allman Brothers with Warren Haynes playing all night in both bands, who had begun carefully coordinating their bookings around their shared guitarist's schedule. Lesh wound up what was essentially three straight months on the road, bringing his tour into Alpine Valley to meet up with the Other Ones and "The Grateful Dead Family Reunion."

They all stitched rehearsals for the Other Ones into busy schedules. RatDog did a European tour before wending their way to Wisconsin. Hart went out with Bembe Orisha, the new band he built around vocalist Bobi Céspedes, blending West African and Cuban music into his own unique brand of world beat. Even Kreutzmann was doing dates with the Tri-Chromes, pretty much a super-charged blues band and an excuse for all involved to consume massive amounts of cannabis. Tri-Chromes was managed by ex-roadie Steve Parish and fronted by lead vocalist Herbie Herbert, the former manager of Journey who now called himself Sy Klopps. A couple of Herbert's musical associates rounded out the band and guitarist Neal Schon of Journey had played on the original sessions, although he couldn't keep up with the prodigious pot smoking.

The locals at Alpine had raised so much alarm, the band took steps. Other dates for November in the Midwest and East were announced to relieve some of the pressure and live Webcasts of the Alpine Valley shows were scheduled. Chicago FM rock radio station WXRT broadcast the show live. Advertisements for the event stressed, "Don't come if you don't have a ticket."

Every tow truck in that corner of the state was aligned along the highway leading to the amphitheater entrance. Cops were everywhere, even mounted police. The threat of a $1,000 fine for illegal vending kept the parking lot scene largely free of paraphernalia and other offensive merchandise (at least openly), although computer-generated artwork by Billy Kreutzmann was on sale from $50 for a commemorative poster to $1,100 for a more elaborate piece.

"We are all under a microscope," read the band's statement to the Deadheads. "If you want more shows, come only with a ticket in hand. Our reputation and our future is on the line."

The Other Ones opened their first set with an instrumental evocation of "He's Gone"—which had usually been sung by Garcia—with the repeated refrain "he's gone, you know he's gone." Striking that sentimental note at the opening released a torrent of pent-up emotions from the Deadheads, who responded with overwhelming fervor that drove the band to even greater heights as they cruised through a crowd-pleasing program of old favorites—"Dark Star," "I Know You Rider," and "Morning Dew" among others. The next night repeated only one number ("Playing in the Band") and came to a serene, satisfying close with Lesh's elegiac "Box of Rain."

All the advance efforts at crowd control proved effective. Few stragglers without tickets showed up at the site. Some of the extra deputies assigned to work all weekend were sent home early. The additional concert dates, which had been announced as provisional depending on the outcome of the Alpine Valley weekend, were on. Mountain Girl and Augustus Owsley Stanley III—the beloved Bear—were on hand backstage to flesh out the family reunion. Mickey Hart told *Billboard* the concert represented nothing less than "victory over adversity."

"We had our own family feud going," Hart said. "See, the music mediates everything in our lives, but once the music stopped, we didn't have that mediation process; we couldn't meet on the stage, look at each other, and renew our vows, as it were. And, so, the business side started overtaking us. We didn't have agreement. There was, like, hard feelings between people. In the back of my mind, I wished we would [reunite]. But I didn't think there would be enough forgiveness and kindness that would rise to the surface."

"We had been disagreeing on a lot of lower level stuff," Lesh told *Billboard.* "And my feeling was that last year, I started really feeling that we needed to reaffirm our relationship on the high level that it started at, and that level was intimately involved with making music, that relationship." "When that's not happening," he continued,

> and everybody's just part of the board of directors that's just doing business, it makes it harder for individuals and passionately committed people like the Grateful Dead guys to work together.

So Bobby and I started communicating, and Bobby sat in with my band, and then RatDog and my band played together on the summer tour. And Bobby sat in with us again. And on New Year's I invited everybody—all the surviving original members—to join my band for our set. I guess that sort of broke the ice, and put it back on the level that it really needs to be at, the high level of making music.

The well-behaved Alpine Valley crowd had given the return of the core four a giant, loving liftoff and the good vibes echoed backstage among the crew and band members. It almost felt like old times. Everybody had a marvelous time. All except one.

Wandering around in the dark, playing an impromptu gig at a local Thai restaurant the night before and a campfire show in the festival campgrounds the night of the show, was onetime band member Vince Welnick, desperately distressed to have been excluded from "The Grateful Dead Family Reunion." He focused on the phrase—along with publicity touting "the surviving members of the Grateful Dead"—and was tearing himself apart at having been left out. Wasn't he a surviving member? Wasn't membership in the Grateful Dead a lifetime thing bestowed on him by Jerry that couldn't be revoked? He came to Wisconsin under the delusion that this terrible mistake would be rectified before it was too late.

Life had not been good to Welnick since he left the RatDog bus. His own band, Missing Man Formation, made a sold-out debut in July 1996 at the Fillmore, but within months, depressive Welnick had alienated his lifelong friend, drummer Prairie Prince from the Tubes, who had put the band together for Welnick, and the group shortly thereafter dissolved in acrimony and incompetence.

By the time Alpine Valley was announced, Welnick had been reduced to playing humiliating shows in small college towns with Dead tribute bands with names like Gent Treadly or Jack Straw in front of sometimes fewer than a dozen patrons. He had successfully battled throat cancer but continued to suffer from emphysema (although that didn't keep him from smoking cigarettes) and sucked on an inhaler all day long.

The Dead had bought out his interest in the band and would not allow him to use the facilities to rehearse his bands or borrow equipment for his recording sessions. He peppered management with phone calls and emails with plans to reunite the band and go out on the road, always with him at the keyboards. He became something of an embarrassing pariah. Not fully understanding, Welnick sat in his motel room at Alpine Valley and waited for a last-minute phone call that never came inviting him to join the band again.

The core four did not give Welnick a second thought—he was only the last of six keyboardists to play in the Grateful Dead—and went along their merry way, riding a wave of bonhomie out of Alpine Valley into a frolicsome performance at Neil Young's annual all-acoustic Bridge School benefit at Shoreline Amphitheatre. In November, the Other Ones headed out on their swing of East Coast basketball arenas and civic centers. Robert Hunter went along and played acoustic between the band's two sets. Vocalist Susan Tedeschi was added to the band on many dates in the second half of the tour.

At the MCI Center in Washington, DC, the band dedicated "New Speedway Boogie" to Speaker of the House Nancy Pelosi, who was watching from the wings. The San Francisco congresswoman and her husband had become almost regular visitors backstage at Dead concerts. Weir and Hart had taken their pal Steve Miller that past February to play a swanky celebration of her elevation to Speaker at the Capitol. The band had come a long way from the ragtag hippie crew that used to crawl the country.

The Other Ones returned home, played a couple of high-spirited nights at Oakland's Henry J. Kaiser Auditorium and, three weeks later, a sold-out concert at the sixteen-thousand-capacity Arena in Oakland on New Year's Eve. As Lesh promised Hart, the good times were back.

Carried along by the glad tidings and good graces they found themselves enjoying, members of the band took yet another step in reclaiming their identity in February 2003. At a board meeting while Weir was out of town—and over his objections—the band voted to officially change their name. "With the greatest possible respect for our collective history," read the announcement posted on the band's

Web site, "we have decided to keep the name 'Grateful Dead' retired in honor of Jerry's memory and call ourselves 'The Dead.'"

The announcement went on to explain that the decision came as a direct result of the "magical" experience at Alpine Valley. "To us, that was the Grateful Dead—without Jerry. We had stopped being the 'Other Ones' and were on our way to becoming something new but at the same time very familiar."

The Dead celebrated the new name with a Valentine's Day concert at the Warfield Theatre where Sammy Hagar joined the band to sing "Loose Lucy" and Joan Osborne, who shared booking agent Jonathan Levine with Phil and Friends, sat in for a few numbers. Warren Haynes finished the night on guitar.

As the band continued to meet the conditions Lesh stipulated for his return to the fold, Cameron Sears came back to work to downsize the operation. The band settled the Irwin suit in January 2003, simply by dropping their conditions and giving up the two guitars, Wolf and Tiger. As expected, Irwin put them immediately up for auction and the two guitars did indeed yield more than $1 million for the destitute guitar maker.

Grateful Dead Merchandise, the goose that laid the golden egg, had been sold to Musictoday, the e-commerce firm founded by Coran Capshaw, manager of the Dave Matthews Band, which already handled the Phil Lesh merchandise account. The remaining dozen employees in Novato were laid off. In August, the old Coca-Cola plant was sold to Marin Mountain Bikes, although the band continued to lease the rehearsal hall/recording studio. The downtown San Francisco property bought with the Terrapin Station museum project in mind was likewise sold (at a tidy profit).

With the band's long-term record contract with Arista Records due to expire, a new deal was being negotiated with Rhino Records, the reissue specialists who had been handling the Dead's Warner Brothers catalog. The agreement with Rhino's corporate owners, Warner Brothers, would include the entire Grateful Dead catalog (the rights to the Arista recording having reverted to the band) and would lavish on the band a multimillion-dollar long-term license. Band members made the head of Rhino audition by singing an obscure Grateful Dead song (he passed). Under the harmonious spirit of the day, they all were on board with the plan.

That would spell the end of Grateful Dead Records, the wholly owned company the band started thirty years before. Lesh had effectively demolished the shared business enterprises between band members. "We want to simplify and play music," Hart told the *San Francisco Chronicle*, "and get rid of all this mumbo-jumbo. That was what got us into trouble."

The band was rehearsing for the 2003 "Summer Getaway" tour when Bob Weir found the magic guitar, a long story that goes back to the circumstances of his birth. Weir was an adopted son. His birth mother sent him a letter many years later in his adult life, and he learned her story. She had gotten pregnant with her college boyfriend in Arizona, gone to San Francisco to have the baby, and given it up for adoption without telling him. She returned to find he had given up on her and moved on with another woman. Their lives never crossed again, she said. She told him the man's name.

At one point, Weir learned that his biological father was a colonel in the Air Force, running the Hamilton Air Force Base in Marin County. A confirmed anti-authoritarian, Weir did nothing with that modestly alarming information. Years later, after the birth of his children, his wife Natascha finally egged him into looking up the man's name in the phone book. When he reached the gentleman and identified himself as Robert Weir of Mill Valley, the man immediately recognized the name. "The only Robert Weir I know plays guitar for the Grateful Dead," he said.

Jack Parber and his wife, Madeline, had raised four sons and they all played music. The eldest took a shot at a career and got as far as playing around Bay Area clubs with a couple of bands before he was struck down with spinal cancer. He moved back in with his parents and spent twelve years in a slow, agonizing death that finally came in 1991. After he died, his brothers all divided his guitars except for one beat-up, broken-down electric. The Weirs became quite close with the Parbers, who were doting grandparents to Weir's two daughters, and they used to spend nights at the Parbers' home, where the guitar was parked in his way in the spare bedroom. After having to practically step over the case, Weir asked the Parbers if they wanted him to take it and they responded enthusiastically.

He brought the old guitar to rehearsal the next day, where one of his equipment people remounted the pickup and put new strings on it, polished it up, and brought it to Weir, who strapped it on and turned back to the rehearsal. As soon as Weir struck the first chord, he knew this was the guitar he had been waiting for. It instantly pulled together the sound of the entire band, the thin, reedy tone slicing through the clutter. After an exhilarating rehearsal with the guitar, they sat around admiring the piece when the guitar tech noticed the five-figure serial number on the back. He called the factory, where he was told that the guitar was a first-run production model Fender Telecaster from 1956 and probably worth more than $75,000. The guitar immediately became Weir's number-one guitar on the tour. James Parber, Jack and Madeline's deceased son, never made the big time, but, in the hands of the brother he never knew, his guitar did.

For the summer tour, the band invited Joan Osborne to join on vocals, putting her sunny alto in the vocal blend, singing a few select lead vocals and lending a touch of unexpected sex appeal to the Dead's stage show with her bare midriff and sensuous dancing. Osborne, who was never a Deadhead and only slightly familiar with the band's music, loaded one of those newfangled Apple iPods with the Dead's catalog and studied. She started out working on a song-book of fifty songs, but every night she found herself having to sing three or four songs she didn't know. By the end of the tour, she was dealing with two hundred songs. The forty-year-old musician had a solid background in folk and blues long before her 1995 number one hit "One of Us," which provided common ground with the other musicians. Her playful personality helped her fit into the boys' club atmosphere backstage. Onstage she liked to kid around with Weir and would even dare to invade the space Lesh held sacred.

Guitarist Jimmy Herring had to walk a thin line between evoking Jerry Garcia and copying him, but he had practice at that by replacing Dicky Betts in the Allman Brothers. The soft-spoken Southern hippie in the lumberjack shirt and the orange-turning-white ponytail first came to attention as lead guitar from the H.O.R.D.E. tour jam band Col. Bruce Hampton and the Aquarium Rescue Unit.

He substituted for Betts one night in Saratoga Springs, New York, in 1993, after Betts had been arrested, and had been offered the job for the rest of the tour, but declined. Seven years later, he did accept their offer to replace Betts for the Allman Brothers 2000 summer tour, where he looked out in the audience at every show and saw WHERE'S DICKY? T-shirts.

In October 2000, he went straight from the Allmans into the first fixed lineup of Phil and Friends—The Q. The forty-one-year-old Berklee-trained guitarist had been studying Garcia since 1998, when he joined the instrumental Dead cover band, Jazz Is Dead, but he, too, had to learn a massive amount of new material in The Dead. Since Lesh concentrated on the Garcia songs, Herring knew nothing from his Phil and Friends work of the Bob Weir side of the equation. Like Osborne, he found himself facing songs he didn't know almost nightly, sometimes vamping the chords and other times decorating the edges to fake his way through.

"I'm not trying to copy," Herring told the *New York Times*. "I just want my playing to sound fairly authentic, as far as the Grateful Dead goes. I don't have to harmonically play what he played. I don't have to copy his riffs and lines. But I'd like for the overall picture to be somewhere within the kingdom."

Herring delivered plenty of big rock thrills during the three-hour shows, capably bolstered by the two keyboardists, Weir's unique rhythm guitar, and the thunderous rhythm section. On good nights, the band could generate genuine Grateful Dead–like flight. On the other hand, this tour was all business, no frills. The backstage guest list was slashed. There was no longer any party going on at the shows. The band stayed at mid-priced hotels. Only the Leshes' accommodations were upscale. In fact, Lesh stayed behind in Boston to hear a symphony matinee, sending his wife and family ahead to New York without him and holding down two big-city luxury hotel suites at once, while Weir didn't bother to get off the bus that night and slept in a parking lot outside the Holiday Inn in Secaucus, New Jersey. A digital clock on the monitor mixing board on the side of the stage stared out at the musicians during their show. If ever there had been a band that didn't need to know what time it was onstage, it was the Grateful Dead, but The Dead was proving to be significantly different than the Grateful Dead.

Still, Weir had come around about the name change by the end of the tour. The band seemed to be thriving and, if he didn't care about taking charge or even greatly influencing the decisions driving the band, he could enjoy playing the music and doing the shows. "I thought we should wait," Weir told the *Los Angeles Times*. "But in retrospect, it was a leap of faith. We said we were going to be the Dead, and we actually are."

Onstage, Lesh acted as bandleader, calling out efficient key changes and melodic transitions through a closed-circuit microphone in the band's earpieces. Having taken charge of creating set lists, he delivered them by five in the afternoon, invariably sending Osborne and Herring back to school until showtime. The tour included Stevie Winwood, Willie Nelson, and Bob Dylan as opening acts at different times along the way, and they always joined the band for a few numbers during The Dead's set. The band drew from the full breadth of the Grateful Dead's catalog, threw in now and again an unexpected Beatles song ("Strawberry Fields Forever," "She Said She Said"), occasionally Lesh's "Night of a Thousand Stars," and Hart's "Only the Strange Remain" from the post-Dead era. Lesh delivered his "donor rap" at the end of every show. It was clearly his band. He was Captain Trips now.

12

Wave That Flag

Wave That Flag

IN 2004, before The Dead went out again, the band adjusted the lineup. With Jimmy Herring from The Q already on board, Lesh wanted to bring in the other guitarist from his favored lineup of Phil and Friends, Warren Haynes. With Haynes capable of covering the Garcia vocals, Joan Osborne was out and, to keep the political balance, Rob Barraco of The Q was given walking papers while Jeff Chimenti of RatDog remained.

Haynes was exploding. He was already firmly planted in his role with the Allman Brothers, and Gov't Mule, his own band, was gaining traction. The forty-four-year-old shaggy Southern hippie, ten years younger than the men of the Dead, brought razor-sharp blues-rooted chops, a sturdy tenor voice, and a handful of songs. He added the unlikely "One" by U2 into the Dead's repertoire.

"I have a brand-new career ahead of me in the same way that a 25-year-old might," he told the *New York Times*. "That's very odd. But it's no more odd than the thought of being in the Grateful Dead and the Allman Brothers at the same time."

Haynes grew up in Asheville, North Carolina, under the spell of Duane Allman and got his start on the road with country music wild man David Allan Coe. He had already written songs and recorded

Furthur Festival—Bruce Hornsby, Bobby Weir, Jorma Kaukonen, and friends, June 1996 *(Photo by Susana Millman)*

David Gans and Phil Lesh with the Broken Angels, December 1997 *(Photo by Susana Millman)*

RatDog: Jay Lane, Rob Wasserman, Johnnie Johnson, Matt Kelly, Bob Weir,
1997 *(Photo by Susana Millman)*

Stan Franks, Phil Lesh—Phil and Friends at Warfield Theatre, February
1998 *(Photo by Susana Millman)*

The Other Ones—Dave Ellis, John Molo, Bruce Hornsby, Phil Lesh, Bob Weir; seated, Mickey Hart, Mark Karan, Steve Kimock, 1998 *(Photo by Susana Millman)*

Artist's rendering of Terrapin Station exterior and lobby

(Environmental Design Archive, UC Berkeley)

Bob Weir wedding; Bob Weir, Natascha Muenter, Phil and Jill Lesh, Mickey and Caryl Hart, July 1999 *(Photo by Susana Millman)*

The Other Ones—Mark Karan, Steve Kimock, Bob Weir, Mickey Hart; seated, Alphonso Johnson, Billy Kreutzmann, Bruce Hornsby, 2000 *(Photo by Susana Millman)*

Phil Lesh, 60th birthday party, Henry J. Kaiser Auditorium, Oakland, March 2000
(Photo by Susana Millman)

Harry Potter float ("Unity is possible"), New Year's Eve, Henry J. Kaiser Auditorium, Oakland, 2001
(Photo by Susana Millman)

Alpine Valley, the core four back together – Billy Kreutzmann, Phil Lesh, Bobby Weir, Mickey Hart, August 2002 *(Photo by Susana Millman)*

The Dead again—Jeff Chimenti (keyboards), Rob Barraco (keyboards), Phil Lesh (bass), Joan Osborne (vocals), Billy Kreutzmann (drums), Bob Weir (guitar), Mickey Hart (drums), Jimmy Herring (guitar), Warren Haynes (guitar), September 2003. Sitting in was violinist Michael Kang of String Cheese Incident. *(Photo by Susana Millman)*

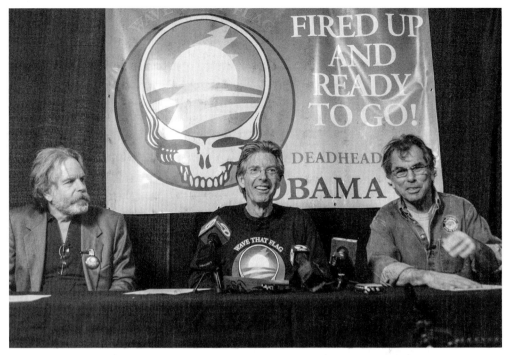

Bob Weir, Phil Lesh, Mickey Hart, press conference backstage
Warfield Theatre night of the California primary, February 2008
(Photo by Susana Millman)

The final show by The Dead at Shoreline Amphitheatre, Mountain
View, May 2009; Phil Lesh, Bob Weir, Billy Kreutzmann, Mickey
Hart, Warren Haynes *(Photo by Bob Minkin)*

Mickey Hart's brain on rhythm, 2014 *(Photo by Susana Millman)*

7 Walkers: Papa Mali, George Porter, Matt Hubbard, Billy Kreutzmann, 2012
(Photo by Michael Weintrob)

Furthur: Phil Lesh, Bob Weir at Coney Island, Brooklyn, 2010
(Photo by Bob Minkin)

Phil Lesh in the Grate Room of Terrapin Crossroads, San Rafael, 2016
(Photo by Bob Minkin)

Bob Weir and the National at TRI Studios, Terre Linda, May 2012
(Photo by Bob Minkin)

"Fare Thee Well" producer Peter Shapiro before the first show at Levi's Stadium, Santa Clara *(Photo by Michael Weintrob)*

"Viola Lee Blues" ending the first set at Levi's Stadium with a rainbow *(Photo by Michael Weintrob)*

Trey Anastasio, Billy Kreutzmann, Phil Lesh, Mickey Hart, Bob Weir, Soldier Field, Chicago *(Photo by Michael Weintrob)*

The stage lit up for the second set at Soldier Field *(Photo by Jeff Kravitz)*

Trey Anastasio, Phil Lesh, Bob Weir at Soldier Field *(Photo by Jeff Kravitz)*

"Fare Thee Well," July 5, 2015 *(Photo by Jeff Kravitz)*

with Gregg Allman and Dicky Betts when he was invited to join the
Allmans for the band's 1989 reunion. He and bassist Allen Woody
left the Allmans to form Gov't Mule in 1997. Woody died in 2000,
and Haynes was invited back into the Allmans fold.

Living in Manhattan's East Village, he had been married for six
years to Stefani Scamardo, who also managed his career. When he
accepted the post with The Dead, he committed to playing thirty-six
dates and fifty shows with the Allmans in 2004, in addition to other
shows with Gov't Mule and solo performances. His new album came
from a solo show he gave the previous year at Bonnaroo ("Live at
Bonnaroo"), and he would be appearing as a solo acoustic opening
act on The Dead tour.

Haynes added a heavier rock sound to The Dead and a third
guitar, which could exponentially increase the spiderweb of criss-
crossing guitar lines in any jam. After the customary wintershow at
the Warfield Theatre (and a surprise guest set at a Gov't Mule show at
the Fillmore in April), The Dead hunkered down for three weeks of
rehearsal at Novato in May. The three-month "Wave That Flag" tour
opened in June with a winning performance headlining the second
night of the Bonnaroo Festival before ninety thousand people. Even
after such a high point, the band and crew quickly realized this summer would not be a repeat of the previous summer's peace and harmony. Almost immediately, Weir chafed under Lesh's authoritarian
leadership. The volume and tempo war began almost from the start.

By playing music together through the earliest years of their career while under the influence of LSD, the members of the Grateful
Dead bonded on a profound nonverbal level. Not only was their music shaped, encouraged, and defined by psychedelics, but the experience imprinted these men with deep, intuitive communication skills,
only made deeper over the years. For musicians to come together
over rhythm and harmony requires empathy, understanding, and a
sense of common purpose. They also needed to listen to each other
carefully to create the proper openness for group thinking. When
these elements are in place, the experience becomes a sort of musical telepathy, a richly nuanced and diverse language shared by the

musicians and audience. With such a dialogue, of course, any emotional undercurrents will come to the surface.

"It's an organic kind of situation," Weir told *Billboard*. "We speak a language that no one else speaks. It comes from all those years on the road; if you piled up the time that we've spent just on stage together, playing, it'd be years. Relationships develop. Feelings develop that I don't think can be found any other ways."

Despite these bonds, Weir and Lesh were not well suited to accommodate one another. Lesh was always strongly anti-authoritarian. At the Fillmore, he would play over Bill Graham while he introduced the band. At the Monterey Pop Festival, after the band endured the indignity of having Peter Tork of the Monkees interrupt their set to tell the crowd that rumors the Beatles would be attending were not true, it was Lesh who invited the overflow crowd outside the arena gates to crash the show, watching in delight as the cyclone fence came tumbling down.

Weir, too, had a strongly contrarian streak. It is said that if he was told to turn left, he would turn right, even if he might have turned left had he been asked. And when Weir was drinking, he could be as obstreperous as Lesh was naturally supercilious. They had a little brother/big brother dynamic that was not always comfortable for either of them.

Weir had come to believe that his job was not singing songs, but storytelling with music. He felt that each song was an audio playlet that needed to sink into the audience's mind. After years of small theater performances with RatDog, he wanted to create that intimacy with the larger audience, drawing them into the musical narrative. To that end, he continually insisted on slowing down the tempo of the band and dropping the volume.

Lesh felt the opposite. He thought Weir's death beat dragged the band down and brisker, more robust tempos were essential in getting the large crowds swept up in the music. With Phil and Friends, he discovered that volume was an important part of the music's impact and he continually pushed up the volume as well as the tempo. The two drummers were caught in the middle of this constant tug-of-war during the performance. With the two musical philosophies competing onstage, the environment grew hostile. The personalities were now clashing while they played music, which had been unheard of in the Grateful Dead.

The rancor had an effect. Weir was slipping deeper in a fog of booze and pills, burying his resentments. Kreutzmann was spending a lot of time in bathrooms. Sober vegetarian Lesh was openly disgusted with his bandmates and he was not above taking his foul moods onstage. Years before, Kreutzmann and Hart had stopped their habit of sharing mushrooms during concerts—"ally" they called it—because Lesh would turn around and scowl at them so furiously, he bummed their trip. During the tempo wars, Lesh could carry his fury into his play, take over the jam, and become the bully of the groove. He made little effort to conceal his anger from the band.

With the two drummers obstinate and impenetrable, caught in a crossfire not of their creation, and Weir dazed and confused, the Leshes struck out, as they saw their power erode and their control slipping. Sternly protective of what she perceived as her husband's interests, the often mercurial Jill Lesh could be calm, efficient, even thoughtful one minute, then turn on a dime into a fit of rage. Stefani Scamardo had to rescue a cowering teenaged Reya Hart, Mickey's daughter, from a Jill Lesh lecture backstage during a concert at the Gorge in Washington. Among other things, she told Reya that she had a horrible childhood and had been raised badly. Young Reya was visibly upset when Scamardo intervened. The two powerful women managers fell into a screaming match before Scamardo took Reya by her arm and led her out of the dressing room. Her father responded by automatically text-messaging photos of his daughter to Jill every hour for the next day. Backstage was a powder keg on the verge of blowing, as Jill reflected Lesh's frustrations among the crew. She had become a problem all her own. And the stage had turned into a battlefield.

Haynes brought a toughness to the sound, but couldn't match the delicacy of some of the music and could get lost in the zone. He stayed rooted in the blues, which was one thing the Dead always did, but only one. Chimenti, the Bill Evans of rock, tended to roll unchecked into strongly bebop-flavored solos. Haynes, Herring, and Weir were constantly butting guitars against each other. Lesh sprinkled gratuitous oldies from other sixties acts in the set lists—the Byrds' "Eight Miles High," the Band's "The Weight," even Donovan's "Sunshine Superman." The band attacked the performances with a crisp efficiency without reaching the critical mass they had managed remarkably often the previous summer, when they were all still getting along. This band never jelled.

Not only was the band not having as much fun, they weren't selling as many tickets. Only three of the five shows in Red Rocks Amphitheatre outside Denver sold out. The band played to half-full houses in Salt Lake City and Phoenix. The band also, for the first time, brought politics into the shows, encouraging voter registration, openly supporting Democratic presidential candidate John Kerry, even playing the occasional "Johnny B. Goode" in his honor. Lesh plastered a KERRY sticker on his bass.

The tour ended in August at HiFi Buys Amphitheatre in Atlanta, on a double bill with the Allman Brothers, who were starting their tour that night. Warren Haynes played three hours with the Dead, did his solo acoustic intermission act, and finished the night with the Allman Brothers. The next morning, he left on the Allmans tour.

A month later, Weir went into rehab. It wasn't his first attempt at sobriety and it wouldn't be his last. He had been the target of an intervention as early as 1986 when he was strung out on white wine and Valium. The entire fall tour by RatDog was cancelled at considerable cost to Weir.

In March 2003, Weir had replaced bassist Rob Wasserman, his original partner in RatDog and close friend, with Robin Sylvester, a low-key, easygoing British expatriate who won the job over former Bobby and the Midnites bassist Bobby Vega. Wasserman's ouster signaled a seriousness of purpose, turning RatDog into more of a rock-and-roll band. The highly accomplished Wasserman always saw his bass playing a much larger role in the ensemble than simple rhythm section work, a vision he shared with Phil Lesh. He was a virtuoso bass player with a grand vision for his instrument and, as a result, often left something to be desired as a timekeeper and rhythm maker.

They broke in Sylvester on a two-month spring run before Weir went out with The Dead for the summer. RatDog managed only a couple of dates in September after Weir's return before it became apparent he could not continue.

Weir's anti-authoritarian proclivities never served him well in the recovery process. He could not even fully process the first of the twelve steps in Alcoholics Anonymous ("admitted we were powerless over alcohol"), let alone the part where you give everything up to a Higher Power. Weir could only absorb so much of the didactic AA orthodoxy and he never attended meetings. He continued a lifelong cycle of going in and out of sobriety. His clean and sober periods could last a long time, but they always ended.

He was living through a more than two-year remodel of the Mill Valley bachelor home he bought thirty years before with inheritance from his parents. He and Natascha were raising two small daughters, and the intense conflict flaring up again on The Dead tour only exacerbated the stress. He could summon Buddha-like acceptance of life-and-death matters and yet would struggle against some of the most basic precepts of reality. He had been on the road so many miles, known so many women, sung so many songs, Weir had become a grizzled veteran, at the height of his significant powers in the prime of his life, but hobbled by his steely insistence on doing things his way for his reasons, whatever they may be. Alcoholics in the recovery community refer to characters like Weir as "terminally special."

Charlie Rose of CBS-TV's *60 Minutes* had shown up at rehearsals in May to grab some footage of the men at work. He filmed Weir, Lesh, Hart, and Kreutzmann busking outside 710 Ashbury, the band's communal headquarters during the Haight-Ashbury days. He caught up with the band in Indianapolis on tour. The resulting piece didn't air until November, by which time the band was off the road with no dates on the calendar. Still, Lesh managed to stir more controversy than he intended among the Deadheads, always a touchy bunch. His anger-tinged comments about Garcia's heroin addiction set off a firestorm on Deadhead bulletin boards across the Internet.

"It's one of the biggest tragedies or the biggest bring-downs of my whole life, to know that he loved the drug more than he loved us," Lesh told *60 Minutes*. "I felt like I had mourned him already when I got the call, and I had been mourning him for years. He was gone for years."

Lesh was giving voice to resentments commonly held by those close to addicts and anger is a frequent response from confused and bereaved family members. On the other hand, among Deadheads, leveling any criticism at Jerry Garcia was touching the third rail. After the broadcast aired in November, Deadheads chattered endlessly among themselves about what they saw as Lesh's gaffe.

At home, the Leshes took note. They had scrupulously studied the Deadhead community to build their own following. From insisting Kimock be included in the first iteration of the Other Ones to reviving old Grateful Dead songs from the sixties in Phil and Friends, the Leshes tested their ideas for Deadhead approval. Feeling that now they alone were proprietors of the soul of the Grateful Dead and held control, the Leshes courted the Deadheads, and it paid off for them. They knew Deadhead loyalty was a valuable commodity and that they owed their status and power to Deadhead approval. They treated the messages they heard on the grapevine seriously. With Lesh's misstep about Jerry, their strategy for domination was immediately weakened, at a time when Lesh was, once again, tired and disgusted with his bandmates.

There had been talk of a New Year's Eve show. Sidemen like Haynes and Herring kept their calendars open. Weir spoke optimistically after the tour about the band's plans for making new music to *Rolling Stone*. "I don't know if albums are the way it's going to be done anymore," he said. "With downloading, the album may be an obsolete concept. If there's some reason to put out a group of songs together, we may do that. We'll be recording all along. We've written a few new songs already."

But any future hinged on Phil Lesh, who again wasn't as interested and couldn't be reached as easily. After his equal share of The Dead tour amounted to substantially less net revenue to Lesh than his Phil and Friends shows, he began to rethink his collaboration with the others. He decided he wanted future income pro-rated with him to receive a larger portion. He reasoned that he was clearly the main attraction in the band, a measurably larger draw than any of the others, and, as such, should be rewarded appropriately. Without him, the others would not make as much money, even with the reduced shares called for in his new plan.

Naturally this did not go over well in the all-for-one/one-for-all world of the Grateful Dead and, as the Leshes grew even more remote, the others slowly began to realize that Lesh had once again taken his ball and gone home, and that the incarnation of the band called The Dead was finished.

13

Jammys
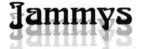

PHIL LESH didn't get out much when he wasn't playing, so the invitation to host the fifth annual Jammy Awards at the Theater at Madison Square Garden in April 2005 was also a welcome opportunity for him to cross paths with a broad cross-section of like-minded musicians. The event, which had graduated the previous year from the much more intimate Roseland Ballroom to the bigger room, was the brainchild of executive producer Peter Shapiro, a rising young impresario who ran a rock club and Deadhead community center in Tribeca called the Wetlands, along with *Relix* editor Dean Budnick. While the bands appearing at Shapiro's club were diverse in style—from Afrobeat to British blues—the common bond between the bands and the audience was a devotion to jamming.

At his club and his Jammy Awards, Shapiro represented this sub-culture of the pop music mainstream, a thriving scene not reflected on the radio or *Billboard* album charts, a genuine underground phenomenon that had been growing quietly over the ten years since Garcia's death in the NSYNC/Backstreet Boys/Britney era of pop. It was a movement that owed its entire existence to the model of the Grateful Dead.

"The Jammy Awards ceremony exists to celebrate the world that was mainly created by the Grateful Dead," said the *New York Times*, "a world of rock-based improvisers, eager to extend their digressive songs by incorporating bits of country and jazz and the blues. The Grateful Dead's leader, Jerry Garcia, died a decade ago, but the group is still at the center of the jam-band universe: the Grateful Dead bassist Phil Lesh served as the evening's host, and Grateful Dead–related projects took home a handful of awards."

In the eight months since the last Dead concert, Lesh had been largely holed up, writing his autobiography, which was published the week before he appeared as host at the sold-out event in New York City. He had been signed to a lucrative book deal the year before by Michael Pietsch, a publishing industry heavyweight running the Little, Brown house at the time. Working without a ghostwriter, Lesh had cranked out *Searching for the Sound: My Life with the Grateful Dead* and had been quiet, save for a couple of one-off Phil and Friends dates around town. The Jammys was kind of a coming-out party for him. None of his bandmates would be around to share the spotlight.

Even if the future of The Dead was in limbo, the band nevertheless won the award for Best Download for the live recording from the 2004 Bonnaroo Festival, and Lesh acted like nothing was wrong, the real first rule of show business. "This proves it is possible not only to survive but prevail," said Lesh, accepting the award.

Lesh presided over an extraordinary evening of music, beginning with his fellow Marin County rock star Huey Lewis, about to make his Broadway debut in the musical *Chicago*, who joined South Bend, Indiana, jam rockers Umphrey's McGee to sing "I'll Take You There" along with Mavis Staples and a subdued Sinead O'Connor, who returned later to join reggae pioneer Burning Spear. Bruce Hornsby sang one of his songs with Yonder Mountain String Band. Peter Frampton reprised his "Do You Feel Like We Do" with alternative rockers Guster. The Disco Biscuits backed country star Travis Tritt in a lengthy exploration of his hit "Honky Tonk History." Lesh anchored the walloping blues jam with drummer ?uestlove and guitarists Buddy Guy and

John Mayer. But the single most mind-boggling moment of the momentous night belonged to Ryan Adams, alt-rock brat with a classic rock swagger, hardly a beloved figure with the jam-band crowd.

Lesh joined Adams and his country-rock-oriented band the Cardinals as the thirty-year-old singer-guitarist, glasses sliding down his nose, hair hanging in his face, took possession of Garcia's "Wharf Rat," pulling it apart and putting it back together in front of Lesh's eyes—bawling, mewling, grating his way through a twelve-minute odyssey before a house full of skeptical Deadheads won over halfway through the first chorus. Lesh struggled to keep up, but stood there, a grin plastered across his face, amazed at what he saw like any other fan, only with a better seat. If he was casting around for a lead vocalist for Phil and Friends that coming summer, he could not have found a better candidate.

Lesh also reacquainted himself backstage with guitarist Larry Campbell, whom he knew from touring with Bob Dylan. After seven years, Campbell had left his post in Dylan's band only four months before. He had been working as the informal musical director of the Midnight Rambles, weekly Saturday concerts held at the barn owned by Levon Helm in Woodstock, New York, as a means of helping cover some of Helm's medical expenses and helping him ease back into playing music after a severe bout with cancer.

He had never been a Deadhead, although *Workingman's Dead* and *American Beauty* had caught the country music–loving Campbell's attention, and he had watched with interest during that first 1999 tour with Dylan when Lesh had Robben Ford and the two guys from Little Feat in his band. When Lesh mentioned backstage at the Jammys that they should play together sometime, Campbell had no idea how few guitar players Lesh knew.

Lesh used guitarist Jimmy Herring for the Phil and Friends show in December 2004 and the February 2005 Mardi Gras shows, Lesh's only public performances since The Dead tour. On both those shows, the band was fronted by the charismatic Chris Robinson of the Black Crowes. Robinson was on the loose, having suddenly scrubbed his fall 2004 tour and fired his band, disappearing except for his two Phil and Friends shows until a showcase with his brother Rich Robinson in February at the Consumer Electronics Show in Las Vegas paved the way for a Black Crowes reunion later in the year. Robinson was not likely to be available again for Lesh anytime soon. With his book hitting the streets, Lesh showed up in New York for the Jammys, ready to consider further musical plans.

The book was a brilliant move that galvanized Lesh's standing as the leading living member of the Grateful Dead. The publishers trumpeted the *New York Times* best-seller as the first inside account, although roadie Steve Parish (of all people) beat Lesh to the market the year before with his memoir of life in the Dead, *Home Before Daylight*. In *Searching for the Sound*, Lesh took charge of the narrative in subtle, telling ways, using a kind of self-serving, faux honesty that impressed reviewers, but not his intimates who had lived these stories with him. It worked. In an article headlined Now the Dead Will Always Be with Us, the *New York Times* credited Lesh, following the death of Garcia, with "reshaping both the band and the public's understanding of its legacy."

Still, Lesh was either playing it cool or keeping his options open regarding the current status of The Dead in his musical life. In the same article, he confirmed there were plans for celebrating the band's fortieth anniversary later in the year, even though he knew that would never happen. "In typical fashion, we don't know what we're going to do yet," he told *The Times*.

Nobody was sitting at home waiting for Lesh. Weir, back on his feet, hit the road with RatDog in March and stayed out for months, rolling into an appearance on the main stage at Bonnaroo in June. Before the massive crowd, Weir played his managers' wet dream of a "greatest hits" set list—starting with "Truckin'," into "Playing in the Band," "Cassidy," "Jack Straw," "St. Stephen," "Sugar Magnolia"— if only to show them he could, but never would again.

In April, Mickey Hart went out with jamtronica specialists Particle, who dubbed the collaboration Hydra. "Hydra is extreme music," Hart said. "Extreme music for extreme people. I need it."

Almost alone among his colleagues, Hart kept his antenna tuned to the contemporary music world, not the pop charts necessarily, but a phenomenon like Particle—live musicians fusing jam-band instrumentals with modern electronic dance music, customarily the product of recording studios—would reach Hart's ears. He had attended raves and kept his eyes on the growth of DJ culture. Formed in Los Angeles in 2000, Particle blew up two years later. In 2002, one of the band's two sets at Bonnaroo started after midnight and was still going strong five hours later at sunrise. A few months later, the band laid waste to the Jammys backing Fred Schneider and Kate Pierson of the B-52s on a romping extended remake of "Love Shack."

Particle brought together strains of funk, jazz, and rock into the world of electronica, also subverting the form by performing primarily in public up to a hundred and fifty concerts a year. This was usually a producer/DJ's game, not a live band's, and was unusual in dance music circles. The jam-band scene embraced the group. Fans of the band dubbed themselves Particle People, attracted to the genre-busting group whose 2004 debut album, *Launchpad*, was a critical and popular success. Particle keyboardist Steve Molitz had joined Phil and Friends in December 2004 at the Warfield, but that had nothing to do with the band's collaboration with Hart, who challenged the group with his polyrhythms and space. Molitz credited Hart with showing the band how to play with more space and patience.

"I have everything all in one place," Hart told the *Santa Cruz Metro*, "all my favorite processors are onstage. I can do things in this band that I couldn't do in the Grateful Dead. These kids were born digital."

While the band members busied themselves with their various projects, Grateful Dead Productions CEO Cameron Sears worked at reducing the overhead and streamlining the operation. Only about twelve employees remained. He kept a skeletal office staff at a small suite on Lucas Valley Road down the highway from Novato. Only the Vault, the studio, and the funky production trailer Ram Rod and Parish kept in the parking lot were still at the old Coca-Cola plant. Sears struggled with the mission, but he plodded on, under the impression he was consolidating operations for sustainability, not closing everything down. Every few months, he would lay off another person or two. With Lesh still refusing to attend board meetings, Sears could call a quorum with the other three, but he had to deal with Lesh through fraught phone calls to Jill, often hearing Lesh in the background offering direction or shouting "No, no, no!"

Lesh did not mount a full-scale Phil and Friends tour that summer, but he did book a July weekend in Denver—one night at the new Denver Fillmore and the next at Red Rocks—and brought along Ryan Adams, his Jammys discovery, as the band's lead vocalist. The Fillmore Auditorium in Denver was an old hall where the Dead played in 1967 when the place was operated in a short-lived, ill-fated venture by Chet Helms of San Francisco's Avalon Ballroom called the Denver Dog. Red Rocks, of course, had been the scene of some of the greatest latter-era Dead concerts.

At Red Rocks, Adams was game, but he never found the intensity of "Wharf Rat" at the Jammys. He flubbed lyrics in virtually every song, even reading from a teleprompter. Adams had not done his homework tackling the massive songbook and his performance teetered on catastrophe. He threw off sparks at points and tried to dig in, but spent most of the three-hour show flailing at the songs. Lesh, in an experimental mood, laughed it off. "Ryan brings the crazy," he said.

If the Deadheads remained unaware of the latest break in the band, the tribute concert, "Comes a Time," to mark the tenth anniversary of Jerry Garcia's death in September at the Greek Theater in Berkeley, should have given them cause to ponder. A five-hour extravaganza and Rex Foundation fundraiser, the concert covered the full expanse of Garcia's career—from his beginnings in the Palo Alto bluegrass scene to his solo bands. A largely disabled Merl Saunders, Garcia's old partner around Bay Area clubs and recent victim of a stroke, hobbled out and sat at the keyboard for a few minutes to receive some applause. RatDog did a short set. The evening built up to a massive Grateful Dead jam session featuring guitarists Warren Haynes and Trey Anastasio of Phish, pianist Bruce Hornsby, and the rest of the Dead guys. Only one was missing.

Nobody knows why Lesh skipped the party. It is not like he wouldn't be missed. He and his wife now had their own nonprofit and it was conceivable that he didn't want to participate in a competing foundation's fundraiser. He never said. What he did say, in a post on his Web site, ever conscious of Deadhead sentiment, was that he could not attend because he would be helping his son move into the dormitory at Stanford University, an hour away, where he was going to be an entering freshman.

Lesh should have known the enterprise of the Deadheads better. In a short time, they had discovered that Stanford ordered parents to leave by 6 p.m. Saturday so their children could start their college careers unimpeded by parental supervision.

On his fall Phil and Friends tour of the East Coast and South, Lesh brought Chris Robinson of the Black Crowes. With Jimmy Herring unavailable, he called Larry Campbell, Dylan's old guitarist he ran into at the Jammys. Campbell fit with the band like a puzzle piece. He was in the guitar chair for Lesh's big New Year's Eve concert at the seven-thousand-seat Bill Graham Civic Auditorium in San Francisco with Ryan Adams back on vocals, Red Rocks all forgiven.

Lesh was still the outlier critic sticking up for the Deadheads in November when Grateful Dead Productions clamped down on the tape traders. It may not have been the smartest move the Dead ever made, but Lesh wasted no time in abandoning any kind of united front. With sales of CDs down dramatically—not just *Dick's Picks*, but the entire industry—the Internet loomed as the new avenue of distribution for recordings. After the introduction of iTunes by Apple in 2001, the music business started to see downloads as the next format, although there were issues around digital rights management that needed to be solved. The Dead began posting concert recordings on the band's Web site and offering downloads for a pricey $18, although the files could be copied. Sometime around Thanksgiving, it occurred to GDP CEO Sears that the band was competing with massive numbers of Dead concerts already posted on the Web and available for free. He contacted the Internet Music Archive (www.archive.net), home to thousands of Dead concert recordings, and asked the site to bar any future downloads.

He might as well have set off a bomb in Deadland. The outrage from Deadheads was instantaneous. Thousands of fans signed an online petition overnight. It wasn't only that the Dead had pulled down the soundboard recordings that were the official property of the band, but they also banned the tapes fans made and traded under the full approval (and even auspices) of the band.

At the heart of the band's complex relationship with their following were the tape traders. For years, the tapers operated with impunity at the shows from a special section set aside exactly for that purpose, a tiny forest of microphones clustered over the crowd. The Dead have always had a loose relationship with their intellectual rights. Garcia's proclamation that whatever the fans wanted to do with the music was OK—"after we're through with it"—was more than authorization; it was the crucial piece in the band's compact with the Deadheads. The tapes fostered new generations of fans and served to create a worldwide community that shared the music and saw these tapes as a product of hippie ideals.

Lesh jumped to the Deadheads' defense. He immediately posted a statement condemning the action on his Web site. "I was not part of this decision-making process and I was not notified that the shows were going to be pulled. I do feel that the music is the Grateful Dead's legacy and I hope that one way or another all of it is available for those who want it," he wrote.

The next day, the band capitulated. They agreed to allow audience-recorded tapes to be freely traded on the site, but reserved the sound board tapes as streaming only. It was not so surprising a teapot tempest in the volatile world of the often-entitled Deadheads, but the attention paid this minor matter was indicative of how mainstream the Dead's following had become in the years since Garcia's death. The august *New York Times* not only devoted two daily news stories to the controversy, but a third think piece by lead pop music critic Jon Pareles explained why it all mattered.

On their own, the band had been meeting with an accountant and financial advisor named Tim Jorstad, who worked with other Marin County rock musicians like the members of Santana, the Doobie Brothers, and Journey. Jorstad had long worked with some of the band and had served as Kreutzmann's proxy at many GDP board meetings. Jorstad counseled the band to cut overhead severely. While Sears was on the East Coast at his family's old summer home dealing with his father's diagnosis of lymphoma, the band met over Italian food in Mill Valley and decided to follow Jorstad's advice. Weir and his wife called Sears in tears to tell him about the meeting. "We're shutting it down," they told him.

While Sears did not understand the urgency, he agreed to Jill Lesh's demand that he take a call with Jorstad to discuss the situation before he returned home two days later. Sears dutifully made the call from a bench at the Boston Science Museum with his kids in tow and reached Jorstad on his phone, driving his Porsche to a dental appointment, seemingly unaware of any urgency, breezy and unconcerned. Sears returned home depressed and discouraged. He had thought he was streamlining the business, not folding it. He felt betrayed.

The band's new record deal neared completion. Rhino Entertainment was changing their business model and targeted the Grateful Dead as a pilot project, putting Sears, John Scher, and Hal Kant in the enviable position of negotiating a beneficial deal. As the revenues from CD sales plummeted, labels were seeking different approaches to dealing with bands. Rhino wanted to assume control of the Dead's entire business, especially the Vault, and demonstrate to other successful classic rock bands how well this kind of an operation could be run. As record sales evaporated, these so-called 360 deals were a new wrinkle in the music business. Rhino was owned by Time Warner Inc., so the label had full access to the Dead's Warner Brothers catalog and had already released two doorstop boxed sets of the band's Warner Brothers releases. Despite Lesh's previous statement about never leasing the Vault, Rhino negotiated a ten-year license to the entire business of the Grateful Dead—all their recordings, merchandise, logos, emblems, intellectual properties, their Web site, the works—for a sum said to approach an astronomical $30 million, $3 million a year.

One morning in May 2006, temperature-controlled moving trucks pulled up in the parking lot at Bel Marin Keys and the Vault was loaded up and shipped off to some Fort Knox–like tape facility Warner Brothers operated in Burbank. The split was leaking into public view.

"I think it was a common thought that if we got rid of the business, we might become friends again," Hart told the *Marin Independent Journal*. "We might actually play again. We really love each other, and, deep down, we're tied at the heart. Our friendship needs to be renewed, but we could never do it around a boardroom table. Now we have nothing to fight over. . . . This is a great load off of me and all of us in general, which is one of the reasons we thought it was a great deal. It had become unmanageable between the four of us. Board meetings were never our thing, even in the best of times."

Rhino hired Grateful Dead merchandising manager Peter McQuaid as a consultant, thinking the company needed someone on their end with intimate knowledge of the Dead. This move did not make the Leshes happy as they had fallen out with McQuaid and no longer wanted him involved in anything Grateful Dead. This time, however, they could not pressure someone to fire him.

In one of those juxtapositions of events that said far more than could be written off to simple coincidence, the same week they came for the Vault, Ram Rod died. He had been on the bus with Ken Kesey and, in strange but important ways, was as much the heart and soul of the Grateful Dead as anyone. The band recognized his stature among them. Back in the giddy early days, before they became big business, the band found it necessary to first incorporate their business affairs. When they had to name officers, for chairman of the board they selected Ram Rod. Lawrence Shurtliff, his given name, came to the band during the first year and stayed for the entire ride. A lifelong smoker, he developed lung cancer and didn't hang around long. Typically he kept it quiet, but band members and crew visited him in the hospital daily. His loss was traumatic to the Dead family. "He was our rock," said Weir.

If that wasn't enough, two weeks later the harried, depressive Vince Welnick, long estranged from his former Dead colleagues, slashed his own throat, in full view of his horrified wife, who was forced to watch him die. The Dead family turned up for support. Parish was on the scene as soon as he got the call. Weir brought his wife and family over to Welnick's house later that day. His friends knew how depressed he had been. Many heard him speak of suicide. He was also in the middle of switching antidepressant medicines, which can be a dangerous time. Still his death came as a harsh shock, a sad end to a turbulent life.

Now that Rhino was minding the store, Hart certainly wasn't sitting around waiting for something to happen. With Kreutzmann living in Marin and the two of them getting along especially well, he returned with a new edition of his all-percussion band Planet Drum with Dead mate and rhythm partner Kreutzmann beside him. Along with bassist Mike Gordon of Phish and guitarist Steve Kimock, Hart brought North Indian tabla master Zakir Hussain, Nigerian hand-drummer Sikiru Adepoju, and Puerto Rican percussionist Giovanni Hidalgo.

With Kreutzmann on board, they called the band the Rhythm Devils, a term that dated back to their drum solos during the seventies, made official by director Francis Ford Coppola when he hired them to produce a combustive percussion piece for the soundtrack to his 1980 film *Apocalypse Now*. After test-driving the unit at the Jammys in April (right before he went on tour with Particle), Hart booked a full-scale nationwide tour in July and talked again with the *Marin IJ* before the band's appearance as the opening act of the annual San Francisco Jazz Festival in September. He didn't sound especially hopeful when asked about the Dead playing together again. "The healing has begun," he said.

> Once we got rid of the business, we don't have anything to argue about anymore really. Hopefully, we'll renew our friendships. We're starting to get together again socially. Because in order to make Grateful Dead music, you've got to really love each other. To do it really successfully and right, it's not about the music, it's about the interpersonal relationships between the players. It's about trust and love and all those crazy things. And that's coming back. So I look forward to some day when we can all be on the same stage and laugh and smile and feel good about each other and play our music. It's not over till it's over, and it ain't over yet. In the meantime, there's Planet Drum and the Rhythm Devils.

Hart exaggerated. The band members weren't speaking. He and Weir talked, but Lesh had nothing to do with them. They all had their own bands. The Vault was gone. Ram Rod was dead. The real estate was sold. The office was closed. The sun had set on the Grateful Dead.

14

Obama

I N AUGUST 2007, Phil Lesh arranged to take his son Brian to New York City for a taping of *The Daily Show* with Jon Stewart. It was Brian's eighteenth birthday. The featured guest was Sen. Barack Obama, a candidate for the Democratic presidential nomination. Brian, a senior at the exclusive Branson School in Ross, was an avid Obama volunteer who attended meetings run by the national high school campaign director in her Palo Alto bedroom. He went to a three-day "Camp Obama" that summer to train organizers and campaign workers. His rock star father pulled a few strings and scored the tickets to the TV taping.

At the show, Obama shook hands briefly with Lesh and his family as he left, but later that evening the Leshes attended an Obama rally before an overflow audience at the New York Marriott Hotel at the Brooklyn Bridge. The forty-six-year-old junior senator from Illinois, lean, poised, and relaxed, electrified the crowd. He warmed up with folksy recollections of his student days living in an apartment in the recently gentrified Park Slope neighborhood ("I couldn't afford it now") before turning to rallying cries for health care, against the Iraq war ("It's not going well"), seeking Osama Bin Laden, and emptying Guantánamo ("I want to restore habeas corpus"). He was firm, fair, measured, but the speech was shot through with his unique understated charisma. He led the crowd to a rousing finale, getting them to scream and holler with him like a Baptist preacher: "Fired up . . . ready to go . . . fired up . . . ready to go . . . fired up . . . ready to go . . . Thank you, Brooklyn. Let's go change the world."

Lesh was swept up by the performance, the hairs on his neck standing on end. Since Brian was an official in the Obama youth organization, he was invited backstage to meet Obama, who then came back out with Brian to meet his parents. They engaged in small talk and Obama asked about Lesh's profession.

"I played bass in the Grateful Dead for thirty years," Lesh said.

Obama brightened. "I enjoy your music very much," he said.

Lesh asked if he had ever attended any Dead concerts and Obama told Lesh he had not seen the band, but he had their music on his iPod. The Leshes glowed at this moment. Jill Lesh, as taken by the experience as her son and husband, spoke up.

"We can get the hippie vote for you," she said.

Obama smiled and her husband echoed his wife and offered to help any way he could. Within days, Obama's staff reached out to speak with Lesh. He started to make plans to hold a Phil and Friends benefit for the Obama campaign, but Brian wouldn't hear of it. "No," he told his father, "you've got to get the Dead together because it will be much more meaningful and important."

Nobody had been thinking about playing music together again. Everybody was actively pursuing projects on their own, freed from the Grateful Dead and not even really in touch with one another. Another reunion wasn't something anybody had even considered. The other three might have thought about it if they were speaking with Lesh. Things did not end well between them. Lesh had recently run into Weir shopping at the Apple store in Marin, so they were talking again, to a degree, but Hart was a different matter. Lesh, who spent a weekend in January canvassing Obama voters (and going unrecognized) in Nevada, bravely put in a call.

"I was about to call you for the same reason," said Hart, whose intense political enthusiasms had already led him to Obama.

On Monday, February 4, 2008, the eve of the California primary, a key state in the Super Tuesday delegate sweepstakes where Obama trailed rival Hillary Clinton in the polls by as much as ten points, "Deadheads for Obama" drew a raving full house to the Warfield Theatre in San Francisco where Bobby Weir, Mickey Hart, and Phil Lesh were going to perform together on behalf of the Obama campaign. Kreutzmann, who had moved back to Hawaii the previous year, was not available. Obama wanted to bring America together and he was going to start with the Grateful Dead.

Outside on the sidewalk, people were offering as much as $300 for a ticket. Inside, the tie-dyed Deadheads were waving Obama signs. Because this was the big event of the night for the campaign in town, every political reporter and television crew assigned to the Obama beat in Northern California crowded into the tiny basement area outside the dressing rooms for a press conference before the show. Lesh extolled the virtues of their candidate and talked about how the Dead men were bonded as brothers. He told about calling and soliciting Hart, as if they spoke every day. As the political reporters, unfamiliar with the personalities involved, dutifully scribbled down Lesh's proclamations of unity, one of the town's music writers stepped out from behind a camera and asked Hart how long it had actually been since the three of them had even seen each other.

"I see Bobby every week," Hart said. "Phil . . . it's been years and years."

The evening opened with a video message from the candidate himself on a screen in the middle of the stage as the band members milled around and watched. "Hi everybody—this is Barack Obama," he said. "and I just want to thank Phil and Bob and Mickey for helping pull this together. You know, Phil's son Brian cut his summer short to join this campaign for change. It's young people like that all across the country who are rediscovering a sense of idealism and possibility. For all of you to come together and help put on this concert to encourage people to vote is extraordinary. So I want to say thank you to all of you. I want everybody to sit down and enjoy the music"—Deadheads smothered the instructions to "sit down" with jeers—"and make sure you vote tomorrow, because if we vote, we not only got a chance to win the election, but we got a chance to change the country and change the world."

With un-Dead-like surgical timing, as applause died for Obama's video, the band rolled into "Playing in the Band" and the place exploded. It was a makeshift Dead—the current edition of Phil and Friends plus Weir, Hart, and RatDog guitarist Karan, but the band was on fire, everybody clearly pumped by the three-quarters reunion and the excitement of the occasion. Lesh's latest band not only included drummer Molo and guitarist Larry Campbell, but singer-songwriter-guitarist Jackie Greene, keyboardist Steve Molitz of Particle, and steel guitarist Barry Sless.

The band brought the brief opening set to a close with the Beatles' "Come Together," a most appropriate selection that RatDog had been performing, but Lesh's band took pains to learn that evening during sound check. At the end of the forty-minute set, Lesh read a campaign speech clearly crafted by the campaign for him full of "Yes we can" and "fired up . . . ready to go." Hart echoed the endorsement and Weir took a poll from the crowd to find out when were they going to vote the next day—in the morning, lunchtime, or after work.

The seven-piece band returned for two more dazzling sets. Greene mowed down "Sugaree," a song he had been performing not only with Phil and Friends but in his own shows as well. At the close of the thrilling evening, Lesh appended his customary donor rap with an appeal for fans to volunteer the next day to help get out the vote. The final song was—what else?—"U.S. Blues." While the band played, some crazy hippie dashed back and forth at the back of the stage waving a giant American flag. By the time he reached the front of the stage and the band charged into the song's final choruses, the hippie had changed his flag to one with the peace sign where the stars usually are. The Deadheads burst into cheers.

The next day, Obama punched his way to an eight-point loss to Clinton. The Deadhead vote Jill Lesh promised to deliver did not swing the day, but The Dead's drawing power on the East Coast was not lost on the Obama campaign who, in the fall election, smelling victory in the perennial swing state of Pennsylvania and looking to load up resources in the state, asked Lesh if the band might be able to hold a fundraiser. By this time, plans were already quietly under way to mount a full-scale Dead reunion the following year, although the official word from the Dead camp was that this would be a one-time-only event and any future reunions would wait until after Pennsylvania. Behind the scenes, Live Nation had made an attractive offer for a modest number of dates with a guarantee of $1 million per show. Only the details remained to be ironed out.

On October 13 at the Bryce Jordan Center at Pennsylvania State University, with Billy Kreutzmann on board, the fully reformed Dead played a concert called "Change Rocks" with the Allman Brothers opening that raised $500,000 for the campaign. Guitarist Warren Haynes played in both bands and stayed on the stage all night. "It's a beautiful night," he told the crowd during the Allmans' opening set. "It's an historic night. Don't forget to vote."

This would be the sixth new edition of the Grateful Dead since Garcia died. It had been almost four years since the four had last performed together. They had all followed different individual paths in the intervening years, but nobody had found the same kind of connection—with the crowd or other musicians—as they did when they played together.

"We're all deeply into this," Hart said to *Rolling Stone* backstage, "into Barack Obama and the thought of taking this country back in some shape or form, what's left of it. It's probably one thing we can all agree on. It's funny that an Obama event would do that, but that's how important and critical this election is. It's our call to arms, or call to music, which is the way we arm ourselves."

After another Obama video speech during the break—"For twenty months, I've been traveling this country from town to town—even developing a 'Touch of Grey' of my own," Obama said. "On November 5th, I hope to announce that we 'Ain't Wasting Time No More.'"—the band swung into immediate action with "Truckin'" stretched into a delirious ten-minute romp, which led to a rollicking "U.S. Blues," an almost ridiculously upbeat opening segment that soon veered into less productive areas. The band lost its footing and never regained the altitude. There had been no real rehearsals. Lesh squeezed in the show between Phil and Friends dates on an East Coast tour; RatDog had been out all summer with more dates starting later in October; both Hart and Kreutzmann had been touring with their own bands that summer. Coming together between all their own tours and projects, the Pennsylvania show by the revived Dead might have suffered as a consequence.

Weir followed Lesh's donor rap with remarks of his own. He quoted gonzo journalist Hunter Thompson: "If every Deadhead who lived in Florida had voted in 2000, it would be a very different world today." The band then launched into "Touch of Grey" followed by a thunderous "Not Fade Away" to bring the two-hour concert to a close. In the end, the band weathered the rough spots to rediscover their primal connection. Lesh raved about Weir's vocal prowess and Kreutzmann boasted he and Hart were clicking again. "Mickey and I are getting along better now," he told *Rolling Stone*. "The egos are out of the way."

Since closing the office and parting ways in 2006, both Lesh and Weir had been keeping busy schedules with their individual bands. Over the past several years, RatDog had grown in popularity and Phil and Friends, at the least, had leveled off. Since Robin Sylvester replaced Rob Wasserman in the band and RatDog took a sharp turn into serious jamming and hard rocking, the crowds had been building. At the same time, the revolving cast of Phil and Friends—plus the band's decreasing novelty—was losing ground with the Deadheads. Guitarist Larry Campbell, who replaced Herring as his main guitarist, was not as beloved by the audience, and the addition of guests like the arcane jazz guitarist John Scofield, however entertaining he may have been for Lesh, left the fans somewhat less enthusiastic. RatDog had developed a serious following after years of dogged touring and evolving the band. In April 2008, for the third year in a row, RatDog sold out three nights at the Beacon Theatre in New York.

Although Weir worked out daily and had a health regime that extended to esoteric ginseng extracts that cost hundreds of dollars a bottle he took before shows, he was a mess. He was drinking heavily, often to a near-comatose state, made all the more dangerous by his fondness for pharmaceuticals. He often complained of shoulder pain from throwing a football—he played with the same bunch of local guys at public parks around Mill Valley every weekend he was in town—or hanging a guitar from his shoulder, and he took painkillers. Booze and downers. In July, after he played a local benefit, a friend found him collapsed, trembling, and unable to speak on the front bench outside the 2 AM Club, a well-known Mill Valley watering hole. The bar owner called an ambulance.

Weir toured almost compulsively. He went out for three six-week tours a year and, in between, played festivals and weekend gigs. During his infrequent stays at home, he could be found sitting in with other bands around town or playing benefit concerts for environmental or political causes. RatDog played the band's 850th show New Year's Eve 2008 at the Bill Graham Civic Auditorium in San Francisco (headlined by Phil and Friends) with the band's roster undisturbed since bassist Sylvester joined five years before.

Lesh also had learned the benefits of having, at least, a longer-term band. Guitarist Larry Campbell continued to serve as his musical *consiglieri* and Particle's Steve Molitz was holding down the keyboard chair with Molo at the drum kit. In July 2007, Lesh added twenty-six-year-old Jackie Greene to his Phil and Friends repertory company. Greene was a promising Dylanesque singer-songwriter and a musical throwback to his parents' generation, who released his major label debut, *American Myth*, on Verve/Forecast in 2006. Raised in the gold rush town of Placerville in the Sierra Nevada foothills, young Greene absorbed his parents' record collection at an early age and recorded his own debut CD in a home studio while still in high school. His 2002 *Gone Wanderin'* album on a Sacramento-based independent label won widespread acclaim and some airplay across Northern California. His major label outing featured Elvis Costello's rhythm section and was produced by Steve Berlin of Los Lobos, but failed to launch.

Lesh first heard Greene's title song from *Gone Wanderin'* on KFOG, the San Francisco rock radio station, and checked out his set at Bonnaroo in 2007. A month or so later, Lesh phoned Greene and asked if he would be interested in helping him make some music. Greene, who knew nothing of the Grateful Dead's music, leaped at the opportunity.

His major label release was a stiff. Greene, who had moved to San Francisco, was sleeping in the equipment locker of the Mission District recording studio he shared with Tim Bluhm of Mother Hips and Dave Brogan of Animal Liberation Orchestra. His '94 Jetta was falling apart. When he landed the job with Phil and Friends, he was finally able to afford his own small apartment.

The next month, he was dropped onstage before a capacity crowd at Red Rocks singing his "Tell Me Mama, Tell Me Right" along with the Dead material with Phil and Friends. Greene brought youthful good looks and enthusiasm, a handful of his songs, a few more Dylan tunes, and his own classic rock sensibilities. With Larry Campbell adding judicious touches of mandolin and even fiddle to the band, Greene's backwoods holler and acoustic guitar made this version of Phil and Friends an entirely more flexible band than the storied Q, even if the latest edition lacked The Q's firepower.

This new reunion of The Dead came at a curious juncture in the schedules of the four principals. Even Kreutzmann was working. After The Dead splintered in 2006, he had joined up with Hart to revive the Rhythm Devils with Steve Kimock, Phish bassist Mike Gordon, African talking drummer Sikiru Adepoju, and a few new Robert Hunter songs. He had moved back to Hawaii in 2007 after divorcing his fourth wife. It was bassist Gordon who introduced Kreutzmann to guitarist Scott Murawski of Max Creek when the three performed together at a benefit concert in Costa Rica. When Kreutzmann suggested a more permanent arrangement, Gordon bowed out, but Allman Brothers bassist Oteil Burbridge accepted. Originally called the Bill Kreutzmann Trio but soon shortened to BK3, the band mixed Dead covers with old Max Creek songs, new originals by Murawski, and a couple of new Hunter songs and played a Northeast tour in summer 2008 and a round of West Coast dates in early 2009.

Kreutzmann was also cooking up music with another associate. He first heard Louisiana native Papa Mali at the Oregon Country Fair in summer 2008 and joined the eccentric guitarist and vocalist for a New Year's Eve gig with Bonnie Raitt bassist Hutch Hutchinson, who also lives in Hawaii, at the Pauela Cannery in upcountry Maui.

Hart was also busy, as usual. He had the Mickey Hart Band on tour all summer 2008 whose returning members included Kimock and Adepoju alongside New Orleans r&b bassist George Porter of the Meters, drummer Walfredo Reyes Jr. and keyboardist Kyle Hollingsworth from String Cheese Incident. Hart also picked up his second Grammy Award for his latest world beat percussion album, *Global Drum Project.*

With RatDog and Phil and Friends also in action, all four had full dance cards when they paused in spring 2009 to play the short but lucrative tour for Live Nation as The Dead. The originally planned fourteen dates were expanded to twenty-three cities over five weeks in April and May 2009. After the Penn State debacle during the Obama campaign, they managed to squeeze in eleven days' rehearsal at Weir's rented studio in San Rafael in February.

The mission was to return with as much money as possible. The coffers were empty. After four years of working their solo acts, the four men's revenue stream had thinned out considerably. Their big money deal with Rhino turned out to return about half what the band had been making on Grateful Dead Records. The Leshes suggested that the members' personal managers sit out the tour and it was agreed. Other options were explored. At first, the band considered hiring mega-manager Irving Azoff, who handled the Eagles and other top rock acts, after Hart was introduced to Azoff by Sammy Hagar (Azoff had managed Van Halen when Hagar rejoined for the 2005 reunion tour), but that unlikely association never happened. Coran Capshaw, manager of the Dave Matthews Band, was dying to handle the tour, but the band members ultimately agreed to work without management to avoid paying commissions, instead hiring Tim Jorstad to work as a consultant paid a $500 hourly fee.

Caryl Hart took time out from studying for her PhD at UC Berkeley to act as her husband's surrogate, understanding that she wouldn't be paid. Taking that role also meant she had to interact regularly with Jill Lesh, who was Phil's manager. Caryl didn't see that as a problem as she considered Jill a friend who had even thrown her a baby shower when she was pregnant with her daughter Reya. But

the Jill she encountered now was a different woman: harsh, antagonistic, and controlling. She quickly tired of being on the receiving
end of screaming phone calls from Jill, who could take issue with
the smallest things. This was not the way the Dead handled things. It
was the Leshes who had declared themselves keepers of the soul of
the Grateful Dead. More importantly, the Leshes were indisputably in
charge of The Dead.

Caryl came to dread interactions with the Leshes. She began to
pop Valiums before taking business meetings to help cope with Jill's
nonstop talking. Relations were also strained—to say the least—by the
Leshes' constant complaints and demands for more money. Their
past threats the previous couple of years to sue the other partners
over business issues didn't help. If Lesh envisioned himself as a
leader who would take over after Garcia and direct the band's for-
tunes, nobody was following him. Not voluntarily, at least.

On the eve of the reunion announcement planned for New Year's
Eve 2008, Jorstad received a 3 a.m. email from Kreutzmann in Hawaii.
"I want nothing more to do with the Grateful Dead," he wrote. "Leave
me out of it." Jorstad, who never knew who was authoring recent
emails from Hawaii, Kreutzmann or his new girlfriend, Aimee More-
head, called the Leshes to ask if the email sounded like Kreutzmann.
They assured him it did indeed sound like Kreutzmann, so Jorstad
now had to quickly contemplate the announcement he and Live Nation were planning to make the next day. There would be a giant
difference between a reunion of the surviving original members—the
so-called core four—and three out of four.

In a panic, Jorstad dispatched Kreutzmann's grown filmmaker
son, Justin Kreutzmann, to Hawaii to get his father to call Jorstad.
When he finally spoke to him, Kreutzmann claimed the email was
nothing more than a joke. Kreutzmann may have relented, but he
maintained a dark, sulky mood for the duration of the tour. He
showed up in poor physical condition and struggled to keep up with
the much more physically fit Hart for the whole tour.

The band hoped to unveil the new edition at a free concert in
New York City on March 30, but weather and city permits scotched
that plan in favor of three shows in one night at small Manhattan

venues. The four thousand tickets were distributed to fans through an online lottery. The morning began with Weir, Lesh, and touring guitarist Warren Haynes playing "Friend of the Devil" on morning TV talk show *The View* (host Whoopi Goldberg was a longtime Dead fan). At five in the afternoon, the same three gave a rare acoustic performance at a former Lower East Side synagogue called Angel Orensanz that focused on *Workingman's Dead* and *American Beauty* material, although the highlight of the hour-long set was a near-twenty-minute, largely instrumental version of "Bird Song."

At eight o'clock that night, drummers Hart and Kreutzmann with keyboardist Jeff Chimenti joined the three guitarists at Gramercy Theater on East 23rd Street for a full electric band romp that began with a half-hour jam and "Playing in the Band." The evening ended with a two-hour session uptown at the Roseland Ballroom, where three thousand fans were treated to a rocking set of fan favorites such as "Eyes of the World," "Cassidy," "St. Stephen," a twisting, turning "Dark Star," and a celebratory "Sugar Magnolia" finale, Haynes topping the mix with Chuck Berry riffs. "It's just like playing a three-hour show," Weir told *Rolling Stone*, "but it's broken up by cab rides."

The tour began two weeks later in Greensboro, North Carolina, and almost immediately tempo wars broke out onstage. Weir and Kreutzmann would engage in duels—Weir fighting to slow the rhythm, Kreutzmann trying to drive the beat back up. The next day was a day off before appearing at the Verizon Center in Washington, DC, and the band accepted an invitation to meet with President Obama in the Oval Office of the White House. Band members and wives talked history with the down-to-earth president. Jill Lesh spotted a vase of scarlet begonias on the way out of the Oval Office, to everyone's delight. After all, it was Obama's campaign that had fostered this current reunion and the place was lousy with Deadheads. They were ushered into Chief of Staff David Axelrod's office to meet with the senior Deadheads on the staff, all of whom intended to attend the concert the following night, where Tipper Gore sat in on drums.

After the first week, Jorstad went home, but a week later he received an aggrieved phone call from Lesh, who demanded that he return immediately to the tour and straighten out the situation. Lesh was unhappy with the musical performances and wanted Jorstad to settle the problems. Jorstad flew from California straight to backstage at Madison Square Garden in New York. He feared the tour would be canceled and the money would have to be returned to Live Nation. With tickets costing as much as $100, sales had not been as brisk as Live Nation had hoped. Although the last tour in 2004 had earned $18 million, the current tour could wind up losing money for the company and they were getting nervous. Jorstad did not want to give them an excuse to cancel. The next night, he brought all four together in a backstage room before the show and explained the financial realities and possible consequences of their disputes.

Jorstad counseled the band to resolve their differences. He knew Weir thought Lesh played so loud, he had to scream to sing. He knew Lesh thought Kreutzmann was rushing the beat. Jorstad advised the band to keep in mind they had not been playing together for more than five years. "I don't know what your expectations were," he told them, "but perfection is not on the menu."

Jorstad reiterated the complaints band members had expressed to him—but not each other—about one another. These feelings needed to be aired, he said, but he also reminded the band that their fans, in the middle of a severe economic recession, had paid big money to attend these shows and the band owed these people a good show. Jorstad resolved to stay with the band for the duration of the tour, even though it would increase his fee.

Thinking it would be shrewd to keep her busy, Jorstad gave various minor duties to Jill Lesh. She was smart and capable enough and took care of some of the details for him, although he knew it could cause huge trouble if other band members found out. She had been working the Phil and Friends tours for ten years, which made her far more experienced than Jorstad. She also had a close working relationship with Matt Busch, the young RatDog road manager who came to Phil and Friends with Warren Haynes in 1999 at age twenty-five. He went to work for Weir in 2005 with the blessing of the Leshes and remained one of the few insiders who stayed on good terms with everybody. Jorstad had to rely on Busch and Jill Lesh. It seemed like a good idea at the time, but he knew better than to tell Kreutzmann.

Jill took her responsibilities seriously. As the tour neared the end, she became enraged at Stefani Scamardo, Warren Haynes's wife and manager, onstage at Shoreline Amphitheatre in Mountain View during sound check. Her beef was the amount of attention Haynes was getting onstage. She attacked Scamardo, criticizing her husband for taking too much prominence. She then dismissed Haynes as hired help. Scamardo, not a timid woman herself, refused to back down as the two women got into it in full view of band and crew.

Backstage, Jill wouldn't stop. She had decided that her contributions to the tour should be compensated, even though the band had decided not to pay managers. She confronted Jorstad over money, demanding a commission for the management work she had done on the tour. "The drummers don't bring anything to the table," she said. "They have to pay."

Fearful of Kreutzmann's reaction if he ever discovered Jill Lesh had assumed anything resembling official duties on his watch, Jorstad counseled her to drop the matter. She would not hear of it. Jorstad even pointed out that she and her husband would be paying a quarter of the fee to her out of their own take and that wouldn't be worth the trouble it would cause. Still, Jill Lesh was determined to extract a fee from the band.

The Shoreline show was highlighted by a troupe of fire dancers from Kauai, friends of Kreutzmann, who lit up the traditional drums/space interlude with fiery acrobatics that linked the Dead's underground roots to the modern-day Burning Man culture. Weir squirmed in the wings. "Is this what we've become?" he muttered to Jorstad. Lesh also hated the display, but Hart thought it was sensational and Kreutzmann was only sorry his friends didn't play every show on the tour.

Of course, the ongoing musical tension between Lesh and the two drummers carried into their relationship offstage. Band members were not speaking and the Leshes had turned against the drummers, especially Kreutzmann. Many years before, in a drunken moment,

Kreutzmann had squeezed Jill Lesh's breasts backstage. The incident had never been forgotten or forgiven. Lesh was not happy with Kreutzmann's playing. He even secretly kept Molo on call throughout the tour in case there was an opportunity to use him. Lesh approached a startled and appalled Mickey Hart before the tour's final show at the Gorge Amphitheatre outside Seattle about substituting Molo for Kreutzmann. The answer was a firm, resolute no, but Lesh was not someone to take no for an answer.

One big money date remained on the calendar, the Fourth of July at the Rothbury Music Festival in western Michigan. The band was scheduled to received $2.5 million for a headline performance with a bonus based on ticket sales. When Jill Lesh discovered the promoters had opened a third gate for tickets not shown on the manifest, she held back the band from taking the stage until the promoters agreed to pay the full amount they owed. With Jorstad not on the trip, she acted as manager. The show started a half-hour late. Instead of that making her a hero with Kreutzmann, he was furious that she would get involved and thought taking the stage late was disrespectful to the fans. Kreutzmann simmered with anger and frustration.

15

Furthur

HE BAND members arrived at Tim Jorstad's office in downtown San Rafael for the final settlement conference after the tour. It had been successful and as much as a million dollars in residual funds needed to be distributed. Jorstad, who managed the tour, something he had never done before, had also represented some of the members as accountant and financial advisor for years, acting as Kreutzmann's proxy for the GDP board when Kreutzmann was in Hawaii. Although he was financial consultant to other Marin County rock stars such as Carlos Santana and Grace Slick, Jorstad was no hippie. He was a small-town boy who graduated from the University of Northern Colorado and had owned his own bank, a straitlaced financial consultant. He was not accustomed to the rough-and-ready rock-and-roll world of the Dead or the complicated personal relationships that extended back more than forty years.

He had attended many performances by his clients over the years and enjoyed concerts as much as anyone, but Jorstad had never gone out on the road with his acts before. The experience on this tour had been revelatory, to say the least. No longer were the sales and revenues simply figures on a page; now he was conducting nightly settlements and paying out crew expenses. In addition, he was constantly negotiating among band members who could no longer communicate among themselves. Even with his hourly fees soaring, he felt compelled to stay on the road, for fear that without him the tour would fall apart. When the tour ended, he was relieved. Jorstad had witnessed many dire scenes in client meetings over divorces and other financial hardships over the years, but nothing had prepared him for dealing with the Dead.

In August 2009, after playing the final, one-off Fourth of July date at the Rothbury Music Festival, all four members of the band presented themselves in Jorstad's office. Jorstad knew that the Leshes were still pissed off at the drummers and planning to extract their pound of flesh via a commission for Jill. Phil and Jill had taken him to lunch and ranted the entire meal over their perceived injustices. Jorstad was clear they were not going to let the matter drop. Finally, before the meeting, he told Hart and Kreutzmann about the Leshes' demands. Kreutzmann exploded at Jorstad for keeping him in the dark about Jill's work on the road and raged that the Leshes thought they could hold up the band for a commission at the end of the tour.

In Jorstad's office with the four members, all the frustration, all the veiled resentments, all the years of being lashed together erupted, and Kreutzmann went off like a geyser. The furious drummer leveled his accusations at Jorstad before turning his attention to Lesh, whose haughty response caused Kreutzmann to explode out of his chair and go for Lesh with his hands. Lesh was no match for the enraged bull, but Kreutzmann was quickly pulled off. He sputtered in anger at Lesh.

"I never want to see you again," he said. "I never want to play with you again. I don't want to have anything to do with you."

Then Kreutzmann stormed out and, once again, closed the door on the Dead.

Lesh, on the other hand, was fine with that. He saw a future without the drummers. He moved quickly behind the scenes with Weir, taking a cutthroat approach to relations in the band, harsh by even his standards. For Lesh, this day had been a long time coming.

Weir sounded sheepish on the telephone talking to John Scher, who had comanaged Weir with Cameron Sears since Garcia died. "I did something last night you're not going to like," he told Scher.

Weir explained that he and Natascha had spent the evening before dining with Phil and Jill and got "knee-crawling drunk." Vegetarian Lesh had stopped drinking many years before and only sneaked occasional puffs of pot out of the purview of his vigilant wife, so this was quite the occasion. Lesh made Weir a proposal. He suggested they combine forces in a new band. He explained to Weir the financial reality: it would take a whole bunch of RatDog shows to earn the same amount he would in a single show if they played together. Without the pesky drummers/partners, they could have a better band, play before bigger audiences, and keep a larger share of the greater spoils.

Weir, who was certainly attracted by the money and the crowds, was also still angry with the drummers from the tour. He could remember specific moments like car crashes during ballads he thought the drummers ruined with their overplaying. In a weak moment, without considering the full ramifications of his decision, he said yes to Lesh. There would, however, be conditions.

Weir would have to dissolve RatDog and jettison his current management. Jill and RatDog road manager Matt Busch would handle the new band and Lesh's booking agent, Jonathan Levine, would represent the act. While it might be possible to save some of his people's jobs under the new conditions, Weir was going to have to fire Scher and Sears, two longtime, close personal associates. Scher began producing Grateful Dead concerts on the East Coast more than thirty years before. Garcia called him their "Jewish cousin" in New York.

With Sears, it was even more complicated. Not only had Sears handled all of Weir's business since Garcia died, his wife was Cassidy Law, daughter of longtime Grateful Dead staffer Eileen Law. Cassidy happened to be born in Weir's bed. The same night, he wrote the song "Cassidy." He was thinking both about the newborn girl Cassidy, whose mother had already decided on the name from the movie *Butch Cassidy and the Sundance Kid,* and Neal Cassady, the bull goose looney of the Merry Pranksters, Weir's onetime roommate and a major figure in Dead circles whose dead body had been found that same day in Mexico. That night was an electric storm of emotion and events in Mill Valley. Weir deeded a portion of the song's copyright to the baby, who grew up like a stepdaughter to him. This cut was going to sacrifice tissue.

As for Hart, Weir called him and gave him the news regretfully. Lesh had approached Hart about going out without Kreutzmann, but Hart's refusal had been absolute. He would not betray his brother. Weir extended the possibility that once he and Lesh went out on the road, Weir could work on Lesh, soften his attitude. Hart remained unconvinced. He was mystified that Lesh and Weir had cut him out. "You're collateral damage," Weir told him.

Lesh and Weir laid plans and quickly assembled their band. Jay Lane from RatDog joined Joe Russo, another young drummer known in jam-band circles for the Benevento/Russo Duo (Phil and Friends regular Molo was unavailable due to a long-term commitment with Roger McNamee's new band, Moonalice). Jeff Chimenti from RatDog (and the Other Ones and the Dead) took the keyboard spot. Guitarist John Kadlecik was a telling pick for the Garcia chair. His band, the Dark Star Orchestra, specialized in performing entire Grateful Dead concerts from the band's history, playing the same songs in the same order. Kadlecik could be scholarly in his efforts at re-creating Garcia's sound in exact detail. He was known as "fake Jerry" and he would go so far as to adjust his amplifiers and other equipment to the period from the show being played. Formed in Chicago in 1997, Dark Star Orchestra were anointed in a late-night jam at a small Chicago club with Phish members Mike Gordon and Jon Fishman just prior to DSO's first anniversary.

In the wake of Garcia's death, the band quickly became known as the leading Dead tribute band, playing as many as two hundred shows a year, polishing their cunning re-creation. In 2008, DSO played a hundred and fifty shows. Given his oft-expressed displeasure with the tribute bands, Lesh's pick of Kadlecik to join his new band served two purposes: it effectively crippled the top tribute band by taking their guitarist and it signaled Lesh's intent to tool his new band into the ultimate Grateful Dead tribute band. Playing with a "fake Jerry" would have been the last thing any of the Dead musicians would have considered in the wake of Garcia's death. Anything but that.

The musicians were assembled at Weir's San Rafael studios. They were not told anything about a new band; they were simply invited to jam with an eye toward performing a benefit concert together at the end of the month. After the third day, the musicians were informed that they were starting a band. They met for dinner at the Leshes' home the next night to talk about a name. That was settled early on by Weir. "How about 'Furthur'?" he said.

On September 18, about a month after the fractious meeting at Jorstad's office, Furthur made the band's debut in three nights at the Fox Oakland, a Gilded Age movie palace whose multimillion-dollar restoration was the cornerstone project of a downtown Oakland redevelopment. The ornate twenty-eight-hundred-seat hall had only opened for concerts a few months before, and Furthur's opening weekend qualified as something of an event in Dead circles, given the band practically dropped out of the sky. The Deadheads knew nothing of backstage infighting. To most of the fans at the Fox Oakland, this was Phil and Bobby with DSO.

The show started with a trifling eight-minute jam between Weir and Lesh, as the rest of the band stood by and watched, effectively isolating the axis on which Furthur would revolve, before the entire band slammed into a hearty "The Other One" for the next fifteen minutes. Kadlecik received a rousing welcome when he stepped to the mike to deliver his first Garcia vocal on "Bird Song."

In explaining the concept behind the surprise new band, Weir reached beyond the interpersonal issues, which he no doubt cared not to express. "Once you add Mickey and Billy to the mix—and this is more real than one might imagine—you add a layer of expectation," Weir told *Relix* magazine. "A lot of folks in the audience are looking for a walk down memory lane and they're disappointed if they don't get that. That's cumbersome. So Phil and I decided to start fresh with the material and with an outfit that didn't carry those expectations."

Lesh also explained the decision to break off from the drummers as a creative choice. "One of the reasons that Bob and I wanted to go ahead with this band was to bring fresh approaches to the tunes, like he was doing with RatDog and I did with Phil and Friends," he told *Relix*. "We treat it as repertoire. In Grateful Dead terms, that means every performance can be different. All versions of the songs are true, just like a fairy tale."

In October, Lesh and Weir previewed the East Coast tour with a brief appearance at a VIP reception for an exhibit about the Grateful Dead in, of all places, the stately New-York Historical Society across the street from Central Park. About three hundred donors and pa-trons milled in the upstairs hall hung with giant antique paintings. "Who knew we would ever be historic," Lesh told the crowd, as he introduced his "best friend and brother" Bob Weir, who arrived on the small stage guitar in hand. The pair played a short set, beginning with a Dylan song undoubtedly selected for the surroundings, "When I Paint My Masterpiece."

Back home in Marin County in November, Furthur played a se-cret show at the tiny 19 Broadway in Fairfax, deep in the bowels of the county, announced only the day of the show. The live rehearsals continued in December with a quick swing through five East Coast small theaters and two nights at Mill Valley's three-hundred-capacity Masonic Hall before ramping up to a full-scale two-night New Year's Eve run at the Bill Graham Civic Auditorium in San Francisco.

In January 2010, Furthur announced the band would do a se-ries of ten consecutive shows at both the Masonic Hall and the 142 Throckmorton Theatre. Deadheads swamped the elite enclave of Mill Valley, filling the quaint town square with panhandlers and camp followers, vans and campers, thoroughly disrupting the up-scale community after the shows in December had caught the lit-tle town by surprise, but the invasion that accompanied the January run was something the burghers were entirely unprepared for. The redwood-covered town center was overrun with hippies and not the bucolic, easygoing California brand, but the more seedy and conten-tious Deadheads from the East Coast. Ticket sales were limited to one ticket per customer and the press was barred from what was being advertised as live rehearsal sessions. Dozens of people waited in line all day on the sidewalks outside the halls. There were complaints of public urination. People were astonished to hear of a knife fight in the Throckmorton lobby.

When the band announced the first extensive national tour for February, the two background vocalists—Zoe Ellis, younger sister of RatDog's Dave Ellis, and Sunshine Garcia Becker, no relation to the guitarist—who were both young mothers with infant children, begged off. Stellar road mother Jill Lesh swung into action, ordered a separate bus and a pair of nannies, and the girls signed back up.

With all this youthful energy behind the grand old men of the Dead, Furthur brought a new vitality to the music. Kadlecik slowly eased his way into his own personal style and away from a more exact re-creation of Garcia solos. Chimenti, always among the most solid musicians on any bandstand, came into his own in this ensemble. Russo was a powerful, supple drummer, and Lane had become thoroughly schooled in the songbook through his years in RatDog. Lesh and Weir even introduced new material. Weir brought "Ashes and Glass" from RatDog. Lesh dusted off an old song Garcia started with David Crosby more than thirty years before called "The Mountain Song," messed around with it himself before giving it to his younger son Brian to finish the lyrics. The Princeton undergrad also worked on lyrics with Robert Hunter for a piece of music by his dad called "Welcome to the Dance" that Furthur introduced as early as the initial Fox Oakland run. Furthur was fresh and confident right from the start. Lesh had taken all the lessons he learned from Phil and Friends and put them to work. Plus he had Weir with him. The Deadheads embraced Furthur immediately.

Matt Busch, Weir's tour manager, and Jill Lesh shared duties comfortably backstage. Busch was calm, capable, and fair. The two camps—Lesh and Weir—did not mingle much. Weir and the Leshes alternated writing the set lists and the loose duties of the bandleader went with whoever wrote the sets that day. They set up backstage tents on opposite sides of the stage and while Weir's was always party central, the Lesh tent was often empty and quiet. The brotherly dynamic between the two principals could shift suddenly from loving and harmonious to chilly and antagonistic without the other band members knowing what happened. At first, Weir was doing fine, enjoying himself, singing and playing great, holding court backstage endlessly. Lesh was bubbly, chipper, surprisingly energetic, although the crew whispered rumors attributing his stamina to anti-rejection steroids he took for his transplant. They also wondered if Jill didn't sometimes take the same drugs.

The good vibes didn't last. Lesh's mercurial wife exploded all over the background vocalists after the next-to-last show on the tour in Colorado. The band had just finished one of the hottest shows they had ever played. Zoe Ellis's father had attended and watched from a strategic seat on the stage. Jill had taken a special interest in the two women vocalists from the start and, with her official duties largely handled by her competent partner, she focused extra attention on them. Then following this exhausting and satisfying show, after weeks together on the road, Ellis found herself facing a livid Jill Lesh, who was furious over some minor misuse of a van and errand runner backstage. Jill further shocked Zoe by lashing into both her and Sunshine personally.

"You are nobodies," she screamed at them. "Less than nobodies. All the years these guys have put in paying their dues—"

"You have no right to speak to me like that," Ellis interrupted. "You don't know anything about what dues I've paid."

Ellis quickly turned and left the room. She was hurt and deeply embarrassed to be spoken to that way in front of her daughter, even if she was an infant. She had to learn twenty-three songs in two days for the first show. While she had come to appreciate the music—especially Hunter's lyrics—she was no Deadhead like her singing partner Sunshine Becker. Furthur had been a fun, fairly well-paying job. She went home after the next concert and sent the Leshes the most polite, kindly letter of resignation she could write.

As it happened, that first tour was also the end of the Furthur road for drummer Jay Lane. After fifteen years of following Weir's leadership, he found himself relegated to a secondary role in a band where Weir also seemed relegated to a secondary role. Where he had been the sole driving force of RatDog, in Furthur, Lane was accenting and decorating Joe Russo's playing. He was the Mickey Hart of Furthur. Lane had no real complaints—he was playing a job any drummer in the world would want—but then Les Claypool called and said he wanted to put Primus back together. Now Lane faced a dilemma. He held long talks on the bus with Weir and came to the decision to leave Furthur, only informing Lesh the day before his final gig. Lesh posted a magnanimous adieu to Lane on his Web site. "Over the past year, Jill and I have come to know and love Jay for the great guy he is," Lesh wrote. He would not be replaced. Russo would remain the sole drummer of the band.

Jeff Pehrson was drafted to replace Zoe Ellis. He was one-half of an acoustic folk-pop duo called Box Set and he auditioned by singing a few Dead songs with Sunshine Becker at a local studio for Lesh and a few others. He got the nod but was told there would be no rehearsals before the Memorial Day weekend date. "Trial by fire," he was told. His future with the band would depend on his performance at that gig. Pehrson passed the test.

The Furthur Festival was an ambitious three-day event that May staged in Calaveras County Fairgrounds in sleepy Angels Camp in the Sierra Nevada foothills. This was not the touring Furthur Festival that Scher and Sears had produced in the late nineties. Angels Camp had been the scene of an annual rock show in the seventies and eighties called Mountain Aire Festival and subsequent performances by both the Grateful Dead in 1987 and Phil and Friends in 1999. Not only did Furthur play note-for-note recitations of six full-length Grateful Dead albums over the three nights, but Larry Campbell and his wife, Teresa Williams, both Phil and Friends veterans, wrangled a second, largely acoustic stage where Campbell, Jackie Greene, and others combined for a middle-of-the-night Phil and Friends mini-reunion. Campbell and his wife augmented Furthur prominently during acoustic-flavored *Workingman's Dead* and *American Beauty* segments of the program. Band members held question-and-answer sessions during the day in a room displaying old photos and memorabilia, including a giant blowup photo of the Dead playing there. Other groups appearing over the weekend included Brian Lesh's band, Blue Light River, and Mark Karan's band, Jemimah Puddleduck.

While Weir and Lesh were launching Furthur, the drummers were not staying home crying in their bongs. Kreutzmann was involved in the most serious non-Dead musical project of his life, a

New Orleans–oriented jam band called 7 Walkers featuring guitarist-songwriter Papa Mali. As bassist for the New Orleans r&b instrumental group the Meters, 7 Walkers bassist George Porter was one of the most influential players in his field. Mississippi-born Malcolm Welbourne—who goes by the name Papa Mali—wrote the band's original material with lyrics from Robert Hunter, mixed at shows with old New Orleans r&b, Papa Mali originals, and, of course, a few Dead covers.

Drummer Hart has never slowed down—from ancillary projects like an art exhibit of slices of bark from redwood trees he found on his morning walks around his Sonoma ranch to a deep plunge into astrophysics with Nobel laureate George Smoot, manipulating sounds recorded from deep in space. Using UC Berkeley's supercomputer, Smoot and his team showed Hart waveforms millions of years old and he turned them into sound files—sonifications—to use in recordings. Hart was literally playing with the Big Bang.

Hart took time to write the score for a ballet by the Alonzo King Company. He was also putting together another edition of the Rhythm Devils, his percussion orchestra, this time featuring the young blues-rock phenom from England, guitarist Davy Knowles of Back Door Slam, and guitarist Keller Williams, headed out on tour in the spring. He and Kreutzmann were still drum brothers, a celebrated percussion team, and Kreutzmann rejoined the band for a handful of dates in the summer, including the Gathering of the Vibes hippie fest in Bridgeport, Connecticut, the night after Further played. Like ships passing in the night.

16

Crossroads

L EVON HELM was a leathery survivor. In 1991, on his Woodstock, New York farm, his beloved barn and recording studio along with all of his gear burned to the ground in an electrical fire. He promptly rebuilt it. In 1998, he was diagnosed with throat cancer and advised to get a laryngectomy. He opted for twenty-seven radiation treatments at Sloan-Kettering Hospital in New York City, which killed the tumor but also destroyed his voice. After several years of writing notes and hoarse whispers, Helm regained his voice, but now he faced foreclosure on his rebuilt barn and home. In 2003, Helm decided to throw a rent party. He tabbed Larry Campbell and guitarist Jimmy Vivino of *The Tonight Show with Conan O'Brien* to put together a hot house band and began holding informal weekly gatherings called Midnight Rambles at his barn. Helm likened the affairs to the late-night sessions held by minstrel shows he attended as a youth in Arkansas.

As drummer and vocalist with the Band, Helm knew something about disputes over control of a storied rock band's legacy. He alone was the holdout when Band guitarist Robbie Robertson purchased the other members' interests in their partnership. Helm and Robertson didn't speak for years. Long after *The Last Waltz*, the concert

extravaganza film by Martin Scorsese that marked the group's retire-
ment from touring, Helm continued to plow that field, leading various versions of the supposedly defunct group as long as he could.
When keyboardist Richard Manuel hanged himself in a sleazy motel
room after one more shitty gig in Florida in 1986 and bassist Rick
Danko died in his sleep in 1999, Helm retreated to Woodstock, where
his credit was always good at Vince's Meat Market.

These Rambles were distinctly low-key affairs. Campbell switched
off between fiddle, mandolin, pedal steel, and guitar. His wife, Teresa
Williams, sang in the band and Helm's daughter, Amy Helm, played.
The barn held two hundred spectators and tickets cost a whopping
hundred dollars apiece, but once Helms' friends like Elvis Costello,
Emmylou Harris, and Dr. John started turning up, there was a line of
cars from his place to the highway every Saturday night.

In July 2010, the night after finishing a sold-out run at Nokia
Theater in Times Square to culminate a successful six-week tour by
Furthur, Phil Lesh and his family headed up to Woodstock to be
guests at the Midnight Ramble. The Levon Helm Studio sat atop a
breathtaking vista of mountain greenery. The refurbished barn had
the clean, wholesome air of a cabin in the woods. The intimate audience included actresses Jane Fonda and Catherine Keener and Phish
bassist Mike Gordon. Lesh was greeted with thunderous applause.

"This is so cool," he said. "Thank you, Levon, for getting this
together—absolutely."

With Phil and Friends veterans Campbell and his wife in the band,
Lesh brought out his two sons, Grahame and Brian, and dug into a set
of Dead tunes like "Deal," "Dire Wolf," "I Know You Rider," and "Friend
of the Devil," Lesh's seismic bass notes shaking the barn floor. Lesh and
his sons' harmonies lit up the songs. The boys showed off their guitar
chops. Lesh glowed. He choked up introducing his sons to the crowd.
"I have to say," he said, "this is the proudest moment of my life."

During the Levon Helm Band set, Lesh sat prominently behind
Helm's drum kit and sang along to "Deep Elem Blues," a song the
Grateful Dead also used to play. Donald Fagen of Steely Dan was
playing keyboards, as he often did with the Helm Band, and Lesh
took up bass for a couple of Dead songs. "Tennessee Jed" was a

song Helm recorded for his Grammy-winning 2007 comeback album on his own label, *Dirt Farmer*, after he got his voice (mostly) back. "Shakedown Street" was sung by Fagen, a great convergence considering the sleek, carefully manicured Steely Dan may have been the polar opposite of the Grateful Dead when both operations were at their peaks. Lesh also joined Campbell, Teresa Williams, and Amy Helm for the Dead's "Attics of My Life" and the entire Lesh clan chimed in on the finale of "The Weight," Grahame and Brian each tackling a verse. It was an evening Lesh would not soon forget.

Furthur finished out the year with a triumphant headline performance at the Outside Lands Festival in San Francisco's Golden Gate Park in August, where the Grateful Dead once played for the Human Be-In and where the band and Deadheads gathered after Garcia's death, as well as tours in September through the West Coast and November through the East, ending with two sold-out shows at Madison Square Garden. By the time Furthur celebrated New Year's Eve in a two-night run for the second year at the Bill Graham Civic in San Francisco, the band had done a massive seventy-seven shows—not including eighteen public rehearsals—since the previous September.

With Furthur, Lesh had taken complete charge of the legacy, in short order establishing the new band as the heirs to the throne and doing the roadwork to back up the claim. As the band swept through the markets, every nascent Deadhead in the nation bought a ticket—the old guard was slow to adopt Furthur—and young people barely out of diapers when Garcia died were discovering the music and joining up.

While Weir relished the road so much he would sometimes ride the bus home at the end of the tour instead of flying to spend a couple of extra days out, Lesh had long hated the touring routine. At age seventy-one, he felt the immense exhaustion of the first year of Furthur settle in mind, body, and spirit. The experience at Levon's Midnight Ramble had reignited thoughts in his mind lying dormant since he abandoned the Terrapin Station museum project ten years before.

In March 2010, the Leshes began talking publicly about buying the real estate where the Good Earth Organic & Natural Food Store stood in Fairfax. The popular grocery store was planning to move to a nearby vacant supermarket in the fall and the Leshes eyed the property as a possible location for a barn of their own. Lesh posted a note about his intentions on his Web site: "We're taking the first steps to make a long time dream—a permanent musical home—come true," he said. "Our goal is to create a vibrant community gathering place: beautiful, comfortable, welcoming—for members of the community to commingle and enjoy good music."

He went on to say they would be purchasing a building that would be remodeled to feel like an old barn and they would begin to present "West Coast Rambles." He indicated Helm had given his blessing to what Lesh was planning to call Terrapin Landing.

Although he raised his family in the nearby upscale town of Ross, Lesh lived in Fairfax for many years before he was married, which is a small town with a mind of its own. Several miles up Sir Francis Drake Boulevard from San Rafael, Fairfax is the last town before the woods overtake the road. A longtime hippie outpost, the city only had one rock club through the seventies, the Sleeping Lady, an organic juice bar that served no alcohol and didn't allow smoking. Van Morrison had lived in town and even bought his parents a small record store in the strip of stores that passed for downtown Fairfax. Lesh knew he would have to ease on in. "There would be a Fairfax-style collaboration between him and the neighborhood in order to work things out," the town's mayor told the *Marin IJ*.

In August, the Leshes filed a permit application for a different, adjacent piece of property. They changed their minds about the old market, checking out the location after closing one night and realizing the corner location would be a problem for a music club in a residential neighborhood. The new site was on the other side of the market, away from houses. "It's solidly on Drake, not on a residential corner," Jill Lesh said to the *Marin IJ*. "The performance space will be concrete clad in wood, so it will be completely soundproof. You would not be able to hear anything outside. Obviously, we have to deal with parking and traffic and other issues, and that's what the use permit process is for. We have a lot of work to do to see if we can address all those concerns."

The property was in escrow pending permit approval and plans called to tear down the old garage and build a 5,400-foot two-story barn with a 2,800-foot performance space to be called the Grate Room, openly modeled on the Helms' place in Woodstock. Lesh had been converted by his visit to Helm's Midnight Ramble. "It was like going to church," he told the *Marin IJ*. "I knew immediately that was something I wanted to do at home, to have a place like that. It's small enough and intimate enough that it gives the music more meaning."

While Leshes were consulting architects and contractors, Weir was up to his eyeballs into high-tech musical real estate development himself, having bought a huge corner building in a San Rafael industrial park, gutted the insides, and built a space-age recording studio designed to host Webcasts like the world had never seen before. This was his new Tamalpais Research Institute—TRI Studios. Weir had a couple of investor partners, but he poured much of his own money into the project, where costs ran more than $3 million. It was a peculiar corner of an otherwise colorless and anonymous collection of warehouses and offices off the freeway. On the other side of the TRI wall was the chop shop where James Hetfield of Metallica worked on his hot rods. Across the street was a rehearsal hall and studio for Sammy Hagar, where the Red Rocker also parked his collection of Ferraris.

"Some guys, when they have a little success in life, they go out and buy a yacht or a fancy car," Weir told the *Marin IJ*. "What I did was build a flying saucer."

The main room of the 11,500-square-foot complex contained a Meyer Sound Constellation, a highly refined audio sound system advancement by the famed Berkeley speaker manufacturer John Meyer. The few Constellations that Meyer had sold at that point had gone to classical music chamber orchestras and the like; Weir was his first customer in the rock/pop field. The room was dotted with as many as eighty small speakers and a couple of dozen microphones to further pick up and disperse sound. The entire system was designed to run through simple computer software that Weir could operate himself from an iPad onstage, bypassing the necessity of mixing engineers. At the touch of a finger, the room could sound like a cathedral or somebody's living room, a baseball stadium or a bathroom. The Constellation was a modern technological miracle, clean, crisp, resonant audio that enveloped the listener without fatigue or strain, like being dipped in a river of sound.

In addition to the futuristic audio, Weir and longtime Dead sound man John Cutler stocked the room with all the toys they wanted, including massive amounts of server space to facilitate plans to support the investment in the studio through pay-per-view Webcasts. Weir knew no such business model existed and that recording studios themselves were going out of business on practically a daily basis, but he was intent on testing his hypothesis. As Lesh had done, it was his way of trying to figure out a way to make music without touring. Even for road-loving Bobby Weir, forty years was taking its toll.

In May 2011, Weir held the first Webcast at TRI the same week he finally appeared with the Marin Symphony Orchestra. Weir had agreed to appear in a fundraiser for the orchestra but insisted they cede creative control. His vision turned into an elaborate and expensive event originally scheduled for 2010. Weir finally made the show in May 2011. He did an opening set backed by ex-RatDog musicians (including both Robin Sylvester on electric bass and Rob Wasserman on acoustic bass) with a quartet of the classical musicians playing some arrangements and—at Weir's impish insistence—a little ham-fisted improvising. For the second half of the concert, the full orchestra played elegantly realized symphonic arrangements of Grateful Dead songs written by Stanford University composition instructor Giancarlo Aquilanti. To debut his Webcast series few days later, Weir re-created the concert's opening segment for the benefit of Web viewers live from TRI Studios.

If he was not busy enough, after a solo appearance at the Sundance Film Festival in February for the release of the dramatic film featuring a Grateful Dead soundtrack, *The Music Never Stopped*, Weir also announced his first-ever solo tour, a handful of East Coast dates in August.

In June, Weir brought Furthur into TRI for a two-and-a-half-hour Webcast concert, offered to pay-per-view subscribers for $19.95. Demand was great enough to crash the TRI servers, meaning many people couldn't sign on the site. The full Webcast was posted as a continuous

loop a couple of days later to make up for the technical problems people experienced. As this was a new technology, these kinds of bumps
in the road had to be expected. It probably didn't help that nobody
on the TRI staff had ever run a Webcast before.

In the meantime, Lesh was having his own problems getting his
project green-lighted by the Fairfax city council. The day before it was
to be considered, Lesh pulled his permit approval from the agenda
after being unnerved by signs posted strategically along the route of
his morning walk reading "No Terrapin, Please." "They must have
done it in the middle of the night after watching where he walks," Jill
Lesh told the *Marin IJ*. "It felt a little weird and creepy."

Jill Lesh also told the paper that she and her husband were disturbed by anonymous opponents who put negative fliers on cars that
were parked at St. Rita's Church in Fairfax during a child's funeral.
The Leshes had proposed paying St. Rita's to use some of its parking
during performances at their planned club. "We didn't want to start
off this way," she said. "There are lots of other places we could go.
We just really like Fairfax. We thought we could really do some things
that would benefit the town."

Weeks before the Leshes announced in November they were
scrubbing the Fairfax project, they had already been meeting with
city officials of San Rafael to check the lay of the land. Lesh had been
reading the Bob Dylan memoir, *Chronicles*, and reminiscing with his
wife. He took her on a drive past the band's old San Rafael rehearsal
hall, Club Front, by the waterfront. "We were having lunch in the area
one afternoon and decided to take a drive by the old studio," Lesh
recalled on his Web site.

> While we were driving around we went by the Seafood Peddler,
> where Furthur did some rehearsal shows a couple years ago in
> their Palm Ballroom. We pulled into the rear parking lot and
> we saw a large painted Grateful Dead/Steal Your Face logo with
> the words "Buckle Up Kidz" above it. We looked at each other
> and both had the same flash—that the Seafood Peddler had the
> foundation for us to realize our long-held dream of finding
> a place in Marin County to make music. It was one of those

wonderful moments in life when it all converges and you can see the path that lies ahead.

In January 2012, the Leshes announced they had purchased the Seafood Peddler, a landmark wharfside eaterie with a trademark sign of a ship atop a flagpole visible from the freeway. The longtime owner simply stepped aside and relocated his business when he heard the Leshes wanted to buy the spot. It was all too perfect. Lesh changed his plan for the name, having decided it was not a landing, but a new beginning. He called it Terrapin Crossroads.

At almost the exact same time Lesh was announcing his new club in San Rafael, oddly enough, a few exits down the freeway Weir was ballyhooing the reopening of a Mill Valley club in which he was an investor, the Sweetwater Music Hall. The miniscule eighty-seat original club was the jewel of Marin County nightlife, a community center to the local rock crowd where Lesh and Weir staged the Crusader Rabbit Stealth Band comeback. After changing hands, a dispute with the landlords, and several years of not being open, a new set of investors acquired the name and pumped a cool $3 million into remodeling the 107-year-old Masonic Hall just off the town square. Weir supervised the installation of a pristine audio system from Meyer Sound Laboratories. If Lesh was going to build himself a playhouse, Weir had staked out some territory for himself at another playground down the way.

"For years, Sweetwater was the place many of us local and visiting musicians headed to when we were looking to play for fun," Weir told the *Marin IJ*. "Well, our clubhouse is back—and it belongs to all of us. Woo-hoo—Mill Valley finally has its playpen back!"

While the soft opening of Sweetwater in January 2012 featured the Southern rock band the Outlaws, the initial calendar leaned heavily toward the Deadhead clientele that Lesh would also hope to attract with bands featuring Mark Karan, Steve Kimock, and other Dead acolytes. Weir played the opening with Sammy Hagar and Jerry Harrison of the Talking Heads, came back a couple of nights later to sit in with Steve Kimock, and then disappeared from public view for the next six weeks.

17

Capitol

"AFTER FORTY-FIVE years, I'm done touring," Phil Lesh told the *Marin IJ*. Eating a "Phil's Scramble" of egg whites, avocado, scallions, cheddar cheese, and tomatoes off the brunch menu on the porch of his new San Rafael club Terrapin Crossroads, a few weeks after the official March 2012 opening, Lesh surveyed his new domain and professed his satisfaction. "This all came together in six weeks," he told the reporter, as Bob Dylan records played on the house sound system. "It's astonishing after the debacle in Fairfax."

A sign outside with the dancing turtles from the *Terrapin Station* album cover could be seen from the freeway. The interior had been paneled in vintage barn wood and the walls were covered with photographs and memorabilia from the Dead. Upstairs was a quiet room full of overstuffed easy chairs and homey couches and downstairs was another lounge across from the bar. Bands played free shows on a small stage in the bar. The big shows took place in the Grate Room, the former ballroom adjacent to the main dining room, where the Lesh family could often be seen eating dinner together before a show.

Lesh would make his way out of the dining room, shaking hands and exchanging pleasantries with his patrons. Jill Lesh was around the club nightly, overseeing details and running the staff. She could be capricious, once pulling Deadhead journalist Blair Jackson—who was more fan than critic—into her office at set break to berate him for not being more supportive of their efforts in the community. Although stung, Jackson, true to Deadhead form, returned to the hall to enjoy the second set. Club staff wore work shirts emblazoned with the stealie and slogan "Buckle Up, Kidz" from the graffiti the Leshes had first spied as an omen of the location's suitability.

Before the official opening, Lesh tried out both the club and a new rendition of Phil and Friends for one night in February before taking the band on weekend dates in Colorado. It was the first appearance of Phil and Friends since the formation of Furthur, a sign of Lesh's growing discontent with Furthur. Soon after, Terrapin Crossroads announced a twelve-show run in March by Phil and Friends with tickets at $150 apiece ($300 VIP tickets were also available), setting off the inevitable protest squealing in Deadhead circles. The club's own Web site agreed the ticket prices were "quite high." However, the site continued, "the reality of bringing a major rock show to an intimate venue is that tickets will cost a few bucks more than usual. It costs a lot to put on a big show in a small space! Rest assured, though, as we get rolling there will be shows and ticket prices for all budgets. We don't want to exclude anyone from what we're building here."

Prices notwithstanding, demand for VIP tickets crashed the club's computers as soon as tickets went on sale. The additional fee included food, drink, an exclusive tent, and a private after-show performance. All twelve shows sold out.

Lesh used a revolving crew for the opening shows that included Phil and Friends veterans Jackie Greene and Jimmy Herring, mixed with Furthur players like Jeff Chimenti, John Kadlecik, Joe Russo, and others. Chris Robinson of the Black Crowes showed up. Larry Campbell and his wife, Teresa Williams, came in for the second weekend. Lesh's son Grahame played on every show. Bob Weir joined one night early in the run.

In April, after a walloping fourteen-show East Coast tour by Furthur that included an eight-night run at New York's Beacon Theatre, the band's longest residency to date, and co-headlining the Wanee Festival in Florida with the Allman Brothers, Lesh presided over the reunion of The Q in four nights at Terrapin Crossroads. He was drawing from a pool of jam-minded younger musicians such as Jackie Greene's pal Tim Bluhm of Mother Hips and his wife, Nicki Bluhm, or members of Ryan Adams's band the Cardinals, or Railroad Earth. Lesh had discovered an array of willing participants in his experiments closer to the age of his son Grahame. Lesh himself played practically every night at the club during May and June, either in the four-hundred-seat Grate Room or in a free show at the smaller lounge.

In May, he officially introduced what he called the "West Coast Ramble" and dedicated not merely the series of performances but his entire nightclub/restaurant operation to Levon Helm, who had died from cancer the previous month. In New York with Furthur in April, Lesh had phoned the hospital and spoke to Helm's daughter Amy. At Terrapin, prior to performing a song-by-song rendition of the second album by the Band, Lesh recalled visiting and performing at Helm's Midnight Ramble.

"So much of our vision comes from there," Lesh said, "an intimate setting, collaboration with different musicians, multi-generationally friendly. It's safe to say that this place would not exist if not for Levon's example and encouragement. I'd like to dedicate not just the show, or the next show, or everything we do here, but the whole place, to Levon Helm."

If Lesh and Weir were building themselves clubhouses, they were also experimenting with building community, which had been the great lesson of the post-Garcia years. While the Sweetwater represented the return of a cherished Mill Valley institution and appealed to a broader cross-section of the community—which fit egalitarian Weir—the club certainly created a wide berth for the Deadheads. Lesh's place was more Deadcentric—or, more specifically, Lesh-centric—and may have actually extended and promoted Dead culture. Most importantly, they both created spaces where community could develop.

At his TRI Studios, Weir was also dealing with community, trying to harness the power of the Internet to support—or, at least, partly support—the space-age studio through regular pay-per-view concerts on the Web. He had remodeled the large building to his exact specifications. Longtime Dead engineer John Cutler and mad audio scientist John Meyer went to town building the most advanced studio in the world, capable of broadcasting heretofore impossible levels of video and audio quality on the Internet. The million-dollar recording console was obtained at a substantial accommodation price after Weir traded a private performance with the company. In addition to two other smaller studios, the main room was two thousand square feet and contained the miraculous Constellation sound system. This kind of technological experiment was in keeping with long-held Grateful Dead tradition. Almost alone among their peers, the Dead devoted large amounts of time and money to research and development. The band put their money where their sound equipment was. Grateful Dead audio innovations over the years have benefitted many people besides the Dead—from the design of large public address systems to tiny hearing aids. The band's first resident audio wizard, Owsley Stanley, invented modern concert sound and monitor speakers for bands to hear themselves sing. The so-called Wall of Sound system the band developed in the early seventies was probably their most well-known experiment—a massive and complex network of speakers that took hundreds of man-hours to erect and take down. The Wall proved to be impractical to the extreme, cost a ton of money, and only was in operation a short time, but the Dead learned lessons from the experience that informed all their future thinking. The Dead never earned a penny from their efforts, only better sound. In the grand Grateful Dead audio research style, Weir knew TRI was a gamble on the future and he ran through all his own money before taking on partners. He never once penciled out the investment.

In March, a free broadcast with the National, the Brooklyn-based alt-Americana band who brought along other musicians, introduced the TRI Webcasts. The resulting performance was exactly what Weir had in mind—a meeting of like-minded musicians, drawing on each other's repertoires and styles to create something fresh in the moment. The National had requested "My Brother Esau," a song Weir hadn't played since 1987. He and lyricist John Barlow fiddled with the lyrics in the days before the show. Weir also sang a National song, "Daughter of the SoHo Riots." The show ended with the entire studio audience standing around the musicians in the center of the room—there is no stage at TRI—while they sang around one microphone "Ripple," "Uncle John's Band," and "Brokedown Palace."

Weir was again throwing himself into work. With Furthur increasingly dominated by the Leshes and tension between them growing louder every show, he sought other outlets. The week after the TRI Webcast with the National, he was back at Sweetwater sitting in with Lukas Nelson, son of Willie, and his band Promise of the Real. That weekend, he played two shows at the Fox Oakland with Bruce Hornsby, two solo sets capped by a duo appearance. Two days later, he left for the Furthur tour and stayed out after Furthur came home to do a round of solo dates on the East Coast. Three weeks later, he was back out doing nine dates in a trio with Chris Robinson and Jackie Greene.

While Weir was doing all this work and Lesh spending most of his time in between Furthur tours at his Terrapin Crossroads, Mickey Hart was touring with his new Mickey Hart Band behind the release in April of a new album, *Mysterium Tremendum,* sizzling, smoldering slow, fat grooves of electrofunk that featured exquisite new Robert Hunter songs such as "Slow Joe Rain." The carefully layered instrumental tracks contained large helpings of Hart's sonifications from the astrophysicists—sound waves he converted using sophisticated algorithms from data collected from planets, stars, entire galaxies.

At the same time Hart was working out with Deadhead astrophysicists, he came together with Dr. Adam Gazzaley of UCSF, a pioneer in bridging neuroscience and technology. The neuroscientist wired him with electrodes and used him as a guinea pig/research associate on serious explorations of the relationship between cognition and rhythm. With signals coming from wires attached to a cap Hart wore while he played drums, x-rays of his brain lit up with different colors as he drummed his way through the rhythms. He was the perfect lab rat. He had long understood the significance of the vibratory universe and had spent considerable time studying the chemical and physical ramifications of sound and music.

"It's the most exciting frontier in music in this century," Hart told an interviewer.

This is what music was meant to do, to be. It was medicinal at first with the shamanic traditions. Then it became entertainment, people paid money to see it performed. Then it became religion again with the church, different kinds of religious prayer. And now it's becoming medicinal again, people are understanding its powers. Now science is going to understand it. The practitioners, we knew it. That was easy. You always come off a stage, if you play halfway decently, elated, with elevated consciousness. It's elevating the consciousness, that's what music does.

If that wasn't enough, Hart also commissioned a twenty-three-foot replica of the Golden Gate Bridge to be used in a performance on the seventy-fifth anniversary of the bridge in May. Twenty-five years before, when there had been big plans for celebrating the bridge's fiftieth anniversary, Hart developed an idea to play the actual bridge like a giant wind harp and percussion instrument. He was going to plant tiny microphones on each of the span's cables and amplify the signals. Those grand plans fell through at the last minute, but twenty-five years later, he adapted that vision—recording vibrations from the bridge and running the sound files through his computers to create "sonifications" of the bridge. Outside the Palace of Fine Arts, in the shadow of the bridge, backed by his band, Hart used those sonifications plucking and pounding on his mini–Golden Gate Bridge.

As busy as he was, Hart was all but completely estranged from his erstwhile bandmates and business partners. "I had dinner with Bob a few weeks ago," he told *Rolling Stone* in April. "We correspond."

Hart's drumming brother Kreutzmann was also on the road that spring with his swampadelic band 7 Walkers. Playing a sturdy hybrid of Louisiana funk and Dead looseness, the group worked small clubs in the cities and hippie halls in the outlying areas. Guitarist Papa Mali brought an agreeable, laconic vocal style to Hunter's evocative lyrics on songs such as "King Cotton Blues" or "Evangeline." In concert, the band mixed Dead staples such as "Bertha" or "Deal" that were given a Gulf Coast rinse, a little New Orleans, a little Jamaica. The band was something of a gem, an authentic blend of Dead and Mardi Gras, but the small audience was not going to pay for Kreutzmann's hillside home in Kauai.

Kreutzmann didn't disguise his contempt for the Lesh and Weir collaboration in interviews. "I haven't really got much interest in them," he told one reporter. "They sound just like the other bands out there doing it. What do you call those bands that copy other bands. . . . Anyways, I don't feel they're doing anything really new with their music."

Furthur had achieved world domination in Deadland. Lesh had marginalized the drummers, co-opted Weir, and crushed the other tribute bands. For all the band's instant success, Furthur also came with the built-in conflicts that extended back to the Summer of Love and beyond. In some ways, the musical battle over tempo and volume was a simple extension of personal conflicts. On the other hand, the fight over creative issues went to the heart of the personal relationships among these men. With improvisational music, the emotions between musicians will play out on a nonverbal level. They take their battles into the jams.

For Weir and Lesh, there was a dichotomy that could never be solved because they viewed their work in such basically different ways. Weir was painting sound pictures in his audience's mind and he was in no hurry for the images to evaporate. He wanted his parables to unspool like movies in the mind.

Lesh, on the other hand, wanted to explore the possibilities of the repertoire, expand on the material, thrust it into new shapes by pushing, prodding, and pulling at the sonics. He sought visceral impact, which required driving tempos and loud volume, especially bass volume. He liked to feel the rumble. Lesh saw himself as a conductor leading an orchestra through repertoire. Interpretation was everything.

These two approaches were bound to conflict, but they also represented a deep divide between the personalities involved that could not be reconciled any easier than the creative issues. The titans of the band did not want the same thing; friction was inevitable.

Weir took action. He shifted his gear from the center of the stage plot to the far side, as far away from Lesh as he could get. He hated screaming over the bass when he was singing. Ostensibly the move was to lessen the roar and thunder of Lesh's powerful bass amps, but the effect was also to isolate the two principals and keep all the hired hands between them as a buffer zone. It was a metaphor that signaled the state of the band.

Weir's friends openly worried about his health. Out of rehab again, he picked up where he left off. He could be uncharacteristically short-tempered, annoyed, and disgusted. Even so, he remained the most unpretentious rock star. He still played football every Saturday he could in the town's public park with his long-standing team, the Tamalpais Chiefs. He was tiring of Furthur and he was squirming under Lesh's thumb. He was growing even more disconnected and alienated from Lesh in the band, which only increased in the imbalance of power. But Weir was nonconfrontational to the extreme and his discontent only fueled more intoxication and resentment. Lesh was also growing tired of Furthur, Weir's drinking and spacey intransigence, not to mention all the travel. Plus he was captivated by the tiny realm he and his wife had created at Terrapin Crossroads. On the heels of the summer Furthur tour in July, Lesh took a Phil and Friends that not only included Jackie Greene and Larry Campbell but his two sons, Grahame and Brian, to play two big music festivals and a Midnight Ramble in Woodstock. He was clearly losing interest in any kind of collaboration with his old bandmates.

Furthur had taken off the runway so smoothly, from the uplifting Fox Oakland opening weekend through the low-key rehearsal shows at small halls around the Bay Area into full launch on East Coast tours. The Furthur Festival at Mountain Aire in that first year seemed like a glowing coronation. Furthur made deliberate efforts to connect to the Dead's legacy like the Valentine's Day 2010 concert at Barton Hall at Cornell University, returning to the scene of a 1977 Grateful Dead concert immortalized on one of the most highly traded tapes from the band's history.

The band was capable of toying playfully with the audience, for instance performing the Beatles album *Abbey Road* one song at a time over the first few shows of the spring 2011 East Coast tour to the delight of the Deadheads, who got the joke immediately. Or arranging a set list where the first letters of the songs would spell out a code—a trick they borrowed from Phish, who had spelled out the Phish song "Fuck Your Face" in a set list a couple of weeks before at Red Rocks. Two weeks later at Red Rocks, the Furthur set list spelled out "Steal Your Face." For the concert on November 11, 2011— 11-11-11—background vocalist Sunshine Becker wore a dress festooned with eleven lightning bolts made by a seamstress she knew from the lots (although she knew it would be considered out of bounds, as Jill strongly encouraged background singers to dress in all black). Over the course of four years, hundreds of shows on nineteen tours, the band had brought tens of thousands of people together to hear their music. Every concert was like a celebration. But the happy early days were long past.

Lesh had enjoyed playing with Weir without the distraction of the Dead drummers, but now Weir was wearing on him, too. Weir likewise had retreated from the warm, brotherly feelings toward Lesh that informed the first several months of the enterprise and had now settled into a sullen acceptance of the Lesh regime, occasionally flashing rebellious rebukes. And drinking. "I've rarely known an interesting man who didn't drink," Weir liked to say. Lesh didn't drink.

It all came crashing down April 25, 2013, at the end of a nine-show run at the Capitol Theatre in Port Chester, New York, a near-hundred-year-old vaudeville house where, as a run-down movie theater, the Dead played eighteen memorable shows in 1970 and 1971. The band loved the sound of the room. With Furthur that night, Weir wobbled his way unsteadily onstage the first set, but his road crew swapped the set list for the second half, eliminating any Weir lead vocals. Early in the second set, it became apparent something was wrong. He blew the vocals to "Eyes of the World" and stumbled toward the amplifiers. He looked dazed and uncertain. Toward the end of the set, as the band was deep in "Unbroken Chain," Weir looked so woozy, his road crew brought out a red plastic chair for him. He kicked the chair out of his way and staggered, continuing to play. He took a few uncertain steps, leaning precariously to his left, then suddenly fell over on his right side. He crashed to the stage like a bag of sand at the feet of guitarist Kadlecik, who had to step back out of the way.

The two roadies rushed to their fallen boss, took off his guitar, and helped him to his feet. They planted him in the plastic chair and handed him back his guitar with the steely patience of two long-suffering loyal squires who had seen their knight toe the abyss many times in the past and attended this latest calamity without a shred of alarm. Lesh never dropped a beat, and hardly looked in Weir's direction. He led the band through to the end of the song, Weir gamely strumming to some rhythm only he heard until his roadies pulled the plug to his amplifier. At the end of the song, the house lights went up and the band trudged off. Weir remained seated until his guys emerged and helped him off. Backstage, at his request, he was given a beer.

Lesh and the band returned to the stage without Weir. Lesh told the crowd Weir had been to the doctor earlier in the day for a shoulder injury. His shoulder had been aggravated on the tour and he had been playing a special lightweight guitar already for the past few nights. The shoulder pain was chronic. So were the painkillers. Vicodin was a favorite. What felled Weir so dramatically was he accidently mistook a sleeping pill, the potent Ambien, for more painkillers. It knocked him crossways.

"You could see Bob is having some problems," Lesh told the crowd. "He hurt his shoulder and had to see the doctor. We're going to finish the set for you." Without Weir, the band did another few songs and returned for an encore of "Built to Last."

Trixie Garcia was at the Capitol that night to dedicate the bar, Garcia's, to her father's memory, but in the end her appearance was vastly overshadowed by the Weir debacle.

Furthur immediately cancelled a big money headline appearance at the Bottlerock Festival in the Napa Valley over Memorial Day weekend ("Grateful Dead and Furthur co-founder Bob Weir is unable to perform in any capacity for the next several weeks," said the band's Web site). Weir typically treated the incident lightly. He wrote an email the next day to his friend Tim Flannery, third-base coach of the San Francisco Giants and amateur songwriter. "I'm doing fine," Weir wrote, "just a bit too much work and especially travel. I put in more miles in the first six months than I normally do in a year. Taking some time off, which I haven't done in 50 years." He managed one last, fairly feeble performance with Furthur in Atlantic City two days after his embarrassing collapse had been broadcast on video clips across the Internet. After that, Weir, once again, disappeared from public view, and Lesh returned to performances at Terrapin Crossroads.

18

Shapiro

Shapiro

P ETER SHAPIRO spent two years negotiating a twenty-year lease on the historic Capitol Theatre in Port Chester, New York, which had lain essentially empty for a quarter-century. He poured more than $3 million into refurbishing the old movie palace and opened the hall for concerts in September 2012 for the first time since its glory years in the early seventies. Bob Dylan was his opening attraction. He had wanted to hold the opening on his fortieth birthday, but Dylan wasn't available on that date and he had to move the launch to three days earlier. For Shapiro, the Capitol would be the new, palatial home court to his growing enterprise.

Shapiro was the leading entrepreneur of jam-band nation. From the beginning of his career, his enthusiasm and ever-present optimism allowed him to plunge ahead fearlessly in enterprises he knew nothing about. Having never operated any kind of bar or nightclub in his young life, twenty-four-year-old Shapiro started out by taking over the operation in 1996 of the Wetlands Preserve, a Deadcentric rock club in lower Manhattan. Shapiro convinced the original owner, a hippie visionary who ran the club with an environmental and social justice angle, that he knew enough about the scene to keep the club's unique program running. Ignoring other big money offers, the hippie sold him the lease for "basically nothing," according to Shapiro.

After closing the club in 2001, unable to afford the rising Tribeca rents, Shapiro concentrated on his work as an independent concert producer who presented everything from the Green Apple Music Festival on Earth Day to concerts for President Obama's first inauguration to his annual jam-band award show, the Jammys. In 2009, he opened the Brooklyn Bowl, which quickly became the nerve center of the entire jam-band movement. As it grew to be phenomenally successful, Shapiro opened subsequent branches in London and Las Vegas. He also bought *Relix* magazine, the mouthpiece of the scene. Shapiro was building a jam empire.

Ebullient, chatty, and eternally boyish, Shapiro was a born schmoozer. Raised in New York City's Upper East Side, he comes from a family of Jewish philanthropists. He never cared much about music as a youth, but was pursuing his undergraduate studies in film and media at Northwestern University when he stumbled across the Grateful Dead. Combining his first LSD experience and his first Grateful Dead concert was a zeitgeist moment for Shapiro, who felt instantly comfortable in the parking lot scene that snowy March 1993 at the Rosemont Horizon outside Chicago. He saw the drum circles and the hippie school buses and realized these people were seeking something they couldn't find at home. As soon as he could, he joined them.

On the road in the parking lots that summer, without any previous experience, Shapiro shot a documentary film about the Deadheads for school credit, and the film landed him a job as associate producer on *Tie-Died: Rock 'n Roll's Most Deadicated Fans*, which debuted at Sundance in 1995 only a few months before Garcia died.

What Shapiro had stumbled across in those final months of the Grateful Dead was nothing less than a sprawling subculture that was quietly spreading further and deeper into a growing movement. Garcia's death threw an unexpected spotlight on Shapiro's little *Tie-Died* movie. He was working as an intern at New Line Cinema in New York and showing his films alongside a Grateful Dead cover band when he heard the Wetlands owner wanted to sell. The owner wanted out.

Shapiro agreed to operate the place through the end of the existing lease and the club was his. He quickly assessed the situation and realized the growth potential. As the entrepreneurial leader of this new generation of Deadheads, Shapiro was uniquely positioned to lead this rapidly evolving audience to Deadland.

In the wake of Garcia's death, as the shadow of the Grateful Dead at first flickered off the scene, the jam-band audience began to factionalize. The New England Dead-inspired jam band Phish was the most immediate and obvious beneficiary. The band jumped from arenas to stadiums almost immediately. Some fans leaned toward the jazz-jam bands like Medeski Martin and Wood, and others went for the electro-bluegrass groups like Leftover Salmon. At Wetlands, the wellspring of the H.O.R.D.E. bands and fountainhead of the nineties jam-band scene, Shapiro worked at extending and expanding on the club's original vision. In the course of his five years running Wetlands, Shapiro booked virtually every act associated with the jam underground. He studied the scene and grew intimately acquainted with the details. He understood the crowd because he was part of the crowd. He was another psychedelicized Deadhead looking for something he couldn't find at home, only he was the Boy Scout troop leader. With his trademark pluck, ambition, and drive, Shapiro quickly established himself as the key mover and shaker behind the scenes in jam-band world.

Every one of the jam bands traced their heritage directly from the Grateful Dead. In a sense, it is like the music played around the Western world these days called Gypsy Jazz. That is nothing but music derived from the French jazz guitarist Django Reinhardt. There is no Gypsy Jazz—it is all Django. He has become an idiom and so did the Dead. Given that in any night the Dead's music could touch upon Chuck Berry, Ornette Coleman, Bill Monroe, and Django himself, they staked their boundaries far enough apart to support and encourage experiments in practically any realm of American music. The progeny of the Dead range as far and wide, from the Dave Matthews Band to String Cheese Incident and beyond. Even bands that don't sound remotely like the Dead—like Widespread Panic or Umphrey's McGee— have borrowed crucial conceptual components from the band. So, while the Dead have been largely absent from this expanding community for almost twenty years, the band's presence in this world, rather than go away, only enlarged. Tapes of old Dead shows constitute the standard indoctrination ritual for all who enter here. The band's songs serve as common literature. Even in their absence, the Grateful Dead ruled the jam-band scene with an invisible authority.

As the scene spread out, Shapiro could track the various tributaries, but he never lost sight of the fact that all streams flowed from the long-lost Dead. While the record industry, mainstream concert business, and broadcast media roundly ignored the movement, in many ways this outlier appeal made the scene all the more attractive to the newcomers. The breadth and depth of this audience consequently were obscured from view, but Shapiro could see it clearly.

He and his partners started the Lockn' Festival in Arrington, Virginia in September 2013, and Shapiro hired Furthur to headline all three nights. After having passed out on the disastrous spring tour, Weir had disappeared for several weeks. He went completely incommunicado; nobody seemed to know where he was. His friends presumed he had been steered—where else?—into rehab, but he was back by June sitting in with friends at shows around Marin.

He took a crack at resuming his Internet-based talk and music show, *Weir Here*, from TRI, a loose, decidedly informal little party mixing talk and music that showed off the host's natural charms to excellent effect: warm, witty, and intelligent, not to mention musical to the bone. Steve Parish played the sidekick who stole every show from his seat on the couch. Weir and the TRI staff had turned out more than a dozen episodes with a wide variety of guests before the April crash. He also made a rare appearance at Terrapin Crossroads, although, for some reason, Lesh did not join him that night. Weir also managed to squeeze in a handful of solo gigs on the road before the Furthur tour in July. So much for taking time off.

At Lockn', musicians from the other bands watched from the wings as Furthur romped through three nighttime headline shows. Maverick country musician Zac Brown joined the band the first night. The second night, Furthur began by playing the *Workingman's Dead* album song by song only to be joined on the final track, "Casey Jones," by

Phish guitarist Trey Anastasio, who stayed for the rest of their set. It was his first time sitting in with Furthur, a jam-band summit meeting.

Furthur was coming to an end anyway. By the time the band headed out to play Shapiro's Lockn' Festival and another handful of East Coast dates, Lesh had secretly secured his future. He and Shapiro had come to terms on a long-term exclusive agreement for Lesh to play thirty concerts in the next year at the Capitol Theatre. The multimillion-dollar deal called for Lesh to make a few additional performances at Shapiro concerts (Brooklyn Bowl in Las Vegas, Lockn' Festival), but the only other performances Lesh would do would be at Terrapin Crossroads.

Shapiro spent weeks negotiating this huge agreement with Jill Lesh and her husband. To Shapiro, this galvanized his position with the Capitol Theatre and ensured the venue's status, but this was a masterstroke of liberation for Lesh. In a single sweeping motion, he rid himself of any further need to be in the music business. He could play music, make millions, and not tour. He would play with his rotating cast at the same spots and the audience would come to him. Shapiro had acquired Lesh's entire career outside Terrapin. He owned the merchandising rights. He owned the recording rights. He had bought Lesh and paid handsomely.

And for Lesh, it would seem his dream was coming true. He was free of erratic Bobby Weir. He was free of booking agent Jonathan Levine, who drove around in a Porsche with a customized license plate reading THANXPHIL. Levine, who had been Lesh's booking agent since the beginning of Phil and Friends, was cut out of these negotiations so there was no agent to commission the deal. Lesh gave Levine the word backstage at Lockn'—an unceremonious end to what had been a long and fruitful association.

Without agents or managers or other partners to pay, the Leshes would net 100 percent. But more than a lavish payday, it was Lesh's ultimate triumph. He was now completely autonomous, free to fashion the legacy in his own image, in total command of his own destiny, unencumbered by responsibility to anyone outside his own family. He no longer had to share any of the revenue with anyone. He held off a public announcement. First, he had to finish off Furthur.

The next week, he announced that Furthur was going on "hiatus" on the band's Facebook page:

> After more than four years of heavy, year-round touring, Phil Lesh and Bob Weir have decided to put their band Furthur on hiatus in 2014. After the four night Furthur run in Mexico in January, the band will take the rest of 2014 off so that Phil and Bob can focus on their countless solo projects. . . . The last time the word "hiatus" was used in regards to the Grateful Dead world was in 1974, and we all know how much good that break inspired. They returned a year and a half later, stronger than ever, and for another 20 years. Furthur's not breaking up; they're simply taking a much-needed break. One way or another, we'll see you around.

A couple of weeks after that, Lesh teased the audience of the syndicated Deadhead radio show *Tales from the Golden Road* in an interview with host Gary Lambert. "I'm getting tired after forty-eight years on the road," Lesh said. "After this tour I'm basically 'off the bus,' I won't be doing any tours per se. Phil Lesh and Friends has a really great setup going for next year for performances outside of Terrapin and we'll make an announcement about it this tour . . . We've got the whole year of 2014 locked in for a really cool way. We'll expand the horizons of the whole scene. Phil Lesh and Friends will actually expand its membership into new areas."

In November, Lesh and Shapiro announced the agreement a week before the inaugural show under the deal at the Brooklyn Bowl. "I'm not retiring, and I'm not slowing down," Lesh told the *New York Times.* "I'm pretty sure I want to make music till I can't breathe anymore. I just want to do it within the most focused possible way. The future looks really exciting."

How could Lesh excuse the unfaithful behavior he had showed his brothers-in-arms? He had been at points cold, uncaring, even cruel, but he didn't seem to hesitate. One by one, he had discarded the drummers Kreutzmann and Hart and, now, Weir. His actions disguised a moral superiority that could have never existed in the group under Garcia's egalitarian leadership. He had long before abandoned the one-for-all/all-for-one philosophy that had sustained the band through long years.

In many ways, Lesh was now free of them all—Garcia included—ending knotted, convoluted entanglements that had pervaded his life for more than forty years. He didn't owe anybody anything. His time had come.

Lesh, it seems, had become the dark knight of the kingdom. He would do what needed to be done. He had a resolute, clear vision and he would do his duty to see that vision through. He was done ceding territory to the other knaves in the court. He appeared to see himself as the one true, capable keeper of the flame. His only loyalty was family. Once again, he would forge ahead on his own.

The end of Furthur came as no surprise to the members. When the band first formed, they had been told it might last a couple of years. The last year, the strain had been showing, although the other musicians were largely unaware of the trauma behind the scenes. After Weir passed out at the Capitol in April, the fans were no longer surprised, either. It had been an amazing band and an action-packed four years. The songbook contained more than two hundred and fifty songs. The band's incessant touring pulled thousands of new people into the audience in every market. Furthur had restored the Grateful Dead catalog to active rotation in summer amphitheater concerts and allowed the Deadhead subculture to grow younger audiences and to multiply across the nation.

But for Weir, Furthur had been costly. He had aggravated his shoulder injury to the point that it was becoming disabling. That, along with his high stress levels, contributed to substance abuse. He had given up his flagship RatDog. Without Furthur, his income would plummet. His high-tech studio was draining funds. He kept TRI fully staffed, operating full-time. They abandoned the *Weir Here* Webcast. Weir kept guitarist Mark Karan on the payroll through his yearlong battle with cancer. He had reformed RatDog for one of the Webcasts and did a couple of other dates with his old band, but after Furthur came back from Lockn' in September, Weir did not play music in public again until the end of the year.

19

Mexico

"PARADISE WAITS," the final gig on the Furthur calendar, turned out to be anything but. In January 2014, a travel outfit called Cloud 9 Adventures organized a four-night excursion for twenty-five-hundred fans to the new Hard Rock Hotel in Maya Riviera on the Yucatán peninsula. The pricey tickets sold out months before. Relations between the band's principals notwithstanding, rain or shine, the show must go on.

It certainly sounded promising—open bars, swimming pools, spas and salons, buffets of tropical food, nighttime concerts at an ocean-side stage. Reality, however, was anything but paradise. Deadheads were distressed to arrive and find the hotel only half-finished. Construction and painting were going on all over the site. Plumbing was broken. In some rooms, toilets had not yet been installed and many bathtubs were filled with mud. No landscaping had been planted. Room reservations were all screwed up and guests were forced to wait in line for hours to speak with someone about the problem. The keylock machine was broken and unlocked rooms were burglarized. People were crying in the lobby.

Never underestimate the Deadheads' ability to ignore circumstances. They came to party and when the sun went down, that's what they did. No funereal air attended the final Furthur shows; the fans knew that Furthur had run its course and that the musicians would be back in one configuration or another. For their part, the band tried to muster the spirit. This last time out, Furthur spread out the riches, mixing material across four nights for a truly panoramic look at the band's songbook, sprinkled with Latin accents like "Mexicali Blues" or a spontaneous "La Bamba" sandwiched in the middle of "Good Lovin'" on the first night. There was an icy chill between Weir and Lesh, who couldn't look at each other. Weir largely went through the motions while Lesh tried vainly to pump life into the performance. "Nice to see all of you South of the Border," said Lesh.

On the last afternoon of the run, Bobby Weir gave a surprise acoustic show from the open-air pavilion in the middle of the hotel's lagoon to an enthralled throng spread out over the grounds. At the beginning of the final show that last night, the group huddled on-stage before, as was their custom, ocean breezes cooling the tropical night air. Lesh looked all the band members in the eye. "What we've done here is really special," he said, a benediction that would frame the band's final performance.

At the end of the night, after the band left, the exit music piped through the speakers as the crowd departed was Taylor Swift's "We Are Never Ever Getting Back Together." Insiders suspected the hand of Weir in the selection; he was father of two young Swift fans and had recently taken his daughters to a Taylor Swift concert.

With another tour group arriving the next day for a "My Morning Jacket" three-day event, Weir, in no hurry to go home, hung around, extended his vacation another few days, and sat in with both MMJ and the Preservation Hall Jazz Band.

But even as this Furthur chapter was closing, with all four of the living Dead as far apart as they had ever been, Weir still knew this Grateful Dead thing had larger, mystical implications for all of them. He may have been tired and disgusted with Lesh, but he could see beyond those temporary feelings to a larger, shared future. The tangled personal relations, power games, and money trips—all very un–Grateful Dead—meant nothing compared to what these four men had achieved in their lives together. They had done something lasting, not that they meant to, but having done so, they had created a body of work and a legacy that they had to live up to. Tired, wasted, and left on his own in Mexico, Weir still knew that.

On his day off in Maya Riviera, lounging around poolside, Weir sat for an interview with *Rolling Stone* and inevitably the question of the band's upcoming fiftieth anniversary the next year came up. Weir didn't flinch. In his easy drawl, he could have been speaking directly to his other bandmates, not some interviewer, and, in fact, he probably was.

"We have to do something commemorative," he said. "I think we owe it to the fans, we owe it to the songs, we owe it to ourselves. If there are issues we have to get past, I think that we owe it to ourselves to man up and get past them. If there are hatchets to be buried, then let's get to work. Let's start digging. I'll just say, to my delicate sensibilities, that it would be wrong to let that go by un-commemorated."

Lesh went home from Mexico with even more reasons not to leave home and his new playpen in San Rafael. His first grandson, Levon Lesh, had been born in January to his son Brian and a woman he met after breaking up with his girlfriend. The Leshes decided to rear the baby. Lesh's deal with Shapiro would keep him away from home plenty, but he played all through February and March at Terrapin Crossroads several times a week before he did his first Capitol Theatre run with Phil and Friends in April.

Terrapin Crossroads had turned into a happening scene with live music in the bar almost every night of the week. With a weighty daily nut of $5,000 just to open the doors, the club was expensive, but crowds flocked to hear different sets of local musicians tackle the Dead repertoire with the likelihood of a guest appearance on any given night by Lesh himself. Other visiting firemen, from Gregg Allman to B. B. King, stopped by the club. Lesh came to the club almost daily in the morning, took a healthy lunch from the nearby Whole Foods, and practiced before the club opened for business. His Maserati could be seen in his reserved parking place whenever he was there.

Weir, on the other hand, came home from Mexico in time to take RatDog out of its Lesh-imposed hiatus with Steve Kimock on guitar and both Robin Sylvester on electric bass and Rob Wasserman on acoustic bass. He gave the rusty band a one-night test drive at the Sweetwater and headed back out for six weeks to tour theaters in the East, Midwest, and South. He was home and gone again within days.

Weir was headed for another crash. People around him saw it coming. He had been the subject of interventions many times. He had been in and out of rehab. He had tried experimental programs, but nothing stuck. After Furthur, he went back out too soon. The immense pressure of his relations with Lesh had driven him back to bad habits. He needed a break. He needed to get healthy again. He needed to stop drinking.

Weir took it all in stride, showing up for rehearsal in a T-shirt that read REHAB IS FOR QUITTERS. He kept himself in shape with rigorous daily workouts, steam baths, and yoga. He ate a healthy diet. When drinking, however, he could grow opaque, less abundantly verbal. Ordinarily generous, supportive, and forgiving, under the influence he could be surly and short. "I don't want to hear any more better ideas," he snapped at the band one night.

A teenager when he joined the band, Weir quickly adopted Jerry Garcia as a surrogate older brother and father figure. Garcia clearly helped shape Weir's values. He learned music from Garcia, but he also absorbed Garcia's character and, in his absence, Weir was often the sole remaining conscience of the Dead. Weir echoed Garcia's passivity. They were both constitutionally incapable of confrontation. As a result, Weir could temporarily get lost in the crossfire, but he always followed his own path. He insisted on it. Weir didn't admit mistakes or apologize. He only moved forward. Furthur had been traumatizing in the long run, but he emerged more than ever convinced of the enduring impact of the Dead's work.

He was now certain that the Grateful Dead's enduring legacy was in the songs. They were only the messengers, and ultimately it was not about them. He longed for the connection he could only sporadically find in Furthur and, failing that, retreated to his local neighborhood band, RatDog.

Weir was a musical savant. As the youngest member of the band, he long before gave up expecting to be taken seriously by his bandmates, but he learned how to get his points across. He was also dyslexic, and reading was a labor, but he always found ways to get the information he needed. He developed powerful nonverbal communication skills on the bandstand, part telepathy, part prestidigitation, part speaking in code. And when Weir bears down and puts his considerable skills to use as a vocalist, he can detail out a song with the kind of artistry found in the great country singers like Merle Haggard or Willie Nelson.

Weir had become a modern-day troubadour—an ancient archetype certain to be recognized by Joseph Campbell, the myth expert and author of *Hero with a Thousand Faces*, the book on which film director George Lucas partially based his *Star Wars* trilogy. Campbell was one of dozens of unlikely people to stumble into the Dead camp. At Mickey Hart's invitation, Campbell attended a Grateful Dead concert. Campbell told Hart he could tell "the band is tied at the heart. You are shaking hands with the ancients." Campbell was guest of honor at a dinner party Hart threw at his home that Weir also attended.

In April, Weir attended the premiere of a documentary about his life and career, *The Other One*, at the Tribeca Film Festival in New York. The feel-good movie ended on an upbeat note of Weir the happy husband and father and his rediscovery of his own biological father, Jack Parber, all heartstring stuff for a straight-to-Internet release on Netflix. A younger generation of rock musicians from Sonic Youth, the National, and other groups testified that Weir was as much a legend as Garcia, only he was still alive. Shot more than a year before it was released, the film caught a happier, more carefree Weir than he was by the time the film came out.

The film was a brief light in a dark time for Weir. His shoulder injury wouldn't heal. He was back touring with RatDog. TRI was closed. Weir suspended his ambitious schedule of Webcasts, cut down the staff to almost nothing, and cut his losses. His business plan was ahead of its time, but the technological marvel and exquisite audio capabilities of the studio remained, if not entirely abandoned, at least neglected. The studio had drained his finances and RatDog was not going to earn the same kind of money Furthur did. Weir was lost and his only answer was to go back on the road and play music. This time, it wouldn't work.

In July, after a month on the road, RatDog pulled into Las Vegas for a show at the Palms Casino Resort. Weir told the band he didn't feel well at sound check and was going back to his room. That night, a half-hour past showtime, when Weir didn't show, a hotel official told the crowd that doctors had been checking on Weir, and he would not be able to perform that night. The spokesman offered refunds and added that since everybody was here, RatDog had volunteered to play without Weir. Drummer Jay Lane handled all the lead vocals, singing from lyrics on a music stand.

The story would have held water if Deadheads hadn't seen Weir drinking all afternoon at the hotel bar and posted photos of him on the Internet. His wife and manager flew in the next day. He finished the few dates remaining on the tour, went home, cancelled all his dates for the rest of the year—a huge financial loss—and, once again, disappeared from public view.

At the bottom of all his problems was his bad back. The damage to his muscles and tendons had been years in the making. Spending his entire adult life standing up for hours in front of microphones and strumming heavy guitars, his rhomboid muscle was one long, gnarled strip of gristle. Playing music had become almost too painful to bear. By the end of the first set of the night, he would be in such pain that the entire second set would feel like playing with a knife in his back. Pain medication just sent him back to rehab. He needed to solve the problem or he could not continue.

Weir delved seriously into his medical issues looking for a cure. For Weir to go six months without playing music in public—not dropping by the Sweetwater on the way home a single time—is evidence of how seriously he followed that path. After endless rounds of doctors, physical therapists, and trainers, he finally found an exercise regimen involving swinging heavy objects that proved effective therapy. He underwent surgery on his neck and had to train himself not to look down at his guitar while he played. For a while, he practiced blind-folded. He devoted himself to healing with a missionary zeal. With the next year's fiftieth anniversary looming, he wanted to be ready for whatever was going to happen.

In the meantime, wheels were turning in the music industry to capitalize on the coming anniversary of the Grateful Dead. In the twenty years since Garcia died, the myth of the Dead had only spread. Prep school students in the band's eighties prime, heavy tape traders, were now running Wall Street firms. And a whole new generation of hippie spawn had embraced the ethos and adopted the mythology. A tidal wave of consumer demand could be envisioned. Every major player in the concert business caught the scent.

In July, Dick Clark Productions, the Hollywood television production company run by the old host of *American Bandstand*, stepped forward with an offer to produce an all-star celebration of the Grateful Dead's fiftieth anniversary in a concert to be held in Golden Gate Park in San Francisco and filmed for a television special. The producers wanted to bring in special guests and create a network television–style extravaganza. Lady Gaga was mentioned as a possible guest star. The offer caught the band members by surprise and jarred management into starting to take the prospects seriously. Having gotten wind about the Dick Clark people looking into renting the park, San Francisco concert producer Gregg Perloff, a veteran of Bill Graham Presents—the firm that threw more Grateful Dead shows than anyone—also whipped up an offer to present the reunited band in Golden Gate Park. Perloff's company, Another Planet Productions, presented the annual Outside Lands festival for as many as sixty thousand paying customers every year in the park.

Coran Capshaw wanted to pay the band $3 million to reunite at his Bonnaroo Festival. Live Nation pitched a nationwide tour. The producers of the annual Coachella Festival envisioned a weekend event at their polo fields in the California desert. Without any business entity or any representatives for the Dead, nobody could even tell where to submit offers. Some were accepted by the band's attorney at a law office in Culver City. Others were received by Jonathan Levine in Nashville, no longer officially representing Lesh, but still the last Dead agent standing. There was a lot of interest, but, at this point, the band members weren't even all speaking. All involved, however, could feel the will of the Deadheads.

The fans knew nothing. These confidential maneuvers were happening behind the scenes. In November, an announcement posted on the Internet brought an end to Furthur, which Lesh had put on "hiatus" since 2013. With this post, he put the band out of its misery with certain finality. "We'll all be keeping very busy over the foreseeable future, and it's time to let Furthur take a bow," the statement read. "We enjoyed the ride more than we can possibly express." The death notice came while Lesh was in the middle of a ten-show run at the Capitol. With Weir still missing in action, the grim post sent a shiver through the Deadhead community, who were beginning to wonder about the pending anniversary and hoping for word of some celebration in the works.

Around the same time, Hart and Kreutzmann went to dinner at Weir's Mill Valley home specifically to talk about the fiftieth anniversary. They each came with their managers. Matt Busch had already held talks with Shapiro, who called wanting to know what Weir was thinking. The three bandmates and their associates brainstormed for several hours about the coming anniversary. They all wanted to do something. The question mark was Lesh.

Weir was still in touch with Lesh—they had sung the National Anthem together at the Giants game in October and watched the game with each other in the stands as the Giants won—but he sagely declined to put himself in the middle. Hart and Kreutzmann, on the other hand, hadn't spoken to Lesh in years and weren't about to start now.

They talked about what they thought it would take to convince Lesh to join them. They talked about what to do if he refused. They agreed that they only wanted one additional guitarist and talked about possible guitar players. Trey Anastasio of Phish was everybody's first choice. The idea of using a rotating cast of guitarists came up and the names Kimock, Kadlecik, and Haynes were mentioned. Even with all the talk, they were so distant from their lifelong colleague Lesh, they had no idea whether he would join them or not. They parted ways that night having agreed they would do something, just not knowing exactly what.

Peter Shapiro had the inside track. Lesh was going to be the key and the other offers were coming largely from people the Leshes didn't know personally. Since his days at Wetlands, Shapiro had been working with all four members. He came from the parking lots, not the corporate music business. He understood the audience and he knew the band members. Shapiro had developed an especially good rapport with the Leshes. He had worked closely with them on the Capitol Theatre deal and, as they came east in October and November to play Phil and Friends shows for Shapiro at the Brooklyn Bowl and the Capitol, he worked on them. Initially, Jill Lesh was adamantly opposed to any reunion, but Shapiro was able to bring her around. With plentiful private time and comfortable surroundings to hold discussions, Shapiro could feel out the Leshes and craft a proposal he could feel confident would be accepted. His first plan involved multiple dates at Madison Square Garden in New York and Oakland Arena in Oakland.

There were many issues facing Shapiro. Lesh would not tour, so the concert would have to take place in a single city. The economics worked against a festival setting like Golden Gate Park, where the expenses of setting up the concert site would eat into the revenue. Also, the Leshes did not want to play on the West Coast. They liked Chicago. Although no reasons were ever given, they refused to entertain other options.

Among other demands, Lesh insisted on reading a manuscript copy of Kreutzmann's upcoming autobiography before agreeing. Putting together the right backing ensemble—especially the guitar player—was crucial. The Grateful Dead had a long history of selling tickets independently, and that tradition would have to be preserved to some degree. At no time did the other band members speak directly to their estranged bandmate. Kreutzmann was urged to take up the issue of his book directly with Lesh, but he didn't have Lesh's email address. All the negotiations with the Leshes went on between them and Shapiro or Matt Busch. Weir's affable and capable young manager had forged a smooth working relationship with Jill during their years with Furthur and all the communication between the two camps now went through those back channels.

Shapiro was gradually able to expand the number of shows from one to two and, finally, three. The offer kept growing. There was considerable resistance from the rest of the band to the idea of Soldier Field in Chicago. The Grateful Dead had played the band's final concert before Garcia died there twenty years earlier and that was not a good memory. Chicago had never been a special city for the Dead, but the location did allow people to travel from either coast with equal ease. After some discussion, the band members decided to go back and do it right this time.

All matters were settled except one and arrangements were made for Lesh to read the manuscript of Kreutzmann's book at an attorney's office in Marin County. He was not allowed to bring his cell phone or any writing instruments. Lesh spent a couple of hours reviewing the book and the deal was on.

On January 5, 2015, Trey Anastasio was in Miami recuperating from Phish's annual New Year's run when he received an email from Phil Lesh, officially inviting him to play with the band. Coran Capshaw was instrumental in convincing Anastasio to join the band. Even though he had been a fan since he was a teenager, Anastasio and Phish had always been scrupulous in avoiding comparisons with the Dead. Phish never covered any songs from the Dead's repertoire. Anastasio recognized the once-in-a-lifetime opportunity that had been dropped in his lap. He was not difficult to persuade. Jeff Chimenti and Bruce Hornsby were also added on keyboards.

Ten days later, on January 16, a video of Jerry's daughter Trixie Garcia was posted on the Internet announcing the three shows for July 2–4 at Soldier Field in Chicago. No band name was billed. The concerts were titled "Fare Thee Well: Celebrating 50 Years of the Grateful Dead."

"The great thing about this show happening at Soldier Field on the Fourth of July," she said, "is because this is an amazing American rock band being celebrated on America's birthday. The great things about these shows happening in Chicago, not only is it the central location for all Deadheads to come gather, but it's also the last place the Grateful Dead played together in 1995. Being able to get everyone back together—the fans and the band members—for this special weekend is really a big deal."

Big deal indeed. It had been a big deal to pull together the disparate forces inside the band, and a bigger deal to overcome all the obstacles presented. But nobody had yet quite foreseen how big a deal it would become.

20

Rehearsal

STINSON BEACH is a tiny beach town at the end of a harrowing drive down the cliffs above the Pacific Ocean in western Marin County. The town boasts a full-time population of 632, but is mostly home to vacation houses for well-heeled San Francisco residents a half-hour drive away. Jerry Garcia moved to this remote outpost with Mountain Girl and their girls in 1972. When the Dead set up the band's original mail-order box office, management chose the post office in the oceanside hamlet. Since the eighties, Deadheads had been buying tickets from the Dead's box office, GDTS TOO, at Box 456 in Stinson Beach. The small but experienced staff braced for an onslaught of orders after the announcement of Fare Thee Well and the decision to allow a portion of the tickets to be sold via the traditional Grateful Dead mail-order system. The band had insisted that the Deadheads be allowed to write in for tickets before releasing tickets to the general public, as they always had.

This was no simple matter to negotiate. The stadium had an exclusive agreement with Ticketmaster, the corporate advance ticket agency, and also a deal with season ticket holders for the Chicago Bears football team to offer exclusive access to tickets to other events at the park. For the Dead, maintaining this long-standing direct connection with the fans was important and Shapiro had to jump through hoops to make it happen. Nobody was prepared for what occurred.

An avalanche of mail buried the tiny post office. Inside a few days of the announcement on January 16, 2015, more than seventy thousand letters fell out of the sky onto their heads. As many as one-third were decorated with lavish artwork—it had always been the Deadheads' theory that drawing pictures on the face of the envelope improved the chances of getting tickets and, in fact, it did. Each envelope contained a money order. More than $90 million was received, enough orders to pay for more than three hundred thousand tickets. The Chicago stadium held fifty-five thousand seats and the advance order was already about twice the number of tickets available.

The explosion took everybody's breath away. No concert in history had been the subject of this kind of advance sale. Nothing in the Grateful Dead's experience remotely prepared their staff for the tsunami of orders. To give the ticket office time to deal with this unexpected torrent, Shapiro postponed the official sale date on Ticketmaster to late February. He rejiggered his seating map to make more $199 tickets available for the Dead ticket office. He expanded the stadium capacity to seventy thousand seats by opening seats all the way around, including behind the band. The inexperienced promoter, producing a show on a scale he had never previously attempted, was caught flat-footed with the hottest concert in rock history. Not that he was surprised.

A week after the announcement, Weir and Hart were in Los Angeles for the music industry trade show NAMM, and Weir tagged along when Hart went to meet with Don Was, record producer and Capitol Records executive, about a possible deal for Hart's thirty years of solo recordings at the Capitol Tower in Hollywood. Was had been working on a record with pop star John Mayer and knew of Mayer's fascination with the Dead. Mayer happened to be downstairs in the basement recording studio and Was called him up to meet Weir and Hart.

Mayer was a misunderstood pop star. He vaulted up the pop charts at age nineteen in 2002 with his first album, *Room for Squares*, a

smooth, frankly commercial pop album that threw off several hit sin-
gles, including "Your Body Is a Wonderland," which won a Grammy.
Although success came easily to him, he remained, obviously, someone with something left to prove. His 2006 album, *Continuum*, was
an acclaimed, popular bid to be taken more seriously as a musician,
an aspiration Mayer managed to swiftly undermine with a series of
gaffes, public romances turned ugly, and awkward interviews.

Plagued with medical issues involving his throat, Mayer disappeared with his next album half-finished. He spent more than two
years without singing in public. He relocated to Bozeman, Montana,
and apparently underwent considerable self-examination. When he
returned in April 2013 to induct the late bluesman Albert King into
the Rock and Roll Hall of Fame, Mayer brought his guitar to the po-
dium and gave a short postdoctoral seminar on electric blues guitar
styles, underscoring his emergence as a guitar-playing rock musician
rather than a sulky pop singer.

Don Was produced Mayer's comeback 2013 album, *Paradise Valley*, a sortie into folk rock inspired by the Laurel Canyon scene of the
early seventies, CSN&Y, Joni Mitchell, etc. It was another plea to be
taken more seriously. During the sessions for *Paradise Valley*, Mayer
became obsessed with the Grateful Dead. He stumbled across "Althea" listening to the Internet music service Pandora and, captivated
by Garcia's guitar lick, followed the song down the entire Grateful
Dead rabbit hole. He soon had downloaded every *Dick's Picks* to his
iPod and was compulsively studying the Dead's music. Was, producer
of Mayer's album, had no idea the collaboration he was facilitating in
his office when he called Mayer upstairs to meet his heroes.

Mayer, an intense and articulate young man, bubbled over. He
went into a speech about how much he admired their music. He
told them he came to the music fresh, with no cultural association
(nobody would ever mistake Mayer for a hippie). He wanted them
to understand how he saw their music on its own, free from the tie-
dye and psychedelics. He said the songs took him places he never
went before and now he visited every day. He might have gotten a
little carried away. It sounded a bit like a sermon. "These are songs

for people with homes who every so often don't want those homes," Mayer told them.

"Hey, you wanna do our PR?" said Weir.

After that meeting, Mayer invited Weir to be his guest during a stint as acting host of television's *The Late, Late Show* in February. After the obligatory interview where Mayer explained that he converted to the Dead's music at the height of his vocal cord problems ("I couldn't even speak at the time and the music just found me"), the two picked up guitars and played "Althea," the song that introduced Mayer to the Dead, and "Truckin'." Mayer's liquid guitar lines jelled with Weir's crystalline chording. Weir was taken.

"There's no way I'm not going to play music with that guy again," he told Matt Busch as they left the television studio.

In March, Mayer went to TRI at Weir's invitation for a week of jamming. Dead drummers Hart and Kreutzmann looked at the sessions as an opportunity for a sectional rehearsal in front of Fare Thee Well, since Lesh had decreed there would be only a minimum number of full band rehearsals. With Mike Gordon of Phish on bass and Mayer producer Don Was on keyboards, the band arrived ready to work out on the half-dozen Dead songs that Mayer came prepared to play.

Peter Shapiro was at TRI that morning. The overwhelming demand for the Soldier Field shows had blown everybody away. When tickets for the general public finally went on sale, Fare Thee Well broke the Internet. More than a half-million people were waiting online to buy tickets when Ticketmaster opened for business that morning. Ticketmaster sold out the more than two hundred thousand tickets in less than an hour. It was the biggest single one-day rock concert sale in the company's history. They figured they could have sold six million tickets. Shapiro's $2,200 VIP "Enhanced Experience" packages featuring floor seats, private lounge, and food and drink were snapped up instantly. More than 86 percent of the tickets were sold outside Illinois. The secondary market was sizzling. StubHub featured several sets of tickets to all three shows for $11,000 (a private suite was available for $20,000). The average resale price

was more than $600. Shapiro was scrambling to meet the extraordi-
nary demand and had convinced the band to consider two additional
shows, prior to the Chicago shows as West Coast warmups. Shapiro,
Matt Busch, and Aimee Kreutzmann drove down that morning to
check out the new football stadium built by the San Francisco 49ers
football team in Santa Clara County.

Located in the heart of Silicon Valley near the city of Mountain
View, the billion-dollar Levi's Stadium had only opened the previous
season. No concerts had yet been held in the facility, but country
star Kenny Chesney was booked into the stadium the coming May.
Only a few miles from Palo Alto where the Grateful Dead first came
together, the area had changed dramatically since those sleepy days.
The tech industry that flowered in little cubbyholes around that part
of the peninsula about the same time the Dead did had blossomed
into America's great new industry and radically transformed the surrounding area, partially fueled by the same psychedelic soup as the
Grateful Dead. It was a long way from Magoo's Pizza Parlor on El
Camino Real in Menlo Park now. Shapiro and the party toured the
spanking new stadium and decided they could do the shows there.
When Busch phoned back to TRI to tell Weir they had cut the deal
for the additional concerts, the band was already playing and he left
word with Weir's wife Natascha.

None of the musicians at TRI knew why they were there, but the
music they were making together was convincing. Weir's sonic marvel of a studio allowed them to explore the subtleties of their music
at comfortable volumes and exquisite fidelity. By the end of the week,
they had decided to form a band. On one hand, whatever plans they
would make would have to wait until after the Fare Thee Well shows
in July. On the other hand, if somehow the plans for the reunion
faltered, a possible backup was now in place. While the band members had all agreed to Shapiro's proposals, they had still not come
together in person.

Drummer Kreutzmann and his wife Aimee had temporarily relocated to San Francisco early in the year. They took an apartment in the
former industrial neighborhood turning hip, Dogpatch, a far cry from
the north shore of Kauai. Kreutzmann's book was coming out in May

and the Fare Thee Well event would be in July. He wanted to play music. He had been locked up in Hawaii since 2012 working on the book with journalist Benjy Eisen, who was now serving as Kreutzmann's manager. He had vowed not to play music until the book was done. Outside of one existing obligation in Belize and Costa Rica in January 2013 called "Jungle Jam," for which he fielded a version of BK3, his Bill Kreutzmann Trio, he had been good to his word.

His days in Kauai could be bucolic. He lived with his wife in his rambling former bachelor pad, a pool house set on lush grounds, a couple of miles from where his wife maintained the organic farm she operated before they met. They were building a new home on a lot next to the farm. Kreutzmann liked to get up early and perform light chores around the place. They hired farmworkers for the hard work, but Kreutzmann enjoyed pitching in. When wild pigs became a problem, they set traps and ate boar for weeks. The farm ran a fruit stand and he took a particular interest in its operation. He also liked to go fishing or scuba diving off his boat, typical daily pursuits of life in the Hawaiian paradise, not to mention the occasional psychedelic camping trip. Although he wasn't playing music while he worked on the book, he and Eisen would eat mushrooms and listen to old Dead tapes.

When RatDog had cancelled their tour after Weir's crash the previous summer, an opportunity suddenly arose for Kreutzmann to play the Lockn' Festival. Eisen put him together with keyboardist Aron Manger of the Disco Biscuits, an old friend of Eisen's, and guitarist Tom Hamilton. Kreutzmann brought guitarist Steve Kimock, bassist Oteil Burbridge, and other guests, including Taj Mahal and Col. Bruce Hampton, for what they called the Lockn' Step Allstars. The well-received set was lauded by reviewers as one of the highlights of the festival. Fresh from that triumph, with Manger and Hamilton on board and bassist Reed Mathis of jam band Tea Leaf Green, Kreutzmann started Billy and the Kids early the next year after landing in San Francisco and took the band on the road in April. He also paused for a weekend at New Orleans Jazz Fest in May with a couple of the Little Feat musicians in an impromptu outing they called Dead Feat. On top of all that, he spent two weeks on a book tour in

May doing signings and media interviews for his freshly published memoir, *Deal: My Three Decades of Drumming, Dreams and Drugs with the Grateful Dead*. Experienced touring musicians who meet the book tour are often flabbergasted by how much more exhausting it is than rock tours because, on the road with a rock band, you don't have to get up early to do the morning TV talk shows. After more than two years of quiet isolation on the islands, Kreutzmann was busting out of his rock fever.

Kreutzmann was a primal man. His life in Hawaii was quasi-retirement, a blend of leisure and boredom only available to someone who could afford it. As much as he liked drumming, music was not his lifeblood and, outside of playing drums, there was not much he was driven to do. Life on Kauai could be idyllic, but he had no support system to rival what he left in Marin. Living on the most remote islands on the planet can be confining and depressing, but every day is paradise. Kreutzmann always liked to blur the line between play and work. After Garcia's death, he had gone full tropo and outside of occasional patches of loneliness and isolation, the island lifestyle largely suited him. Only now was he itching for activity.

In May, all four men almost crossed paths at "Dear Jerry," a Garcia commemorative concert held at Merriweather Post Pavilion in Columbia, Maryland. Early on it was decided that they would save any joint appearances for Fare Thee Well so Lesh opened the show as Phil Lesh & Communion (with his sons in the band) and left to catch an early flight. The four-and-a-half-hour all-star concert also featured New Orleans songwriter Allen Toussaint, Garcia bluegrass associate David Grisman, Jamaican reggae star Jimmy Cliff, country singer Eric Church, alt-rock princess Grace Potter, Garcia's favorite East L.A. Mex-rockers Los Lobos, seventies rock hero Peter Frampton, and others. Without Lesh at the end of the show, the other three—Weir, Hart, and Kreutzmann—came together for "Touch of Grey" and the ensemble finale of "Ripple." Early flight or not, Lesh still managed to extend his opening set to the point where the entire day's schedule needed to be adjusted.

Hart had never slowed down, and Fare Thee Well only interrupted his steady stream of activities. He was immersed in consuming, passionate projects at all times. He had begun recording another album, continued to create his artwork, and done "Music and the Brain" work with neurophysicist Dr. Adam Gazzaley. He served on the boards of the National Recording Registry and the Exploratorium, a beloved San Francisco science museum. He was part drummer, part mystic, part swashbuckling Gandalf bravely forging ahead, a force of nature unto himself. He and Kreutzmann were the yin and yang of the beat; Kreutzmann the steady, powerful beat; and Hart the imaginative, irresistible color. They were drum brothers under the hood of the rhythm together, a symphony of percussion at the heart of the Grateful Dead.

Lesh didn't appear to see it that way. In Furthur, he never replaced Jay Lane, indicating he didn't feel the second drummer was necessary to interpret Grateful Dead material. He treated Hart and Kreutzmann with a certain disdain. He seemingly saw the drummers as disposable and made no attempt to disguise his contempt. They returned the disrespect. To the drummers, being left out of Furthur remained a wound that had not entirely healed. But that was hardly the beginning of the clash. This battle extended back through the years, but had only broken into the open when Hart made that "liver of a jerk" comment after Lesh's transplant. After that, relations between the Leshes and the drummers had been at best tenuous, wary, and terse; at worst suspicious, combative, and hostile. A lot of bad blood had been spilled. Coming back together, even for this limited amount of time, was fraught with possible danger.

That morning in June, driving to the first day of rehearsals at the sound stage the band rented in San Rafael, Hart felt undeniable excitement, but he also experienced considerable anxiety. He had not been in the same room with Lesh for a number of years now. They could both still feel the animosity, even at a distance. So much of Lesh's actions and statements had been hurtful, they cut Hart to the bone and he had struck back. The conflict was a deep heartache for Hart because Lesh had been Hart's first friend in the band after Kreutzmann brought him in. He had lived in the Belvedere Street house in the Haight with Lesh, sleeping in a closet. Lesh turned him on to the album *The Music of North India*, a recording that changed

Hart's life and, subsequently, the music of the Grateful Dead. Hart scarred the album cover dripping wax from candles as he struggled to read the liner notes in his dark closet. He and Lesh had shared the rhythm and the great adventure that was the Grateful Dead all their adult lives. Underneath the anger and recriminations were broken hearts. Hart wondered what was waiting for him as he pulled his black Porsche into the studio parking lot.

32TEN Studio in San Rafael was a massive facility built by George Lucas's production company, Industrial Light and Magic. They shot pieces of *Star Wars* and *Indiana Jones* movies there. TRI was too small for the full-scale production they were planning to mount. Their equipment had been loaded in and set up. Vocal rehearsals with Weir, Lesh, Anastasio, and Bruce Hornsby had been taking place the previous four days. The quartet worked out the harmonies using only acoustic guitars and Hornsby on piano, who could feel his keyboards in the intimate, low-key music they were making, helping shape the songs.

Lesh had insisted that he would only play one day of full band rehearsal for each show, a total of five days with the drummers. Considering Anastasio had to learn around one hundred songs, it seemed unnecessarily difficult and more rehearsals might have been indicated, but his bandmates had learned that Lesh would not negotiate. There had always been arguments about how much rehearsal was good for the band. Of course, only the Dead would worry about overrehearsing in the first place. But Weir, Hart, and Kreutzmann were under no illusions that that was Lesh's reasoning on the Fare Thee Well rehearsals. They figured that he simply wanted to avoid spending that much time with them.

When Hart walked into the cavernous studio, his greatest fear materialized. Lesh was the only one who had arrived ahead of him and they were alone. The awkward moment passed quickly. Lesh was immediately cordial and open. They gave each other a hug and exchanged witticisms. Hart felt his doubts ease and sat down behind his drums.

For months, the musicians had been passing around a shared text of a list of songs they wanted to play. There was a second list of songs people didn't want to play, but nothing was ever added to that list. At rehearsal, with limited time to process a massive songbook, many numbers were discarded simply because they were too complex and would eat up too much rehearsal time.

With more than one hundred songs to consider, Lesh had proposed arranging the concerts in a chronological retrospective. Set lists for all the shows were written, although the band would tinker with the selections up to the last minute. Lesh had been experimenting at Terrapin Crossroads with themed presentations concentrating on individual years from the Dead's history, studying the repertoire, using his club as a laboratory for Fare Thee Well. Only the week before, John Mayer had sat in at Terrapin, re-creating two individual 1977 shows. Lesh knew he wanted to open the Soldier Field shows with "Box of Rain," because that was the last song the Dead played at Soldier Field in 1995, and end the entire series of shows with "Attics of My Life."

At the rehearsals, he took charge, strutting around like a rooster, ruling on other people's ideas, snapping off terse orders to his equipment handlers. Lesh was clearly nervous—everyone was. He threw off tense vibes, which were intimidating and uncomfortable to both crew and musicians. The air was fraught with electricity. Hart grew frustrated tinkering with his drum sound and exploded, throwing a stick at his equipment guy. The atmosphere between Weir and Lesh could become charged. Weir balked at Lesh's bullying, clearly still a sore spot from Furthur, but the touch-and-go moments came and went. There was too much work to be done for much disagreement and, for the most part, the musicians concentrated on the daunting enough tasks at hand.

Guitarist Anastasio had been thrown in the briar patch. He started learning the songs on his own almost immediately after accepting the assignment in January, but before long, he hired Broadway pianist Jeff Tanski, who wrote charts for seventy songs and rehearsed daily with Anastasio in a Midtown Manhattan studio they locked out for the duration. He spent three days in March with Weir at his Stinson Beach place, jogging the beach together in the mornings and strumming arch-top guitars long into the night. Weir spent another few days with him in Marin in April and again Manhattan after the "Dear Jerry" concert in May. After that, Anastasio came to Marin County in May for a couple of days playing with Lesh, even sitting in one night at Terrapin Crossroads. Attending a barbecue given by Lesh was Anastasio's first opportunity to witness the little brother/big brother dynamic between Lesh and Weir, even before he played with the two together. In between jams, the three of them sat around a table at Lesh's and worked on the set lists for the shows.

The guitar parts were hard enough, but Anastasio had to practice his vocals without knowing which songs he would be assigned to sing lead or which harmony part he would be singing. Weir sang a lot of the old Garcia songs and Lesh used to cover the high notes on the harmonies, but now he sang lower. Some parts were in different registers. There was no way for him to know until they all came together for rehearsal.

Anastasio could not win. He had been given an impossible task, a job with failure built in. Not only did he have to learn and master a massive number of complicated songs that his bandmates all knew better than he did, he was standing in the place of Jerry Garcia, one of the most distinctive stylists to ever play an electric guitar, before some of the most critical and discriminating fans in rock. He would be faulted either way—if he sounded too much like Garcia or didn't sound enough like Garcia. And as much homework as he had done, it was pure fantasy to think he could ever be adequately prepared with such an extensive and complicated songbook. He was one courageous musician.

Anastasio impressed everyone with his attitude; he proved he was a team player even under such grueling conditions. He behaved like a guest, not the alpha bandleader he was in Phish. On breaks, he fussed endlessly with his guitar tone and swapped out gear in consultation with his guitar tech. Relentlessly upbeat, Anastasio was the kind of person who looked people in the eyes when they spoke, quiet, gentle, and serious. But he was left largely to his own devices. Nobody was communicating with him. Keyboardist Chimenti, who had played in every post-Garcia band, made an effort to be especially helpful with Anastasio and, in fact, could often bring the whole band back to focus when they got lost.

There was considerable debate over the stage plot. Weir wanted to stand beside Anastasio so they could more easily see what each other was doing. But Lesh insisted on holding down center stage. That meant the drummers had to endure the pounding volume of Lesh's amplifier and a Plexiglas divider was positioned between the drummers to partly dampen the sound. Weir reluctantly agreed to the arrangement to keep things running smoothly. Lesh and Weir also agreed to compromise on their volume-versus-tempo argument.

The tension was largely lost in the pressure of rehearsing this enormous amount of material in such a short time. Breaks were short and nobody hung around and socialized afterward. There wasn't a lot of easy camaraderie. The others might make comments about Lesh among themselves, but they would say nothing in front of him. There was a lot of talk about reducing the number of lead vocals Lesh was giving to himself and letting Anastasio sing more, but little came of that. The old animosities may have lingered, but they went unspoken. At this highlight of their careers, they simply would rather let Lesh have his way than possibly ruin everything by tangling with him.

Even more than Hart, Kreutzmann harbored strong feelings toward Lesh. They circled each other warily the first couple of days, but Lesh broke the ice after getting worked into a froth by the pounding beat Kreutzmann was laying down. At the end of the number, Lesh leaped toward Kreutzmann's drum set and reached over for a congratulatory handshake over the kit. It was a small gesture and an awkward moment, but a genuine flush of enthusiasm from Lesh.

At the sight of that exchange, Hart breathed deeply, confident now that they could pull this off.

21

Rainbow

THERE WAS no explaining the rainbow. Some immediately thought it was artificial, created by the wizards of Obscura Digital, the group who designed the magnificent light shows for Fare Thee Well. But it turned out Obscura was not behind it. An artificial rainbow would have to be projected on something and this one was too high in the sky for that. Music industry trade magazine *Billboard* even reported the next day—incorrectly—that producers had paid $50,000 for the spectacle. But to everyone's complete amazement, the rainbow proved to be an authentic phenomenon.

The Grateful Dead had always been a beacon for unexplained phenomena. They all well remembered the Portland, Oregon, concert in June 1980 when nearby Mount St. Helens erupted during the band's concert while they played—no lie—"Fire on the Mountain." Concertgoers were showered in volcanic ash leaving the abruptly canceled show. Or the 1987 concert in Telluride, Colorado, during the Harmonic Convergence. The Dead's cosmic consciousness invoked all kinds of strange and wondrous powers. But if the Deadheads needed a sign of validation to crown this convergence with an omen none could deny, they couldn't have asked for a more startling and satisfying one than the massive, arching rainbow that encompassed the entire scene, a corona ringing the stadium, stage set, and band, its appearance perfectly timed at the climax of the first Fare Thee Well set as the reunited Dead turned the corner and headed for the barn playing "Viola Lee Blues."

The band had arrived at Levi's Stadium outside Santa Clara on Friday afternoon to hold a two-hour sound check that, in addition to a much-needed technical rehearsal, provided another useful practice session for the band. The production had come together quite quickly and rather chaotically in the final few weeks. Longtime Grateful Dead lighting designer Candace Brightman was brought in somewhat late in the day to confer with Shapiro and his production specialists. She found plans in disarray, the chain of command obscure, and a morass of email communications—more than sixty-five a day—that only spread the confusion.

The first proposed stage design came from Mike Tait of Tait Towers, the stage construction and design firm that built massive stage sets for Madonna, the Rolling Stones, and Michael Jackson. Tait envisioned a gigantic, elaborate stage that would have cost more than $1 million. Brightman didn't like the stage design. She thought it was overdone, clumsy, and un–Grateful Dead–like. In spite of that, erroneous emails circulated saying that Brightman endorsed the design.

She was bewildered by the lack of communication. There was no central organization and Brightman could never figure out who was in charge of what. She had been told by management she could not speak to any of the band members unless they were all present, which made knowing their wishes difficult. Word eventually was handed down from the band that they wanted an "industrial look" and Brightman went about a more rudimentary design that incorporated a simple proscenium decorated with roses and a large video screen. Obscura Digital, the high-tech outfit from San Francisco, created luminous, imaginative light projections for the proscenium. A computer model was used to build the stage, sound, and lights and nobody knew how it would work or what it would look like until it was constructed and plugged in at Levi's the day before the first show.

On their drive from Sebastopol where they lived to Levi's Stadium for the Friday afternoon sound check, Mickey Hart and his wife and daughter stopped at the water's edge in the Presidio in San Francisco to draw a deep breath and take a moment's respite before heading into battle. His wife Caryl had to negotiate the time off from her job as park director of Sonoma County. The sun sparkled on the bay and the ocean breeze cooled the air, as the Harts took a break from the three-hour drive for a brief family interlude. Where they were going, such private exchanges were going to be scarce. They were leaving serenity behind.

At sound check, Bob Weir stepped out of the late-afternoon shadows onto the giant stage at the end of the stadium and looked out at the empty field and grandstands yawning before him. It had been many years since the Dead commanded stadiums. He could not escape the feeling that what was about to occur was truly momentous. In many ways, his entire life had led to this place and this hour. More than the culmination of twenty years of struggle, a victory over immense adversity, an exultant triumph of spirit over flesh, this was the peak of a lifetime's path.

Preparing to oversee the storied songbook he so intimately helped to create with his lifelong colleagues for one final remarkable occasion, Weir knew their hard-won rapprochement had brokered this tenuous peace and paved the way for a once-in-a-lifetime experience. In that moment, he stood on top of all that had been accomplished, and he determined to feel it in every cell of his body.

The stadium was eerily quiet. With the perimeter of stadium and parking lots surrounded by cyclone fencing and gates closed until the afternoon of the concert, the only people on the scene were worker bees buzzing around the hive. There were few hangers-on waiting in the wings, as stagehands busily finished preparing the production. No crowds of Deadheads, partying and partaking, camped out in the empty, quiet parking lots.

As the sky turned orange and purple from the tie-dyed sunset, when the band finally assembled onstage and the first belches of electric guitar and eruptions of drums echoed from the stage, barely a soul paused to watch. The band cruised through "Althea" and "Brown

Eyed Woman." They practiced the next night's opening selection, a one-two punch of "Truckin'" and "Uncle John's Band." They tried out "Cumberland Blues" and ran "St. Stephen" with the "William Tell" bridge into "The Eleven." They went over the bridge a few times. The Lesh experimental piece "What's Become of the Baby," a studio track the Dead never performed live, was rehearsed and "Cream Puff War," a song from the band's earliest days, was worked out several times.

These songs all came straight from the Fillmore era and, for good measure, they trotted out the traditional set-closer of the day, "Turn on Your Lovelight," the blues romp that was a specialty of the band's first blues singer and keyboardist, the beloved Pigpen, who died at age twenty-seven in 1973. Weir had handled the song more than capably since 1981, when he reintroduced it to the band's repertoire. They even tried "Alligator," another number from the band's early days the Dead dropped from their songbook in 1971. Clearly, the legacy would be deeply plumbed.

A couple of intrepid Deadheads had sneaked into the stadium yard. In a twenty-first-century touch, they recorded the rehearsal from outside the stadium and posted it on the Internet. Shapiro quickly brought in the Phish security team, and they went nuts racing around the stadium trying to find the source of the broadcast and shut it down, but gave up when they realized it was coming from the parking structure across the street.

On Saturday, the day of the show, with the perimeter fenced off and the lots not open until three in the afternoon, the customary "Shakedown Street" scene moved to a hotel parking lot a mile away. Still, when the fans began to trickle into the empty stadium from the official parking lots in the late afternoon, the crew couldn't help but be struck by what they saw. As these hippies of all ages filed through the turnstiles and onto the field, all hands recognized immediately that this was no ordinary rock concert crowd. It was not simply that they came in colorful raiment, festive moods, and buzzing with anticipation—they did all that—but this crowd was instantly special. Nobody had seen anything like it before. Unlike other concertgoers, they were quiet, peaceful, happy. They radiated joy. Shapiro had colored roses handed out to the first forty-five thousand and that helped set the tone, but it was the Deadheads who brought the party, and that was clear before the band ever set foot onstage.

In fact, it was the Deadheads who willed this concert into existence. Their collective, conscious expectation of a giant celebration in honor of the fiftieth anniversary created the event. The musicians themselves were hardly in a sentimental mood about the good ole Grateful Dead at the time, although they could not fail to notice the looming milestone. The mere fact that they were still alive was amazing enough. It was possible that the four living members had never been further apart in all their adult lives, but the will of the Deadheads pulled them together like an irresistible force. Between the power of the Deadheads and the allure of the music, the band encountered a complex siren song that even the most recalcitrant among them could not resist.

Truth be told, the Deadheads also cast Trey Anastasio in the Garcia chair. All the other guitarists that the Dead had tried after Garcia, to one degree or another, had failed. Nobody could replace Garcia. Anastasio had barely played ten minutes with any of the Dead musicians and didn't know the repertoire, but his status as the lead guitarist/vocalist/Garcia-like figure of the second generation's leading jam band made him the only obvious, noncontroversial choice. In the history of a singular rock band who resolutely followed their own path and kept their own counsel, Fare Thee Well was the first time the Dead made decisions based on focus-group studies, even if they were collected through the ether.

At Levi's Stadium, the sheer size of the seventy-thousand-capacity crowd was staggering enough, but the unified identity of the people attending lent the proceedings the uncanny intimate, familial air of a high school graduation or church social more than a rock concert. Old friends came together. People ran into people they knew from past shows. For this one day, all these people would be friends who never met before, happily sharing this signal event that brought them together and gave them all common purpose. Stockbrokers who came in their Mercedes, street people who picked up a miracle ticket in the lots—everybody was a hippie for the day.

Backstage was swarming with well-wishers, friends, and celebrities such as television's Andy Cohen, Deadhead ex–Speaker of the House Nancy Pelosi, Apple widow Lauren Jobs, rock star John Mayer, whose presence was a mystery to many, although the pending formation of a band between him and three of the core four qualified as one of the worst-kept secrets in Deadland. Mayer, who had hoped to sit in at the shows, had to be told that there would be no special guests on this engagement.

The two camps—the Leshes and the other ones—remained sharply divided. The dressing rooms were a metaphor for how fractured the band had become. In the stadium, signs pointed to dressing rooms for Weir, Hart, and Kreutzmann in one direction and to the Lesh dressing room in the opposite direction.

Walking the short stairs to the huge stage, flanked by VIP viewing areas, the men from the Dead were finally ascending a hill they had spent many long years trudging up. Epiphanies of self-discovery, tests and trials, long days adrift at sea—each man had both lost and found his true self, fought his own dragons, lashed himself to the mast, and ultimately proved his worth. This coming together had been written long before it happened, although it had been far from inevitable. These lost sailors would combine their tempest-tossed crafts for one more voyage. As they gazed out on a sea of tie-dye in the warm California afternoon sunlight, a wave of emotion rippled through the band.

About to embark on a series of five concerts that would recapitulate and summarize a career shared with millions, the seven members of this band arrayed themselves behind their instruments and bobbled, tumbled, and stumbled their way into a soft, rolling groove that picked up steam as it clattered to its feet. Lesh bounced lightly on his heels with a face wreathed in grins, while Weir's expression was set in a gaze of steely determination. Hart and Kreutzmann started out softly, Hart using brushes instead of sticks, slowly powering into the groove. Hornsby and Chimenti, on piano and organ, respectively, could barely be heard in the cacophonous sound mix. When the three vocalists stepped forward to sing the opening lines of Hunter's autobiographical calling card for the band, "Truckin'," the stadium erupted. When they hit the line "what a long, strange trip it's been," the place went nuts all over again.

Following with "Uncle John's Band" sent a warm, comforting signal to the Deadheads that Fare Thee Well would be a feast for the fans. When the band finally chugged to a stop, the song stretched out into a long, largely uneventful jam, the show had been running for a half-hour. With the next selection, "Alligator," a psychedelic-era Pigpen specialty, the band began serious archaeology as Lesh stepped forward with a wobbly, froggy lead vocal.

"Cumberland Blues" gave the band a brisk but supple groove to explore. Weir sunk into the song like a knife. Lesh grinned as they smeared the harmonies out of pitch. The next two songs were authentic antiques. "Born Cross-Eyed" was a track from the band's second album, *Anthem of the Sun*, that the Dead played only a handful of times in 1968, and "Cream Puff War," a song that Garcia always hated off the first album, hadn't been performed since 1967.

The first productive jam of the concert led to "Viola Lee Blues," another staple from the ballroom days that had been abundantly reprised by Phil and Friends. Weir leaned hard into the song and the band burbled along a driving rhythm they took through various detours. Gray clouds now covered the sky and the stadium floor was dark, swept by spotlights. As the band neared the end of the lengthy jam, slowing into some quieter dynamics, the crowd inexplicably burst into cheers. The clouds had parted briefly, and, as a sign of the miracle that these concerts were, the storybook-perfect rainbow appeared in the sky above the eastern end of the stadium like a halo.

The rainbow blazed its arc in the sky as all eyes in the stadium turned up. Unaware of the celestial event transpiring out of sight over their shoulders, the band played on. As the rainbow gradually melted back into the gray clouds, the jam slowly, deliberately disintegrated into a squall of squeaks and squawks and rolling tympani as the first set of Fare Thee Well came to its perfect ending.

The lack of rehearsal showed. They had played plenty of bad notes and missed more than a few vocal cues. Harmonies could be iffy. Anastasio was timid, almost uncertain, not bold and assertive, and his solos never caught fire. At times, he quickly handed off the lead. They might stay on the same riff over and over. Hornsby and Chimenti were tucked over on the side of the stage and almost entirely absent from the house sound mix. People probably forgot they were there and the few solos Hornsby took were lost in the din.

But Weir stoked the fire, continually lighting up the inside of the sound with propulsive strokes on his guitar that found the right spaces. He was singing like a man determined to elevate the stadium single-handedly, sometimes obviously straining his voice. Lesh, cheery and upbeat, braided his thumping bass lines around the beat. It was the two drummers, however, who made it sound like the Grateful Dead. Like prizefighters who fought a busy, tough, but uncertain first round, the musicians retired to backstage for the set break.

The second set dug even deeper into the psychedelic electro-blues Dead catalog, a revisit to the band's sixties heyday when the Dead held forth at Winterland or Fillmore West until the morning sun was in the sky. "Cryptical Envelopment" led to "Dark Star," long one of the Dead's signature pieces they would go years without playing (although it was standard fare for Phil and Friends). A crushing "St. Stephen" and "The Eleven" gave way to Weir leading "Turn on Your Lovelight"—a sequence immortalized on the *Live Dead* album. Hart and Kreutzmann took over for a twenty-minute "Drums/Space" that featured a lot of Hart's prerecorded sonifications triggered from the bandstand.

In the middle of the sonic inventions, Lesh moaned and warbled his way through "What's Become of the Baby," a strange, unlikely piece of dissonance from *Aoxomoxoa* in its live debut. "The Other One" and "Morning Dew," two Fillmore-era standards, brought the show to a joyous, nostalgic close. Hornsby took the lead vocals on the encore, "Casey Jones," the third song of the night from the *Workingman's Dead* album. The fans poured out of the stadium in dazed delight. The entire night had been devoted exclusively to songs from the sixties— Grateful Dead 101, the introductory course. Bob Weir bounced off the stage, pumped up and psyched. "Boy, I sure missed those stadium crowds," he said to Matt Busch as they descended the stairs.

But Weir stormed out of backstage almost immediately. Nobody knew where he was, including his wife. It turned out that he was furious over the stage volume. Later that night, Weir reached Lesh on the phone and angrily complained about how loud he had been playing. His voice was hoarse from screaming over the band and the old battle between them was reignited. Weir let him have it and Lesh agreed to turn down. Of course, that would never happen. Day two was hours away.

On Sunday, the next day, Roger McNamee accepted an offer of tickets from former NBA basketball star Bill Walton, possibly the best-known Deadhead, with more than eight hundred and fifty shows under his belt. McNamee, the tech investor who guided the Dead's aborted foray into the Internet, had made his peace with the post-Garcia bands. As an experienced civilian Deadhead, he loved the music and the culture, but the scene in the audience was not the same as in Garcia's day. Knowing that the band had not had much time to rehearse, he figured it was better to skip Fare Thee Well than be disappointed. McNamee had been playing a hundred concerts a year with his own band, Moonalice, which entertained Deadheads on a regular basis. He kept a lot of connections to the Dead scene— John Molo was his drummer, Barry Sless his lead guitarist, and Jerry's friend Pete Sears played bass. Garcia's equipment manager Steve Parish and several other members of the Dead's crew worked for Moonalice. He had no plans to attend the Fare Thee Well shows until Walton called and insisted he come.

McNamee had no idea what to expect. He went early to scope the scene and found the parking lot merchants were enthusiastic but out of practice. Walking to the stadium, he started meeting people he knew from old Dead shows. Getting into the giant venue went like a breeze. He smoothly found his way to his seats in the crisp, clean white stadium and texted Walton, who came with passes and took him to the roped-off Friends and Family viewing section on the field in front of the soundboard and lighting console.

In the little compound, he saw most of the guitar players from Phil and Friends and Furthur. He said hello to Garcia's widow, Mountain Girl, who was down from Oregon with her daughters. He got a high five from Sen. Al Franken, who hosted Dead concerts with his comic partner Tom Davis in the seventies when they were with *Saturday Night Live*. McNamee's brother had flown out with his kids. He was having a ball and the music hadn't even started. It was just like a Grateful Dead show, he thought.

Before the show, Kreutzmann climbed aboard a golf cart driven by his manager with a security guard on the back and tooled through the parking lots handing out packs of cigarette papers promoting his new book. Excited Deadheads waved and shouted at him, gladly accepting his gifts.

Word on the opening show had been good and the second show was markedly better. The band was improving, not just show by show, but almost song by song, the musicians playing together better at the end of the concert than the beginning. From the first note the second night, the band was looser, more confident, more swinging, less uptight. After concentrating the night before on the Dead's earliest repertoire, opening with "Feel Like a Stranger" planted the band firmly in their eighties peak, reviving a frequent opening number from epic eighties Dead shows. Weir burned his way into the song and Anastasio answered him with a verve and commitment he had been all but entirely lacking the previous night. Weir took a slashing, sterling bottleneck guitar lead on "New Minglewood Blues," and Hornsby handled vocals on "Brown Eyed Woman."

Weir howled "Loose Lucy," serious as a judge, growling over the bar-band riff, driving every line home as hard as he could. In his typical shorts and Birkenstocks, Weir acted like he was carrying the whole show on his back. "Loser" was a Grateful Dead song Hornsby felt enough affinity with to include routinely in his solo performances since his stint with the Dead in the early nineties (although he never performed it with the Dead) and he wrung out the elegance of the lyric with the band at Levi's.

"Row Jimmy," with its tricky extra two-beat phrase, fooled Anastasio every time, but Weir again poured himself into the song. The set hit critical mass with "Alabama Getaway," a house-rocking rendition led by Anastasio on vocals. Weir slowed down the forlorn "Black Peter" to a death march and burrowed into the song with ferocity, picking a perfectly understated guitar solo into the first verse. He and Anastasio fired each other up in heated exchanges on the end of "Hell in a Bucket" to close the first set.

Opening the second set with "Mississippi Half-Step," another frequent opening number during the eighties, plopped the band back into that rich era, Anastasio loose and agile on lead guitar, Lesh halting and uncertain on vocals. Weir's "Wharf Rat" led to an extended jam—Hornsby thought the Ravelesque quality of his piano solo had been lost in the cavernous stadium—out of which the band emerged with "Eyes of the World," which faltered only under Lesh's vocals.

The band was cooking and dropped into a low groove for another Weir dirge beat on "He's Gone," Weir punching every syllable, a song originally written about one of the band's managers ("steal your face right off your head"), a joyful celebration of his departure, but now inevitably seen as a mournful paean to Garcia. This emotional high point swiveled into the nightly drums feature. The previous night, Hart and Kreutzmann had experimented with manufactured sounds and beats they drew from both their interests in electronic dance music—Deadtronica—but tonight Hart brought his Planet Drum associate Sikiru Adepoju on the African hand drums and the percussion symphony went world beat.

The band broke out of the drums with "I Need a Miracle" into "Death Don't Have No Mercy," another relic from the psychedelic era that even longtime Deadheads like McNamee had never heard in concert before, and, finally, a jubilant "Sugar Magnolia." To cap this Deadhead's dream second set, the band returned to encore with "Brokedown Palace."

McNamee wandered out of the stadium, buzzed, bedazzled, and ecstatic. He ran into Howard Cohen, Mickey Hart's manager, and asked if there were any tickets available for Chicago. "Fuck, yeah," said Cohen. McNamee got on his smart phone and quickly found hotel rooms in walking distance of Soldier Field. From what he just saw, he knew he needed to be there. And he knew Steve Parish also had to come.

The next stop was Fourth of July weekend in Chicago.

22

Chicago

SIGNS HUNG from practically every bar, "Welcome Deadheads." Next to Soldier Field, the Field Museum of Natural History got into the act, draping the entrance with three giant banners of dancing tyrannosaurs wearing crowns of roses by psychedelic poster artist Stanley Mouse, who co-created the original skull and roses for the Dead. Old concert tapes blared from portable players. Deadheads in costume were everywhere. A truck selling Grateful Dead merchandise rolled through the Loop, attracting crowds wherever it stopped. Hotel staffs dressed in Dead T-shirts. A local brewery produced an American Beauty Ale. Even the staid old Palmer House offered a special cocktail, the Deadhead, that mixed tequila, vodka, rum, and gin. Fare Thee Well hit town and Chicago rolled over and played Dead.

The chief attraction at "Everything Is Dead," the Field Museum exhibit mounted for the occasion, was Tiger, one of the guitars made for Jerry Garcia by Doug Irwin. The guitar was bought anonymously at auction by Hyatt Hotels heir Dan Pritzker of Chicago, leader of the rock band Sonia Dada. In addition to other Dead memorabilia, the Field featured a large display of decorated ticket envelopes from GDTS TOO in Stinson Beach. Jazz bands played Dead tunes in the museum atrium.

Nightclubs were packed with after-shows featuring acts with known Deadhead appeal like Railroad Earth, Karl Denson's Tiny Universe, Afrobeat rockers Antibalas from Brooklyn, a New Orleans r&b jam band featuring Papa Mali and Ivan Neville. Jackie Greene and Steve Kimock did a Garcia tribute. Garcia's mandolinist buddy David Grisman played a bluegrass brunch. Joan Osborne gave a matinee. Bars and restaurants all over town hosted pay-per-view screenings of the video feed from the sold-out concerts.

The *Chicago Tribune* embraced the event in its editorial pages. "Yes, it's a big deal," they said. On Friday morning before the first show, Peter Shapiro met with Mayor Rahm Emanuel and thanked His Honor for letting him bring the circus to town.

Hotels were bursting. Occupancy was up 120 percent from the Fourth of July the previous year and rates jumped 77 percent. Tickets were selling for astronomical prices on the secondary market, $1,500 for obstructed-view seats. VIP packages ran into the thousands. The *New York Times* noted the upscale nature of the event in an article headlined GRATEFUL DEAD FANS REPLACE VW VANS WITH JETS AND THE RITZ-CARLTON.

Among the most opinionated and entitled fans in rock music, some of the Deadheads raised objections to the massive commercial juggernaut. Stewart Sallo, publisher of the *Boulder Weekly,* wrote a passionate article for *Huffington Post* that received a lot of attention, denouncing the ticket sale system, complaining about choosing Chicago as the location and using Trey Anastasio on guitar. Wrote Sallo: "It's worse than a pity—it's an outright tragedy—that perhaps the most beloved band in history has put itself in a position to be remembered for participating in what may go down as the biggest money grab in music history."

In characteristic openness, Shapiro reacted by locating Sallo's cell phone number. They talked and emailed several times and, after consulting with Sallo and others, Shapiro used a different system to sell tickets to the Santa Clara shows. He literally bought out the Ticketmaster allotment and sold every ticket by lottery through GDTS. Sallo changed his tune. "I am convinced Peter Shapiro's heart is in the right place," he told the *Washington Post*, "and I don't think you can expect these guys to work for free."

The band had cancelled their original plans to fly out immediately following the last Santa Clara show. Instead the musicians and their parties travelled separately to Chicago and assembled for tech rehearsal and sound check on Thursday at Soldier Field. Although the band had agreed on a press blackout before the show, Kreutzmann did a few interviews for his book on the condition that he didn't answer questions about Fare Thee Well, but of course he did. The bright green grassy field would not be covered for the show until the following morning and the band worked out for two hours in the fading afternoon light before an empty stadium. That night, the musicians kept to themselves, although if you looked quickly you could have caught Phil Lesh and his party having drinks in the lobby of the Ritz-Carlton, band headquarters for the weekend.

On Friday, the stadium opened the lots at one o'clock in the afternoon, four hours earlier than they would for tailgating before a Bears game, after rejecting a petition signed by eleven thousand Deadheads asking to allow overnight camping. Shapiro installed tables for select nonprofits in what he called Participation Row, and other authorized vendors found key spots. Kreutzmann was furious to learn the artwork his associates planned to sell had been soaked by late-night automatic sprinklers inside their tent.

Next door, Jerry Garcia's art dealers had erected a small wood building and readied to do land office business. As at Levi's, the parking lot scene was hardly the robust carnival from days of yore, but people were meeting who hadn't seen each other in years. Police averted their gaze as vendors doled out various cannabis edibles. One gentleman openly sold balloons filled with nitrous oxide from a tank.

All afternoon, Deadheads moved like a herd through the park to the stadium. At every downtown traffic light, a cluster waited to cross. Hippies stood all along the way holding up one finger for a "miracle" ticket. The fragrance of burning marijuana was everywhere. The tribe was gathering, coming together in the lakeshore park as they walked to the stadium past Mouse's banners hanging on the front of the Field Museum. As joyful and loving as Santa Clara had been, the Chicago tribe went far beyond that. They had come from all over the country, taken over Chicago as an invading force for the weekend, and transformed the city for their own purposes.

At Soldier Field, security barely checked the crowd while they flooded into the refurbished old football stadium. Shapiro dressed personnel in tie-dye and, once again, handed out fifty-five thousand roses along with printed programs. More than three-quarters of the audience had traveled from out of state. While there were plenty of gray ponytails in the house, more than half the crowd wasn't old enough to have seen Garcia play. The festive audience of more than seventy thousand broke the attendance record set by U2 in 2009.

Fare Thee Well had struck a chord. The concert attracted interest far beyond the commercial appeal of the surviving Dead members in any previous incarnation. Whatever convergence of synchronicity and thinking had transpired to create this enormous cultural moment, it had worked. If there is such a thing as a collective unconscious, it was certainly operating here. The air at Soldier Field was heavy with emotion, rich with consumer satisfaction, before one note of music had been played. These people had come to a historic occasion and they knew it. It was the passing of an era and they were not going to let it pass without them.

The VIP guests included Deadhead Sen. Al Franken, who had also attended Levi's, and *Game of Thrones* author George R. R. Martin. John Mayer knew he wouldn't be invited to play, so he brought his girlfriend Katy Perry. The pop star couple attracted a lot of attention as unlikely backstagers since word about the new band they were going to call Dead & Company hadn't really filtered out. Chicago homeboy Bill Murray was on hand, hanging out with the Los Angeles alt-rock singer-songwriter Jenny Lewis. The rock world was well represented with Perry Farrell of Jane's Addiction, Jon Popper of Blues Traveler, Liz Phair, members of Phish, Disco Biscuits, Wilco, the National, moe. Actor Woody Harrelson and actress Chloe Sevigny attended, as did Indianapolis Colts owner Jim Irsay, who owned Wolf, one of Garcia's Doug Irwin guitars.

The Friends and Family section was crowded with old Dead family members. Mountain Girl was there with all three of her daughters, dropping a little acid for that old-time feeling. Second-generation Dead children were everywhere, not just the Garcia girls, but a passel of young adults who had grown up together backstage, many of them with children of their own. Somebody brought a jar containing Owsley Stanley's ashes and placed it on the soundboard.

Backstage, once again, the dressing rooms were divided with Lesh on one side and the others in the opposite direction. Lesh's accommodations were not only larger than the pipe- and drape-covered locker rooms the others used, but came with a private bathroom. A lengthy afternoon sound check also provided another undercover rehearsal, but sapped the musicians before the show. The mood backstage, while not grim, was businesslike. Weir toyed with his guitar quietly in the corner wearing his serious man-at-work face. Kreutzmann took a few minutes to pose for family photos and cut a birthday cake for his grandson, but otherwise stayed alone and solemn in his private sanctum.

The men from the Dead couldn't escape the weight of the great expectations that awaited them. As the band mounted the stage, the four men knew this was where it all ends. All the struggles, all the heartbreak, all the broken alliances and mended fences no longer mattered. They did what they needed to do to get them to this point. The music would take them the rest of the way now.

They would start where they left off—singing "Box of Rain," Lesh's best-known song for the Dead, which ended the last Soldier Field concert exactly six days short of twenty years before. Whatever powerful emotional weight that might have carried was destroyed almost as soon as Lesh opened his mouth to sing. All the Phil and Friends shows had not turned Lesh into a lead vocalist. The band charged into the song, but Lesh's feeble, strained vocal couldn't match the power of the band. In the record industry, they would say he couldn't sing up to the tracks. He worked his way weakly through the song, hardly the striking, penetrating moment needed to open the show.

On "Jack Straw," Weir took control and slowed the drive into the song down to a syrupy crawl. After some less successful passages, they brought the piece to a substantial finish. Anastasio's first lead vocal, the surefire "Bertha," got better almost line by line. Not only was this the first time he had ever sung it in public, he was doing it in front of a jam-packed football stadium. His guitar solo was more confident. By the end, he was winning everybody over, on the bandstand and off.

Up next, "Passenger" from the *Terrapin Station* album was never more than modest repertoire, even when the band played the song occasionally during the late seventies and early eighties, not some neglected gem, but the band found a nice groove to work. "The Wheel," ostensibly an opportunity for Anastasio to stretch out and shine, would have foundered entirely except for Weir's prodding but elastic rhythm guitar.

Weir led the band directly into a painfully slow, almost unsteady "Crazy Fingers." Even though Anastasio delivered the scrupulous lead vocal, Weir was driving the train. Halfway through the first set at Chicago, the limitations of the band's ability to re-create the authentic Grateful Dead experience without Garcia were already obvious, but that was also beside the point to everybody who was there.

Weir dug into "The Music Never Stopped" with the conviction of someone who was under a spell. He was possessed. Weir and Anastasio tangled their guitars to the close, driving the band to a fierce end of the first set.

Lesh opened the second set with "Mason's Children," a track left off *Workingman's Dead* and performed by the band only a dozen or so times in 1969–1970 that had been a piece of archaeology extensively excavated by Phil and Friends, another number that hardly qualified as a lost classic. Anastasio handled "Scarlet Begonias," his confidence clearly growing set by set, and Hornsby took the reggae-fied "Fire on the Mountain," the band jelling as they went into the evening's drums/space segment.

The space jam led to the complex Lesh psychedelic nugget "New Potato Caboose," which the Dead stopped playing in 1969. The band dissolved into lengthy jamming through a surprisingly tepid "Playing in the Band," where the musicians lost the plot going out too far in the zone, "Let It Grow," with Weir overamping the vocals again, and into the eighties vintage beloved medley "Help On the Way/Slipknot/ Franklin's Tower." Anastasio muttered "sorry" after fluffing some lyrics, but the band built toward a credible climax.

Hornsby, who had not been well versed in the Dead's sixties psychedelic catalog since the band largely avoided that material during his stint, felt right at home swimming in this stream. As he looked across the stage and experienced this palpable sense of power growing, watching everyone onstage, feeling himself rocking the house, he knew this was what he came for and took pause to cherish the moment. He turned and took in the vast crowd, swept with spotlights, dancing and weaving like a roiling sea, and was almost overwhelmed by the whole scene. He knew it would not come again anytime soon.

Lesh returned for his donor rap. "Nobody up here had any idea what response we would get," he told the crowd. "It is stunning to see and experience the love we have for each other." The band encored with a supple "Ripple"—Weir allowing himself a satisfied smile as he slowed down the tempo even more heading into the final verse and chorus—and sent the crowd out into the warm Chicago night humming and buzzing. It may not have been the epic Grateful Dead performance, but the show was not without searing high points and rich emotionalism. Weir poured himself into the music and Lesh, at age seventy-five, showed incredible stamina, barreling through a four-hour show and two-hour sound check like a man half his age.

Roger McNamee missed the first show in Chicago. His band Moonalice had been booked to play after the pay-per-view broadcast on Friday at Mill Valley's Sweetwater, the club Weir helped create. He pulled together his party including Moonalice guitarist Barry Sless and equipment manager Steve Parish. Parish, whose son attended medical school in Chicago, agreed to go only reluctantly. At least he could visit his kid. They flew into Chicago on Saturday. On the flight, Parish, hardly a shrinking violet, complained loudly about his discomfort. He didn't want to go. He was unhappy with the whole deal and convinced he would not be welcome.

Cameron Sears also felt weird about attending. He had managed the Grateful Dead through a procession of stadium tours in the eighties and nineties and had not been part of the scene after getting kicked to the curb by Weir when he and Lesh started Furthur. Sears had taken a job as executive director of the Rex Foundation, the philanthropic concern founded and initially funded by the Dead, but surviving as an independent charity after Garcia's death.

Shapiro gave Rex a slot in Participation Row and Sears had manned the table at the two Santa Clara shows, which he had not enjoyed. It was too weird, standing outside the squeaky-clean, soulless stadium, handing out pamphlets, when he was accustomed to working backstage, supervising the crew, arranging a thousand details, and being in the center of the action. He had not been especially inspired by the music he heard, so Sears also went to Chicago without any high expectations.

But Chicago turned out to be an entirely different experience for Sears. This was a special occasion beyond the scope of the Levi's Stadium shows. He was thronged at his table by old friends he hadn't seen in years. The happy crowd refreshed his recollection of how wonderful Deadheads could be and how powerful their sense of community truly was. He was bowled over and, watching the band, found the spirit of the crowd imbued the concert with such joy, the quality of the music no longer mattered. That night, he got on the phone to his wife, Cassidy, who was on vacation with their two teenage children in Massachusetts, and convinced her to book tickets and fly in for the last show on Sunday.

The Fourth of July on a Saturday and a Grateful Dead concert in the park—all downtown Chicago had been turned into Deadtown, thrumming with the glow from the last night's show. Some Deadhead picked up David Gans's breakfast tab at a downtown restaurant because he recognized the broadcaster's voice from his satellite radio Grateful Dead show. Gans and his business partner Gary Lambert were doing three-hour preview shows from a booth in the lot and color commentary at set break from the Chicago Bears broadcast booth above the fifty-yard line to accompany the live broadcast on Sirius XM, delayed one hour to preserve the video pay-per-view exclusivity. Gans and Lambert had been astonished at how much fun they had with what could have been a bothersome, boring task. Like everybody else, nothing prepared them for the overwhelming good feelings of the weekend.

Everybody knew the circus was in town by the second show. An airplane circled downtown trailing a sign reading GRATEFUL FOREVER. The Direct TV blimp floated above the stadium, flashing dancing bears on its video display. For the second time, they broke the U2 attendance record at Soldier Field. After the brief sound check, Phil and Jill Lesh, like Kreutzmann at Santa Clara, took a golf cart out to tour the lots. Like visiting royalty, they took their star turn with Jill behind the wheel waving to the Deadheads, the exclusive Fare Thee Well photographer Jay Blakesberg capturing it all on video.

Band members rarely ventured into the lots before. Someone took Weir on a quick ride through one of the lots during the nineties and the scene was burned into his brain. They largely averted their eyes from the grimy subculture beyond the gates, especially after the crowds outside the concert grew larger than those inside and caused enormous problems with various civic authorities. The band hated these mob scenes, but Shapiro had fashioned a safer, carefully filtered version of the old parking lots for Fare Thee Well, a modest, curated facsimile of the sprawling underground market that sprung up around Grateful Dead concerts.

Neither Lesh nor any of the Dead would have ventured into those original dens of iniquity. In the intervening years, however, the musicians had grown more respectful of the genuine bond between the Deadheads and the band and come to better understand the nature of the community that grew around their often-insular enterprise. What was happening at Chicago was, for once, the band returning the respect showed them by the Deadheads. These forays by band members into the crowd at Fare Thee Well acknowledged the relationship from this new perspective. The mood in Chicago was just that contagious.

In a sense, the psychedelic extravaganza of the previous night's set list came from Lesh, just as the first night at Levi's had been his. But tonight, as with the second show in Santa Clara, it was all Bobby

Weir. Everybody's fingerprints were on all the set lists, but, switching off as they had in Furthur, Weir and Lesh were the basic architects of the first four shows. The finale was a thoroughly contemplated collaboration, but the penultimate Saturday concert would be on Weir.

He gave his traditional guitar bow to the audience and counted the band into a deliberate "Shakedown Street," Weir singing hard over the funky rhythm, Anastasio burnishing the extended final chorus with tasty counterpoint run through an envelope filter, a piece of gear popularized by funk bassist Bootsy Collins but later adapted by Garcia for one of his signature sounds. Lesh came out of the gate thunderous and Weir was shouting over the band by the second verse. Given that it was the Fourth of July, playing "Liberty" next made perfect sense in the context, although the song is not especially patriotic. Taken from an old Robert Hunter solo album and reworked by Garcia, the number found its way into the band's shows during the nineties and was scheduled for inclusion on the unfinished final album. Weir led the stomping version defiantly, soul-shouting his way to the end. Anastasio carefully, gamely picked his way through "Standing on the Moon," a piece that sorely missed the ethereal delicacy of Garcia.

In relatively short order for this group, the band rattled off "Me and My Uncle," "Tennessee Jed," and "Cumberland Blues," the first song to be repeated from the Santa Clara shows. Weir took out the bottleneck for a deathly slow blues, "Little Red Rooster," but it was Chimenti on organ who took over the song with a rousing, full-throated solo that drew loud cheers. The crowd could be forgiven for failing to notice the band even had an organ player, considering the absence in the sound mix of both Chimenti and Hornsby on grand piano. They were tucked away onstage in the far corner like two little boys, quietly seeing what they could get away with.

Stepping up for his first vocal, Lesh ambled awkwardly through "Friend of the Devil," effectively undermining one of the band's key songs. Weir can sing it like a master, but due to the politics of the Fare Thee Well process, Lesh ended up doing this crucial song in Chicago, despite efforts to limit the number of songs he sang. Lesh and his wife were alone in their appreciation of his vocal skills. The set slowed to a low point.

Without waiting for Weir to count the band in, Anastasio kicked off "Deal," at a decidedly jaunty tempo he learned from a Jerry Garcia Band version. Before Weir could do anything about it, he was off to the races. Anastasio made his way through the vocal well enough, but then lit up the instrumental break with a sprightly, dancing, silvery guitar solo. Hornsby took the second verse as the band continued to gallop along the first charging uptempo drive of the day. The stadium came to life.

For the past three shows, Anastasio stayed in the shadows, following everybody else's lead, but out of nowhere, without even thinking about it, he took the reins of this band and led them into a blasting, rocking, cathartic close to the first set. Although Weir managed to slow it down on the final chorus, it was too late. As the crowd cheered madly, Anastasio skipped offstage to catch up with Weir, slipped his arm over Weir's shoulder as they walked backstage for the set break, and asked if everything was all right. "Cool," said Weir.

Lesh opened the second set with the slow, rolling groove of "Bird Song," Hunter and Garcia's song written after the death of Janis Joplin ("all I know is something like a bird within her sang . . . "), although Lesh changed the pronoun to the masculine. Anastasio riffed lightly over Weir's jazzy chord inversions and Hornsby kept a steady stream of piano tinkling through the jam. An organ swirl from Chimenti—shades of Pigpen—announced "Golden Road (To Unlimited Devotion)," a jaunty piece of long-lost Grateful Dead garage rock straight from the Summer of Love. The crowd leaped into action. The band charged through the song, Hornsby and Anastasio leading the vocal chorus, and then lost their way in a long, pointless jam.

Weir slowed down the introduction to "Lost Sailor" while he was playing it and followed with one of his most mesmerizing vocal performances in the concerts so far. Going straight into "Saint of Circumstance," Weir reprised the pairing of these two songs written by Weir with his lyricist John Perry Barlow common to Dead shows of the early eighties. Hornsby took the plodding "West L.A. Fadeaway." The band picked up and worked over a riff they came up with during the previous night's "Playing in the Band," with Chimenti and Hornsby driving the song to a satisfying close on keyboards.

Anastasio assayed "Foolish Heart," a latter-era Hunter-Garcia gem from the *Built to Last* album, the group's final studio album. They tucked a stinging, productive jam on the end—the band was now playing tight and confident, really swinging—that led into the space/ jam portion of the program. Coming out of the cloud of sound, Weir tried to nudge his compatriots into "Stella Blue" a couple of times before they finally followed his lead. Singing in the original Garcia key, Weir struggled with one of the most poignant songs in the Dead songbook, slowing it down for maximum narrative effect. He put everything he had into each line, like a sculptor chiseling the song lyric by lyric.

Of course, "One More Saturday Night" brought the set to a frothy, rollicking end. Lesh came back. "Fifty years ago, a good friend of mine made me an offer I couldn't refuse," he said, "and he gave me a life I couldn't have imagined. What a long, strange trip it's been."

Since it was not only Saturday night but the Fourth of July, the band returning to encore with "U.S. Blues" came as no surprise. Weir was game, but his voice was shredded from shouting all night over the powerful machine behind him. As the last great American rock band launched their last song of the night, outside on the Chicago skyline, red, white, and blue lights raced up and down the top of the Tribune Building in tribute. When the band left the stage, fireworks filled the night sky.

23

Finale

CARYL HART was back in the hotel room with her husband after the Saturday night show, high and happy, when Jill Lesh called. They had largely avoided one another over the weekend after a brief, unpleasant encounter on the side of the stage, although Phil had been nothing but congenial with Mickey. Jill was calling Caryl as her husband's representative to sternly explain that she would be taking an executive producer credit for the DVD of the concerts. Caryl was offended at her tone and presumption. She knew of no reason why Jill Lesh should receive a credit on the production. The conversation didn't last long, but when Caryl got off the phone, she was no longer floating on the stratospheric experience of the night. She had firmly come back to earth.

The Leshes didn't suddenly become compliant and cooperative once they agreed to do these shows. Even after all their demands had been met, down to and including reading Kreutzmann's manuscript, they continued to find issues that needed to be settled. They went over the budget carefully, trimming expenses wherever they could, maximizing revenue. There would be no complimentary tickets, eliminating the guest list that could run into the hundreds at certain Grateful Dead shows. Mountain Girl ordered a batch of tickets to make sure family members who couldn't afford them would be covered. Jill was not satisfied with her husband's Jumbotron time at the Levi's shows, especially that there were not enough close-ups, and complained to the video director, demanding more camera time for Lesh.

After Caryl Hart told her outraged husband what Jill said in her Saturday night call, word spread rapidly through the rest of the band. By the morning of the final concert, everybody was pissed off at the Leshes all over again.

On Sunday morning, Steve Parish awoke and realized there was no way he could get out of going to the show. He had skipped the concert the day before, spending time with his son instead. He didn't feel good about any of this, but he had accepted McNamee's generous offer and felt obligated to his good friend. Since getting fired from Phil and Friends on the first tour, he had kept his distance from all the foolishness, although he was still lodged deeply in the heart of the Dead world. Parish was a true believer and has been since the day they picked him up off the sidewalk. Now he was dubious, conflicted, and unhappy—with himself and his circumstances.

Parish had never been to a Grateful Dead concert—or any concert, for that matter—through the front door. He had never seen a box office or used a ticket. He had never sat in a seat in the audience. He had no idea what to expect or even what he would have to do and it only added to his discomfort.

He left for the show early with McNamee and Sless, stepping out in the warm Chicago summer to walk through the park to the stadium. Instantly Deadheads recognized the big lummox. They approached him with respect, almost reverence, and talked with him like a cherished old friend. He wasn't two blocks away from the hotel and every few steps another Deadhead would stop and greet him. Parish felt the love and it melted his defenses. By the time he reached the stadium, he was developing a new attitude when he ran into Cameron Sears, who was heading for the Rex Foundation booth. Sears immediately recognized Parish's confusion and shepherded him through the box office to pick up his passes. As soon as they got inside, they encountered Mountain Girl and Caryl Hart, who took over from Sears and escorted an anxious Parish and his party backstage.

Parish was still distressed when Robbie Taylor, Lesh's stage manager, rushed to him as soon as he saw him backstage and embraced his old colleague. Parish was suddenly surrounded by the crew, who were all ecstatic to see him. Ram Rod was dead; Parish was their last link to the glory days of the Grateful Dead road crew when they were grizzled cowboys riding the range. His presence was a touchstone to the crew that brought the spirit of the crowd backstage. Taylor took him to a special chair, placed it in Parish's customary spot in the wings, a few feet offstage, and there he sat like the honored dignitary he was. The tough old bastard, really a softie, was humbled by the reception.

This would be the final show. Whatever these four men would go on to do after this, Fare Thee Well would stand. Lesh may have thought of these shows as one giant encore and the others may have seen the concerts as more of a portal to pass through, but in any case, this was the finale, the last fanfare, the closure that had been sought and denied for twenty years. For both the musicians and the fans.

This was the greatest farewell in rock history since the Band said goodbye at The Last Waltz, and that concert took place before a mere five thousand people, not hundreds of thousands, not only in Chicago, but watching the pay-per-view video feed across the country. The entire nation took note of the final concert by the Grateful Dead, from the highest offices in the land on down. President Obama paid tribute in a statement released by the White House, which Shapiro reprinted in the program for the day's concert.

"Here's to fifty years of the Grateful Dead, an iconic American band that embodies the creativity, passion and ability to bring people together that makes American music so great," Obama wrote. "Enjoy this weekend's celebration of your fans and legacy. And as Jerry would say, 'Let there be songs to fill the air.'"

Lesh, Weir, Hart, and Kreutzmann would take the stage together for the last time in their lives. The four musicians constituted one of the greatest and most original rhythm sections ever. Without Garcia at the center, their gyroscope had wobbled for twenty years, righting just long enough to pull off this extraordinary coup of a finale. Whatever personal problems had plagued them would now be put aside for the music one last time. They owed this to the fans—and themselves. This was anything but just another gig. This needed to be their finest hour. Their emotions ran high as they took the stage with serious looks of intent on their faces.

Cameron Sears had a car waiting for his wife and family at the airport that morning and she rushed with them to the concert, walking in backstage almost at showtime. Cassidy Sears immediately saw Trixie Garcia, with whom she had grown up backstage, and another Dead kid friend, Sage Scully, the daughter of the band's first manager, Rock Scully, who had died only the previous January. She was instantly caught up in the flush of the happy family reunion, besieged by dear old friends she hadn't seen in years, but couldn't stay backstage and catch up because the band was about to start. She hurriedly made her way out into the crowd, getting into place as the band began to play. As soon as they struck up the music, she burst into tears and bawled through the entire first song. She was not the only one weeping in the crowd.

Today, as they went onstage, Lesh summoned everyone to the center to take a bow. The seven acknowledged the crowd, both in front and behind, and basked in the prolonged reception, finally falling into a group hug before taking their places and picking up their instruments. The opening song, "China Cat," has been paired practically since its 1968 introduction with "I Know You Rider," a number in the songbook from the band's earliest days. Anastasio took the Garcia vocal on "China Cat" and the band roared through a lively jam that quickly segued into the inevitable "I Know You Rider," although the musicians stayed on the appealing groove for a long time before Weir stepped forward to sing. The entire stadium sang along— *I know you rider gonna miss me when I'm gone.*

Weir took "Estimated Prophet," his great song from *Terrapin Station,* at a lazy gait over the reggae beat. The song might have fit more comfortably on the second-night set list at Levi's, but Weir gave the song a strong and passionate reading. Anastasio vamped on Garcia's envelope-filter part through a lengthy heated instrumental passage before the band migrated into a spacey jam that brought the song to a close. Hornsby pulled out the surprising "Built to Last," title song of the Dead's final album that the band played a handful of times in 1990 and then discarded, only to have Lesh reprise the number with both Phil and Friends and Furthur. Hunter's lyrics were weirdly appropriate:

All the stars / Are gone but one
Morning breaks / Here comes the sun
Cross the sky / Sinking fast
Show me something / Built to last

"Samson and Delilah" was one of the songs Weir used to bring down the walls at Winterland. He can command the old blues song with the authority of a Viking. At Chicago, he snapped the house to full attention every time he stepped to the mike on a song the band traditionally saved for Sundays. Lesh sang "Mountains of the Moon," a piece from *Aoxomoxoa* the Dead played a few times over a couple of months in 1969, which was primarily a vehicle for a long, spacey jam that gave way to Weir singing a lusty "Throwing Stones." The instrumental passage built to a driving climax, Weir and Anastasio locking together for a piercing, stinging fusillade that had the crowd waving their arms and dancing. With that, the band broke for intermission.

Fireworks covered the sky at the end of set break. As starbursts exploded above them, the band filed onstage to watch. Jill Lesh held baby Levon, wearing protective earphones, in her arms, pointing to the skies. As the last streaks of fireworks disappeared from the sky, the band rumbled into "Truckin'." Unlike the version they played in Santa Clara, the band nailed it hard this time—vocal harmonies on the mark, band pumped up, Chimenti's organ finally fully in the mix, steaming down the groove at a crunching tempo. Anastasio lit up a stinging, piercing guitar solo. The whole band came out on fire. They stretched the song past the ten-minute mark.

Weir sang his song "Cassidy" with his most earnest conviction, the band wrapping around him and lifting him up as he sang, then pouring themselves into a long, fiery jam. In the crowd, Cassidy Sears burst into tears again. It was her birthday song and was also steeped in close personal associations for Weir. He had sung the song several hundred times, but never with any more feeling than he did in Chicago.

Anastasio stood up next to sing "Althea." He had expected the song to show up on the first set and, when it didn't, assumed the number was being dropped entirely. He was somewhat relieved not to have to perform this particular Garcia vocal in front of a million Deadheads, especially after watching Weir and Lesh battle over the song's tempo the day before at sound check. He drew a breath, stepped forward, and—having seen Garcia play this song from the audience a thousand times—counted off the song at the proper tempo while staring Weir straight in the eye. Behind him, the band slammed into the song and he turned and delivered his best vocal performance yet, his confidence having grown immensely seemingly overnight. The band took off on another soaring excursion that led way to the opening notes of the "Terrapin Station" suite, one of the most complex and delicate compositions in the Dead repertoire, where they hit the first speed bump of the set—Lesh's vocals on "Lady with a Fan."

People had tried to persuade Lesh not to attempt this vocal, but he insisted. There had been years in the eighties when Lesh didn't sing with the band and the crew didn't even set up a mike stand for him. Lesh's voice lacks the range and power for truly expressive singing. He labored carefully over the lyrics, rolling on and off pitch, in a voice that was, for the most part, bland and colorless. He couldn't articulate the melody with any precision. He approached the lyrics tentatively and swallowed his consonants. With his stiff delivery and limited skills, he left little room for nuance. And play what you want, a band is only as good as the singer. When Weir took the mike for the main body of the song, the difference was instantly apparent. Weir sang his heart out, crafting each line with supple care.

Even the drum solo by Kreutzmann and Hart was super-charged, the two drummers stirring up a storm of high-powered rhythms on their drum kits before Hart moved to his sequencers, sonifications, and The Beam, the strange giant percussion instrument of his own devising he once described as "doorbells from Mars." Using a driving rhythmic loop, Hart dropped dancing, swimming, flying sparks over the beats. Kreutzmann retreated from his stool and joined in the crazy assortment of percussion instruments and drums arrayed on the stage in the cagelike assemblage known as The Beast. Hart even dragged out the train horns he used to blast out twenty-five years before to announce "Casey Jones" at Dead shows. He got on The Beam and led the reconvened ensemble in a dazzling fog of noises and sonic inventions that paved the approach brilliantly to the ending reprise of "Terrapin Station," Lesh, once again, alas, on vocals.

A stunning, mesmerizing jam where the sound mix and band arrangement finally put Hornsby's piano playing in the foreground gave way to "Unbroken Chain," a Lesh song introduced to the band's repertoire in the final months before Garcia died. Lesh adopted the song, not only as the name of his charity, but as a kind of signature number with Phil and Friends and Furthur that his fans rallied around. Weir followed with the emotional high point of the show, a wrenching version of "Days Between," which the band gave a magnificent, epic thirteen-minute performance.

The song, probably the last Garcia-Hunter masterpiece, introduced by the band in 1992, was a melancholic Hunter ruminating over the past (*and there were days I know/when all we ever wanted/was to learn and love and grow*). The bittersweet mood of the song—whatever is the opposite of nostalgia or a fond feeling for the past—perfectly underscored the moment. The song was autobiography as Weir was singing it. He delivered the sermon with surgical precision and gospel intensity; he was nothing short of amazing. He seized the moment with every ounce of his abilities, his blazing eyes staring intently into the night.

As the last note of "Days Between" hung in the air inviting a solemnity to the proceedings, the drummers began to pound out a familiar jungle tattoo—bump-debump, debump, bump, bump—the call of the introduction to "Not Fade Away." The song's original author, Buddy Holly, borrowed Bo Diddley's beat, and the Rolling Stones compressed his plaintive plea into a tidy rocking beat. But the Dead found the spiritual center of the song and opened it up long ago into a broad, rollicking tribute to everlasting spirit. In the hands of the Dead, the song was no longer about trivial romantic affections. It took on cosmic dimensions.

Never did the song make more sense for the band, never was the message more appropriate. And, for once, Weir set the tempo at a strong, stirring, almost martial upbeat. Off at a gallop, this one he would not slow down. He turned to the crowd and stroked the loud, stinging chords that announced the first verse and, in that instant, pulled the crowd together as one. The three vocalists stepped to their mikes and sang. At the end, as the band faded the song onstage, the audience took it over, clapping the beat behind the singers as the musicians slowly stopped playing, then taking over the singing when they stopped. The drummers jammed with the crowd, adding the beats between the crowd singing "You know our love will not fade away." Eventually, they also stopped and left the stage. But the crowd did not stop. They kept singing, clapping between the lines themselves to keep the beat now. They sang loud and lusty, an entire stadium full of people, and they didn't stop until Lesh reemerged from backstage.

An obviously moved Lesh came out to deliver his donor rap. "Now we've arrived at the point," he said, "we never thought we would get here. I'd like to think of it as a crossroads rather than an ending. I know everybody here is going to walk out tonight and move on with their lives and hopefully, as I am, energized by all the love we've seen in these shows. God bless you. I mean that. We're going to do that. Take some tangents, move in different directions. It's been a long time coming, but I'm grateful for it." He made his standard plea for the audience to pledge to become organ donors. "Long live Terrapin Nation," he said.

The crowd again picked up the chant: "You know our love won't fade away."

Weir emerged from backstage wearing a T-shirt reading LET TREY SING and started snapping off the chords to the introduction for the final song as Anastasio, a huge smile spreading across his face, stepped forward to sing "Touch of Grey." Hornsby handled the second verse, then Weir took over and sang the rest of the song. Photos of the band in their youth splashed on the video screen, as their lives flashed before their eyes. This was it—the last Grateful Dead song at the last Grateful Dead concert. Weir made the most of it.

Lesh always planned to end the concerts with the angelic chorale, "Attics of My Life." It would have been much better if they had taken the time to rehearse the difficult three-part harmonies. Anastasio kept waiting to try out the song in San Rafael, but they only ran it once around a piano. The next time they tried the song, everybody had forgotten their parts and nobody was singing the Garcia part. They ran the song a couple of times in sound checks, but Anastasio was panicked. He called his New York arranger Jeff Tanski and asked him to write charts based on the record. He handed charts to Hornsby and kept one for himself. While a montage of old photos of the band members—living and dead—paraded across the stadium video screens, Weir led the vocal ensemble on acoustic guitar, Chimenti eased in a little organ and sang the melody from his charts. Nobody came in together crisply and the timing, breathing, and pitch varied through the first verse as the little choral group picked up steam. They finally caught up with each other in time for the final crescendo and put the song—and the concert, and the Grateful Dead—to rest.

Lesh summoned the band to center stage for their bow. He and Weir hugged and kissed. Hart slipped under Lesh's other arm as the entire ensemble took their bow. The musicians stood on the stage, talking and hugging, culminating in a giant group hug, broken up by a cheer. The audience picked up the "Not Fade Away" clapping again.

That left it to Mickey Hart to offer the benediction. On his way off the stage, he stopped at the microphone. "Please, the feelings we have here," he said, "remember them, take them home, do some good. Hug your husband, your wife, your kids. I leave you with this— please be kind."

If the entire series at Levi's Stadium began with a rainbow, this was the pot of gold at the end. It was a triumph. The closing set had been everything it needed to be, everything it should have been, everything everybody wanted it to be. It was rich with emotion, hot licks, imaginative improvisations, inspiration, some great singing, and, most of all, the magnificent songs of Jerry Garcia and Robert Hunter, whose name was not mentioned from stage once during all five concerts. Hunter didn't mind. Hunter knew how unsentimental those guys were. He didn't attend the concerts anyway. Despite everything, the musicians had succeeded. Perhaps in the final set they at last did what they came to do. They managed to evoke the mystery, the magic, the adventure of a Grateful Dead concert as well as anyone since the Grateful Dead.

Backstage after the show, Jonathan Levine painfully made his way to Lesh's dressing room. The booking agent who had been such an important part of the Phil Lesh solo career had undergone major spinal surgery six weeks before and he was only able to walk with a great deal of difficulty. He had received a note from Jill inviting him to the Santa Clara shows, but those were out of the question. He managed to pull himself together the next week and fly from Nashville for the final show in Chicago. Twenty years before, he had been changing planes at Chicago's Midway Airport when the Grateful Dead gave their last show at Soldier Field and he briefly considered deplaning and going to the show before deciding to continue his flight. He didn't feel he could miss it this time.

In the spacious dressing room in the bowels of the stadium alone with the Leshes after the show, Levine joined a sentimental champagne toast with Jill and Phil. They were soaking in the glow of this immense accomplishment. They were happy and spent. Levine left them alone and, when he couldn't find a ride back to his nearby hotel, made the excruciatingly slow and painful walk back by himself.

Back at the hotel, Trixie Garcia found herself partying with members of the band, Bill Walton, and other insiders in the lobby of the Ritz-Carlton. Everyone was there except the Leshes and Weir. It had been a draining series of concerts for Jerry's youngest daughter. All five shows had been like a whirlwind. She had been continually swamped by old friends and Deadheads. She gave dozens of interviews. Growing up backstage at Grateful Dead shows, she knew the difference between that band and Fare Thee Well, but she enjoyed the music enough. Mostly, she was connecting dots and looking for some closure of her own. She had spent a lot of time with her two sisters and her mother and she was bone tired. But she was wondering where Weir was when he swooped down on her and carried her away to his own party in his suite.

This was the real after-party. Weir's hotel room was crowded with freaks and characters. The atmosphere was loose and celebratory. Weir was relaxed, feeling good, and holding court. Trixie felt right at home. People were drinking and sharing joints. Everybody was still high from the concert. Movie star Bill Murray rampaged around the room, in a festive mood after staying late to help the grounds crew clean up the trash.

Fifty years later, that's the way it was.

24

Coda

FARE THEE Well was an outsized, unprecedented success by almost any measure. The shows drew more than $50 million at the box office, a record for a concert by a single band. Total attendance was more than 362,000. For the third day in a row, the last Soldier Field concert broke the long-standing attendance record held by U2 with a crowd of 71,000. The band sold $8 million worth of T-shirts and hoodies at the five shows. One concertgoer paid $526,000 in a charity auction over the weekend for a signed guitar Bobby Weir played for a couple of numbers at Levi's Stadium. The pay-per-view broadcast also set a record for a music broadcast with 175,000 streams subscribed.

Over the Fourth of July weekend, the entire nation knew the Grateful Dead was playing the band's final concerts in Chicago. Clubs and theaters all over the country hosted events. Peter Shapiro had crowds every night at both his Brooklyn Bowl and Capitol Theatre. Both the Sweetwater and Terrapin Crossroads held viewings. Even the Empire State Building got in the act, draping its top floors and spire in red, white, and blue lights to celebrate the show in Chicago. Given the men from the Dead had no idea what to expect from the event, the reception was breathtaking. They floated out of Chicago on a cloud.

The reviews treated the musical performances fairly. Jon Pareles, the distinguished pop music critic of the *New York Times*, wrote a review of all three concerts. "'Fare Thee Well: Celebrating 50 Years of the Grateful Dead,'" he wrote, "also revived the band as an enterprise both quixotic and commercial, history-minded and fond of a tall tale, carefully plotted and forever in search of the happy accident. This briefly convened, decisively final incarnation of the Grateful Dead often managed to live up to the band's name with songs that could turn intuitive, down-home, whimsical, haunted, elegant or euphoric."

Greg Kot of the *Chicago Tribune* was less certain. "Without Garcia, this couldn't be the Grateful Dead anymore, no matter what the ticket stub says. Instead, this was—at best—a Grateful Dead tribute show, a celebration of a remarkable legacy," said Kot. Writing in England's *The Guardian*, Mark Guarino was more reasoned. "Expecting the original band would be naïve," Guarino wrote. "Instead, the band that showed up this weekend ignited fresh sparks and induced a few lulls, both with well-intended reverence for a back catalogue that has remained poignant."

Perhaps the most remarkable thing about the shows in Chicago was that the "seventh member" showed up. In the early days of the Grateful Dead, the band would speak of that intangible extra ingredient that made a show great as "the seventh member." Sometimes he would be there at the beginning of a show and leave. Sometimes he would show up in the middle and stay. Sometimes he wouldn't come. He could not be depended on in any way, but when he was there, the gigs were great. The seventh member always brought the party.

At Levi's Stadium, the seventh member flitted in and out of the shows. At Chicago, he made longer appearances in the first two shows, but never settled into his chair. On the final show, he played several numbers with the band during the first set and decided to stay for the rest of the night. The result was that the last set of the last show was on fire, infused with the secret ingredient that was the primary drug of the Deadheads.

Whatever absolution the Fare Thee Well band needed, they more than earned in the tenth set of the five-concert run. With that final pinnacle, they had done what they came to do. And, as only the Grateful Dead could do, they chose to honor their legacy with this extraordinary panoramic retrospective of their glorious career—ten sets, eighty-eight songs (a mere two repeats), more than seventeen hours onstage. They could have played Wagner's complete Ring Cycle in that time.

The grand ambition it required is something that goes to the heart of the Grateful Dead—the band that went to Egypt to play the Great Pyramids, the band that built the Wall of Sound, the band whose manager once posted plans for a flying amphitheater on his office wall. Any other rock band would have simply put together one set of greatest hits and played it five times. But the Grateful Dead were always more than just another rock band.

All of this was nothing short of a miracle, a miracle worked in no small part by Peter Shapiro, a true believer innocent enough to think he could make this happen. Shapiro never lost touch with his fan side. He was one of the crowd and ably represented their audience's point of view to band members. In the entire music business, only Shapiro was positioned to be able to navigate the thorny, twisting, slippery back channels of the Grateful Dead world to bring the fractured group back together just long enough to play these concerts. He also alone knew how successful this reunion would be.

Even more so than the band, Shapiro understood the vast musical and social subculture based on Grateful Dead music that had developed over the years since Garcia's death. Fare Thee Well certainly qualified as a peak, but Shapiro's vision extended into the future. Immediately after the concerts, he announced appearances by all four of the Dead men at his Lockn' Festival in September. Phil and Friends would be joined by guitarist Carlos Santana. Kreutzmann would bring his latest ensemble, Billy and the Kids, and Hart would perform three times, including two late-night concerts in the woods with Steve Kimock. Bob Weir would serve as special guest, sitting in all day with whoever would have him, and many would. Shapiro was in the Grateful Dead business and business was never better.

In August, Weir, Hart, Kreutzmann, and John Mayer announced the Halloween debut performance by Dead & Company in Madison

Square Garden (ironically, Lesh would be playing for Shapiro an hour's drive away at the Capitol Theatre). Oteil Burbridge from the Allman Brothers would play bass and Chimenti would handle keyboards.

Fare Thee Well's impact on everyone involved—the boys of the band, the community of Deadheads, the culture at large, and even their own music—was multilayered and profound. The event was freighted with so much meaning to so many people for so many reasons, resonating far beyond the parochial world of the Deadheads.

In some ways, Fare Thee Well was an echo of Woodstock forty-six years later, a fresh reminder that the ideals represented there would not disappear, no matter how much they had been marginalized, dissolved, derided, and plain laughed off. The same spirit attended both events. The crowds came together in peace and love for the music and understood that, for however long they would be together, they had become a community.

In the twenty-first century, the Grateful Dead were one of the last remnants, the final rallying points, of sixties idealism, long thought to have vanished. The impressive display of community made clear that whatever it was that people called the movement, the underground, the counterculture, Woodstock Nation, or any other name, those values had not only never vanished, they now permeated all ranks and ages of American society. Yet they still stood outside the mainstream, an alternative to the evanescent pop and r&b conventions of the day. The flame was not extinguished. It had many keepers, a silent tribe whose clarion call to assemble one last time would be met with a gathering of Woodstockian proportions.

They came to Chicago to celebrate the music of the Grateful Dead. But they also came for a ceremony, both jubilant and solemn, presided over by the living members of the band. They knew they were all called together to lay the Grateful Dead to rest. Whatever that was onstage playing the music at Fare Thee Well, it was not the Grateful Dead, only an earnest facsimile. To the audience, however, it was enough, symbolic as it was of all they had shared for fifty years, and they combined with the musicians to perform their tribal rites that both acknowledged and reaffirmed the meaning of their community.

Perhaps they understood innately that this was also a symbolic gesture of passing the torch.

Yet it was anything but the end of an era—the era had ended twenty years before. It was more specifically the end of the Grateful Dead as imagined by Jerry Garcia. Whatever these musicians would go on to do with their work, they had loosened themselves from the grip of the Grateful Dead and its legacy. They had finished what they started fifty years before.

With this final punctuation, the legacy was securely defined, illuminated, and, now, handed off to the future. This often brilliant, always evocative reinterpretation of the Dead songbook by the four original members, with the potent symbolism provided by Trey Anastasio from Phish, the leading second-generation Dead acolytes, clearly showed that they left the inheritance in capable hands. They had made their point. The word had been spread. The music would live on.

Early in his post-Garcia education, Lesh figured out that the band's music could have a separate life as repertoire, musical pieces open to reinterpretation, but he missed the importance of the texts. Weir, who saw the songs as the band's body of work, emphasized the texts, which detail the spiritual and philosophic ideas that truly linked the community. In the end, both approaches served to expand and extend the Dead's music into life after Garcia, even if they were bound to conflict.

The Fourth of July was the perfect date for this celebration. In Hunter's lyrics, he paints a history of a different America. He tells stories—gothic, weird, and whimsical—that evoke the dark underbelly of Mark Twain's America, a grotesque cartoon riddled with piercing truth, a prayer for the wicked and the ridiculous, a call for unity, combined always with themes of freedom and adventure. The blend of Hunter's unique and detailed tales of sin and redemption with Garcia's ability to harness the vast abundance of twentieth-century American music—gospel, hillbilly, rhythm and blues, jazz, bluegrass—into one compelling musical landscape is what made the Grateful Dead, alongside the Beach Boys, the greatest of American rock bands.

All four heroes—Weir, Lesh, Kreutzmann, and Hart—found themselves on the long road to Chicago before they knew they were going there. Without Garcia, they all spent too many lost years trying to find their way. The triumph was that, in the end, they did. Fare Thee Well freed them. They found closure to their personal and creative lives. They could now put the Grateful Dead away. They lived up to their pact with the Deadheads. They could live for the first time without the Grateful Dead beast hanging over their heads, only trailing behind them.

So much had changed in fifty years, starting with the scale on which the band operated. They went from a constituency drawn from a small San Francisco neighborhood to a global audience. From the $3 tickets at the Fillmore and Avalon, the band had graduated to luxury boxes and VIP suites costing thousands of dollars in Chicago. The men themselves had grown from young, intrepid innocents to wise tribal elders. The earth had cooled considerably.

Mickey Hart likes to think of the Grateful Dead as a hierophany, a revelation of the sacred, a manifestation of the divine, something that looked like a rock band but was actually something wholly different. Joseph Campbell had called the Dead "an electric gamelan orchestra." The members of the band used to refer to what they did as "diving for pearls." Born of the rich imagination and clear mission of Jerry Garcia, an artist determined to work in a collaborative mode, the other members had followed his lead so completely that after his death they were left scrambling to figure out what it really was.

Each led his own hero's journey on wildly divergent paths to, finally, arrive at the same place at the same time. It was a journey of self-knowledge; they not only had to learn who they were, they had to learn who the Grateful Dead was.

In the end, everybody won. Everybody got what they wanted. Lesh could go home, weary from battle but satisfied with the final encore, and rest easy doing occasional Capitol Theatre gigs and staying busy at Terrapin Crossroads. At age seventy-five, surrounded by family more than friends, he could now hang up his sword and suit of armor and put his adversaries behind him, while enjoying one of the most active retirements a musician could imagine. He earned his respite. Terrapin remains his great gift to the community. In its short time, thousands of shows have been presented, dozens of bands have blossomed, nurturing a wellspring of Dead music for years to come.

Hart went back to both active touring with Dead & Company and his various projects in his typical whirlwind way of creating mania and magic: recording imaginative, complex percussion pieces at his home studio on his Sonoma ranch, studying neuroscience, and serving on nonprofit boards. The mystical drummer does yoga every morning in his Japanese garden and drives everybody who works for him crazy with his unflagging energy.

Kreutzmann returned to Hawaii. Dead & Company tours provided him enough drum time. He needed to restore himself with the long, lazy tropical days in Hawaii, snorkeling, surfing, fishing. His book brought Kreutzmann out of the shadows, and his pride in the Grateful Dead is unquestioned, even if he remains the most aloof of all four from the legacy. His primal needs are less complex, and the once-brutish, angry young man has mellowed into an acerbic but avuncular white-bearded grandfather.

Weir the troubadour dove into Dead & Company and picked up his schedule of guest appearances, dusting off his solo act, appearing regularly at benefits at the Sweetwater and elsewhere. With Fare Thee Well in his rearview mirror, he was free to take the repertoire and be himself. He will stay on the road the rest of his life, spinning tales with his guitar. He found his destiny long before the final Fare Thee Well—merely another adventure in an adventure-filled life—and as always, he will be on his way to the next project.

And, for all the sweat, goofs, blown cues, and impossible tasks, Trey Anastasio got what he came for as much as anybody. He lived out the fantasy of a lifetime. He belonged to the Grateful Dead. The night after the first concert at Levi's Stadium, the most tense and intimidating moment of his career, Anastasio sent his wife a text message: "That was the most fun I've ever had playing music in my whole life."

Certainly, Peter Shapiro got what he wanted. His concert and all the ancillaries couldn't have been more successful. But for Shapiro, the victory was much larger than box-office grosses. He became a made man, the single most important concert producer of his day, "Bill Graham without the yelling," said one Dead associate. He picked his way through a minefield to reach his goals and, in the end, after a series of historic concerts, he could rest gratified that he had done what he set out to do as well as he could have. Shapiro may not have been there when the Dead started, but he was there to help put them away and they couldn't have done it in grander, more extravagant style.

But it was the Deadheads who won the biggest prizes. In a stunning statement of joyful unity, the Deadheads proclaimed their independence over the Fourth of July weekend in Chicago. They celebrated an entire nation of Deadheads and saluted the core four and their associates as the spiritual leaders of a movement they clearly had no intention of abandoning.

In fact, over the twenty years since Garcia died, the band's impact and influence—and their audience—may have grown to an even greater magnitude than when the Dead existed. It is an astonishing phenomenon and this would never happen to, say, the J. Geils Band, or even the Rolling Stones without Jagger. But the Grateful Dead, in spite of everything, continued to have momentum with the combination of a staggering number of great songs the band added to the catalog over the years and the extraordinary revolutionary concepts about the possibilities of a rock band.

The Deadheads won, not only because they summoned forth these concerts and willed them into existence, but because now they were the band. They brought the spirit; the musicians only played the songs. It was the Deadheads who filled the stadiums with the kind of joy they so well remembered and turned the shows into the harmonic convergence they were. Whatever had been lost had been recovered. The truth was what Mickey Hart said in an interview way back at the beginning of this journey, fresh after Garcia's death: the Deadheads are the Grateful Dead now.

These people wanted to go to one more Grateful Dead concert. And they did. It did not matter who was on the bandstand or what they played, Fare Thee Well was a genuine Grateful Dead concert. The last one.

Acknowledgments

Acknowledgments

I AM NO Deadhead. I have never attended consecutive performances by the band, never traded tapes, never twirled in the hallway, and didn't spend much time in the parking lots. On the other hand, there is no other rock band I have seen on as many occasions, and the Grateful Dead have been responsible for some of the finest moments of my music-listening career.

I saw my first Grateful Dead show in April 1966 at the Berkeley Veterans' Auditorium on a bill with another band called the Union Jacks, a teen dance attended by around fifty other people. Over the next few years, it was impossible to go to rock shows in San Francisco and NOT see the Grateful Dead. They played every hall, all the big concerts in the park, political demonstrations, everywhere. They were the utilitarian home team of the San Francisco scene.

My first interview with Jerry Garcia took place in 1970 backstage at a small club called the Matrix where he was playing with organist Howard Wales before a desultory Monday night crowd of a couple of dozen. Over my years as pop music critic for the *San Francisco Chronicle*, I insisted *The Chronicle* be the market leader in Grateful Dead news and came to know the members of the band and their many colorful associates. When Sammy Hagar asked Bob Weir and myself when we first met, I said, "Around 1974, but he didn't notice me for another three or four years."

"Not even then," said Weir.

While I am by no means in the ranks of Dennis McNally, Blair Jackson, David Gans, or the other dedicated journalists who have made the band a specialty, I have watched this enterprise with great interest and amusement for many years from a privileged perspective and come to know something about the scene.

Many of the events portrayed in this book I first covered in the pages of *The Chronicle* (many, but not all—colleagues such as James Sullivan, Joshua Kosman, and others also provided sterling Dead coverage in the pages of the paper). After Garcia's death, I followed with special interest the trials and struggles of the band members as an endless soap opera with surprise twists, shifting alliances, and dramatic reunions. When I left the paper in 2009, I no longer continued to attend the concerts or track the latest permutations, which is where coauthor Pamela Turley enters the picture. She went to more than one hundred and fifty shows by Furthur, Phil and Friends, Rat-Dog, and all the other post-Garcia editions of the band, although she never once saw the Grateful Dead. Her viewpoint was inevitably enlightening.

Even all these years later, the remnants of the band's code of silence remain. People around the musicians continue to be reluctant to openly discuss personal matters or band politics. Many declined the opportunity. Most of the people who did participate would have likely demurred had it not been for long-standing personal relations. The conflicts and adversities of the years after Garcia's death left wounds that have not entirely healed, but Fare Thee Well provided an adequately happy ending and closure enough for the people around the band as well as the musicians themselves.

There are many people to thank. Dead biographer and publicist Dennis McNally patiently, somewhat begrudgingly repeatedly helped navigate many complex details. Cameron Sears revisited memories he would rather have not on several occasions. Roger McNamee was an unflagging supporter and enthusiast. Steve Parish generously shared his unique and sage viewpoint. Bob Weir and Mickey Hart helped explain the perspective from within the band.

The book benefitted from the experience of many of the band's close associates. Tim Jorstad was extremely helpful on numerous occasions. Peter McQuaid patiently detailed his experiences in repeated meetings. Jan Simmons was as candid and forthcoming as always. Jonathan Levine recounted his work with Phil and Friends. John Scher went to lunch in Manhattan and conducted several phone interviews. Thanks also to Nancy Mallonee, Eileen Law, Jacqueline Sabec, Rose Solomon. Caryl Hart sat in on one interview with her husband and gave one on her own. Their daughter Reya Hart also contributed.

Matt Busch, Benjy Eisen, and Howard Cohen offered valuable backstage perspectives. Candace Brightman gave a guided tour of the Fare Thee Well production. Peter Shapiro was abundantly supportive, both in phone conversations and at his New York office. Stefani Scamardo spoke of her time on the road as her husband's manager.

Musicians who contributed include Steve Kimock, Robin Sylvester, Jay Lane, Mark Karan, Bruce Hornsby, Bob Bralove, Henry J. Kaiser III, Robben Ford, Jeff Mattson, Joan Osborne, Scott Amendola, Joe Goldmark, Jack Casady, Jorma Kaukonen, Wes Stace, Rebekah Chase, Dave Ellis, Lauren Ellis, Jeff Pehrson, Zoe Ellis, Sunshine Becker Garcia, Jackie Greene. Nicholas Meriwether, research assistant on my book *Summer of Love*, guided us through the Grateful Dead Archives at UC Santa Cruz. From backstage came Rick Sanchez, Hector Banez. Rick Abelson, Cathy Simon, Steve Spickard, and Neil Cumsky explained the Terrapin Station project. Thanks also to Waverly Lowell of the Environmental Design Archives, UC Berkeley, where the Cathy Simon papers live. Sabila Savage, David Murray, Dave Luce, David Seabury, and Carey Williams helped tell the Stan Franks story. Michael Nash talked about *Satchel*.

Trixie Garcia was a gracious help, as was her mother, the redoubtable Carolyn Garcia. Dead journalists David Gans and Blair Jackson were both generously supportive (Jackson's interviews on www.dead.net were also an invaluable resource). Brian Markovitz of the *Deadheadland* blog shared his knowledge and enthusiasm for

Furthur. Friendly competitor Paul Liberatore directed me to a rich cache of his articles in the *Marin Independent Journal.* Chris Sabec helped navigate the Garcia estate. Robert Hunter even answered a few emails.

Lots of local folks helped out: Herbie Herbert, Larry Lautzker, Scott Mathews, Clare Wasserman, Brian Rohan, Bill Belmont, J. C. Juanis, Gregg Perloff, John (Stewball) Stewart. Charlie Miller located some key tapes. Doug Long discussed the Irwin guitar case. Dave Frey talked about the Lockn' Festival. Steve Hurlburt of Atlanta supplied a steady stream of data and intelligence.

Susannah Millman, Bob Minkin, Jeff Kravitz, and Michael Weintrob provided the photographs. Thanks also to Mark Pincus of Rhino Entertainment. Bill Van Niekerkan of the *San Francisco Chronicle* cheerfully plumbed the paper's clip files.

I always hoped to join the long list of music book authors to work with Ben Schafer at Da Capo Press. Scratching that off the bucket list. Additional thanks are due to the team at Da Capo: Justin Lovell, Kevin Hanover, Matthew Weston, Quinn Fariel, and Michael Giarratano.

As always, my appreciation to long-suffering agent Frank Weimann of the Literary Group, who continues to hope that I will someday write a good book. Special thanks must go to coauthor Pamela Turley, who made a good book great. And, of course, my darling daughter, Carla.

· · · · · ·

Coauthor Pamela Turley would like to thank her partner in crime, Steve Hurlburt, for the sensual and spiritual pleasure of so many hours of Grateful Dead music by an array of incredible musicians, as well as his enthusiasm for this book. Other thanks include the support of friends Lee Gipson, Ed Wier, Tony Oliver and Ellyn Davis, and the unconditional support of the Turley children, David, Jonathan, Olivia, and Isabel. Special appreciation to her coauthor, the irrepressible Joel Selvin.

Bibliography

Books

Alderman, John. *Sonic Boom: Napster, MP3, and the New Pioneers of Music.* Perseus Publishing, 2001.

Allen, Scott W. *Aces Back to Back: The History of the Grateful Dead.* Outskirts Press, 2013.

Bourque, Laura Bloch. *Wetlands NYC History: A Visual Encore.* Frog2Prince Publishing, 2014.

Browne, David. *So Many Roads: The Life and Times of the Grateful Dead.* Da Capo Press, 2015.

Budnick, Dean. *Jambands: The Complete Guide to the Players, Music & Scene.* Backbeat Books, 2003.

Conners, Peter. *JAMerica: The History of the Jam Band and Festival Scene.* Da Capo Press, 2013.

Dodd, David G., and Diana Diana. *The Grateful Dead Reader.* Oxford University Press, 2000.

Dodd, David, commentary. *The Complete Annotated Grateful Dead Lyrics.* Free Press, 2005.

Fitzpatrick, Travis. *Father of Rock & Roll: The Story of Johnnie "B. Goode" Johnson.* Thomas, Cooke & Company, 1999.

Getz, Michel M., and John R. Dwork. *The Deadhead's Taping Compendium,* vol. 3. Owl Books, 2000.

Grushkin, Paul. *Dead Letters: The Very Best of Grateful Dead Fan Mail.* Voyageur Press, 2011.

Hart, Mickey, and Frederic Lieberman. *Spirit into Sound: The Magic of Music.* Grateful Dead Books, 1999.

Hunter, Robert. *A Box of Rain: Lyrics 1965–1993.* Viking Penguin, 1990.

Jackson, Blair. *Garcia: An American Life*. Viking Press, 1999.

———. *Grateful Dead Gear: The Band's Instruments, Sound Systems, and Recording Sessions from 1965 to 1995*. Backbeat Books, 2006.

Jackson, Blair, Dennis McNally, and others. *Grateful Dead: The Illustrated Trip*. DK, 2003.

Knopper, Steve. *Appetite for Self-Destruction: The Spectacular Crash of the Record Industry in the Digital Age*. Free Press, 2009.

Kreutzmann, Bill, and Benjy Eisen. *Deal: My Three Decades of Drumming, Dreams and Drugs with the Grateful Dead*. St. Martin's Press, 2015.

Lesh, Phil. *Searching for the Sound: My Life with the Grateful Dead*. Little, Brown, 2005.

Menn, Joseph. *All the Rave: The Rise and Fall of Shawn Fanning's Napster*. Crown Business, 2003.

Mockingbird Foundation. *The Phish Companion: A Guide to the Band and Their Music*. Backbeat Books, 2004.

Parish, Steve, and Joe Layden. *Home Before Daylight: My Life on the Road with the Grateful Dead*. St. Martin's Press, 2003.

Scott, John, Mike Dolgushkin, and Stu Nixon. *DeadBase IV: The Complete Guide to Grateful Dead Song Lists*. Deadbase, 1990.

Thompson, Dave. *Go Phish*. St. Martin's Press, 2005.

Whitburn, Joel. *Top Pop Records 1955–1972*. Record Research, 1973.

Selected Magazines, Newspapers, and Other Sources

Associated Press. "The Future Is Dead Ahead." October 10, 1995.

Barry, John. "Phil Lesh Jams at Levon Helm's Midnight Ramble." *Rolling Stone*, August 2, 2010.

Bermant, Charlie. "Dylan, Lesh Offer Few Surprises." *Rolling Stone*, June 21, 2000.

Blisten, Jon. "Phil Lesh and Bob Weir Disband Furthur." *Rolling Stone*, November 4, 2014.

Bloom, Steve, and Shirley Halperin. "Grateful Dead Reunion Q&A: Bob Weir and Trey Anastasio." *Billboard*, January 16, 2015.

Botton, Sari. "RCA Trumpets Hornsby with In-Stores." *Billboard*, October 14, 1995.

Browne, David. "Backstage at the Rock & Roll Inauguration: The Dead's Phil Lesh on Obama Gig." *Rolling Stone*, February 5, 2009.

———. "Rolling with the Dead: Legends Rock Three Back-to-Back Shows in New York." *Rolling Stone*, March 31, 2009.

———. "Bob Weir on Dead Reunion, His Doc and Being Jerry's 'Bag Man.'" *Rolling Stone*, May 20, 2015.

———. "Business Is Booming for the Grateful Dead." *Rolling Stone*, January 19, 2012.

Budnick, Dean. "Jimmy Herring Crafts His Own Lifeboat." *Relix*, December/ January 2009.

——. "Dead Behind, Furthur Ahead." *Relix*, September 18, 2013.

Chinen, Nate. "Swirling in and out of Focus as Past and Present Tangle." *New York Times*, April 29, 2009.

Chow, Andrew. "Grateful Dead Break Soldier Field Records." *New York Times*, July 6, 2015.

——. "Fare Thee Well? Not Quite: 3 Members of Dead Uniting Again." *New York Times*, August 5, 2015.

Clarke, John. "Grateful Dead to Play Another Show for Barack Obama." *Rolling Stone*, September 5, 2008.

——. "The Dead Reunite for Obama at Scorching Penn State Benefit Gig." *Rolling Stone*, October 14, 2008.

Correal, Annie. "In Brooklyn, Cheers for Obama." *New York Times*, August 22, 2007.

Coscarelli, Joe. "The Trip Is Ending: Dead Will Play Final Shows in July." *New York Times*, January 16, 2015.

——. "Ticket Resellers Asking High Prices for Final Grateful Dead Shows." *New York Times*, March 2, 2015.

——. "As Grateful Dead Exit, a Debate Will Not Fade Away." *New York Times*, July 2, 2015.

——. "The Grateful Dead Close out Their Final Concert with Music and the Words 'Please, Be Kind'." *New York Times*, July 6, 2015.

Dalton-Beninato, Karen. "Mickey Hart's Brain on Drums." *Huffington Post*, September 23, 2012.

DeCurtis, Anthony. "Music; Everyguitarist." *New York Times*, June 6, 2004.

Dewan, Shaila K.. "Trying to Fill the Void When the Music Stops." *New York Times*, October 17, 2000.

Doyle, Patrick. "Trey Anastasio on Phish's Band, His Man Cave and the Dead's Big Gigs." *Rolling Stone*, June 24, 2015.

Dumas, Alan. "A Grateful Audience." *Rocky Mountain News*, November 28, 1995.

Edgers, Geoff. "Suspicious Deadheads Up in Arms as Grateful Dead Promoter Tries to Fit More Fans into Farewell Concerts." *Washington Post*, June 8, 2015.

Eisen, Benjy. "Deadheads Boycott Dead." *Rolling Stone*, November 29, 2005.

——. "Grateful Dead Drummer: Jerry Garcia 'Wasn't Really Happy' Playing at Band's End." *Rolling Stone*, January 17, 2012.

——. "Grateful Dead's Bob Weir Reopens Landmark Sweetwater Venue." *Rolling Stone*, January 26, 2012.

——. "Grateful Dead: 'We Weren't a Girl Scout Troop.'" *Rolling Stone*, April 16, 2012.

——. "Phil Lesh Dedicates New Ramble Site to Levon Helm." *Rolling Stone*, May 11, 2012.

——. "Grateful Dead's Mickey Hart 'Sonifies' the Golden Gate Bridge." *Rolling Stone*, May 25, 2012.

——. "Bob Weir on the Dead's 50th Anniversary: 'We Owe It to the Songs.'" *Rolling Stone*, January 30, 2014.

Eisler, Peter. "Garcia's Death Led Band to New Musical Paths." *USA Today*, May 31, 1996.

Fimrite, Peter. "Jerry Garcia Guitars in Legal Limbo." *San Francisco Chronicle*, April 22, 2001.

Friar, William. "Deadheads Attend an On-Line Concert." *Oakland Tribune*, December 12, 1995.

Fricke, David. "Post–Grateful Dead Band Furthur Opens Eight-Night Stand in NYC." *Rolling Stone*, April 10, 2012.

———. "Inside the Grateful Dead's Final Ride." *Rolling Stone*, February 13, 2015.

———. "Trey Anastasio on Dead Reunion Shows: 'I Don't Want to Just Copy Jerry.'" *Rolling Stone*, February 17, 2015.

———. "The Grateful Dead Say Farewell: The View from the Balcony." *Rolling Stone*, July 4, 2015.

———. "The Days Between: Trey Anastasio Reflects on His Time in Dead Camp." *Relix*, October 14, 2015.

Gans, David. "Surviving Members Focus on Solo Projects." *Rolling Stone*, January 26, 1996.

Garofoli, Joe. "RatDog Offers Weir Life After Death." *Contra Costa Times*, May 24, 1996.

Gilmore, Mikal. "Life After Garcia." *Rolling Stone*, December 28, 1995.

Golden, Tim. "It Is Money Battles Like These That Make the Dead Truly Grateful." *New York Times*, February 2, 1997.

Graff, Gary. "With Election Looming, the Dead May Rise Again." *Billboard*, March 28, 2008.

———. "Hart: The Dead Happy to Rock Again for Obama." *Billboard*, July 1, 2008.

———. "Dead Tour May Lead to New Music, Recordings." *Billboard*, April 12, 2009.

Greene, Andy. "Grateful Dead Drummer Mickey Hart Unveils New Band." *Rolling Stone*, August 19, 2011.

———. "Mickey Hart: Another Dead Tour Is 'Always a Possibility.'" *Rolling Stone*, August 24, 2011.

Guarino, Mark. "Grateful Dead: Final Concerts Unite Fans and Band as Legends Fade Away." *The Guardian*, July 6, 2015.

Halperin, Shirley. "Grateful Dead Fare Thee Well Soundcheck Report: 'Uncle John's Band,' 'Truckin', 'Althea' on Set List." *Billboard*, June 27, 2015.

———." Grateful Dead Fare Thee Well: Trey Anastasio for the Win on Night Two in Santa Clara." *Billboard*, June 29, 2015.

Halperin, Shirley, and Jeff Cornell. "Grateful Dead Fare Thee Well Kicks Off as Glorious Rainbow Appears & Trey Anastasio Holds His Own." *Billboard*, June 28, 2015.

Halstead, Richard. "Grateful Dead's Lesh Postpones Discussion of Marin Project After Signs Posted Near His Home." *Marin Independent Journal*, August 18, 2011.

———. "Phil Lesh Scraps Plans for Terrapin Crossroads Music Hall in Fairfax." *Marin Independent Journal*, November 8, 2011.

———. "Lesh May Be Considering Music Venue in San Rafael." *Marin Independent Journal*, November 9, 2011.

Hansen, Megan. "San Rafael Considers Leasing Beach Park to Terrapin Crossroads Restaurant." *Marin Independent Journal*, August 26, 2014.

———. "San Rafael Approves Terrapin Crossroads' Plan to Improve Beach Park." *Marin Independent Journal*, March 3, 2015.

Harrison, Eric. "Day of the (Almost) Dead." *Los Angeles Times*, June 22, 1996.

Hermes, Will. "Grateful Dead's Goodbye." *Rolling Stone*, July 4, 2015.

———. "Chemistry Lost, Cash-Grabs Abound." *Rolling Stone*, July 5, 2015.

———. "Grateful Dead End 50-Year Career with Moving, Magnificent Final Show." *Rolling Stone*, July 6, 2015.

———. "How Grateful Dead's 2015 Farewell Became a New Beginning." *Rolling Stone*, December 21, 2015.

Hochman, Steve. "For Dead, the Music Lives On." *Los Angeles Times*, December 11, 1995.

Horowitz, Donna. "Love Light Shines in Jerry Garcia Estate Trial." *San Francisco Examiner*, December 12, 1996.

———. "Grateful Dead's Bassist Recalls a 'Smoky Haze.'" *San Francisco Examiner*, December 28, 1996.

Iams, David. "Sally Kellerman and Grateful Dead's Bob Weir Headline Theater Group's Gala." *Garden State Press*, October 17, 1995.

Itzkoff, Dave. "Grateful Dead to Rise in New York Exhibition." *New York Times*, October 2, 2009.

Jackson, Blair. "New Life for the Dead." *Relix*, June 2003.

Juanis, J. C. "Phil Lesh's 60th Birthday Bash." *Relix*, March 15, 2012.

———. "Phil Lesh on Longtime Bandmates and New Friends." *Relix*, January 22, 2015.

Kane, Rich. "Deadhead, Let's Let Sleeping RatDog Lie." *Orange County Register*, December 11, 1995.

Kava, Brad. "Santana: Long Live the Dead." *San Jose Mercury*, October 21, 1995.

Kosman, Joshua. "Three Ex-Dead Members to Play with Symphony." *San Francisco Chronicle*, December 15, 1995.

———. "Rockers Give Classical Kids a Hand/Ex–Grateful Dead Members Help Youth Orchestra Ease into Improvisation." *San Francisco Chronicle*, June 9, 1996.

Kot, Greg. "Grateful Dead Play Slack Tribute to Legacy." *Chicago Tribune*, July 3, 2015.

Kreps, Daniel. "Grateful Dead to Rock for Obama Again?" *Rolling Stone*, September 2, 2008.

———. "Grateful Dead Reunite for Chicago Farewell Concerts with Trey Anastasio." *Rolling Stone*, January 16, 2015.

———. "Barack Obama Pens Tribute to 'Iconic' Grateful Dead." *Rolling Stone*, July 5, 2015.

Lagasse, Brennan. "Show Review: Furthur Festival, Mountain Aire, CA—5/27–30." *Relix*, June 7, 2010.

La Gorce, Tammy. "A Festival Carries the Torch of the Grateful Dead." *New York Times*, July 15, 2011.

Leeds, Jeff. "Deadheads Outraged over Web Crackdown." *New York Times*, November 30, 2005.

Liberatore, Paul. "High-Tech Exhibit of Grateful Dead Planned." *Marin Independent Journal*, March 29, 1996.

——. "Reuniting Grateful Dead Members, Fans Happy About Tour, but Not Ticket Prices." *Marin Independent Journal*, February 12, 2009.

——. "Dead's Phil Lesh to Open Music Venue at Seafood Peddler Site in San Rafael." *Marin Independent Journal*, January 4, 2012.

——. "Dead's Weir Heralds January Opening of Sweetwater Music Hall in Mill Valley." *Marin Independent Journal*, January 11, 2012.

——. "Lib at Large: Sound and Serendipity for Weir and Mill Valley's Sweetwater." *Marin Independent Journal*, January 20, 2012.

——. "$150 Tickets for Phil Lesh's Terrapin Crossroads Opening Has Fans Grumbling." *Marin Independent Journal*, February 18, 2012.

——. "Lib at Large: Grateful Dead's Lesh Fulfills a Dream in Terrapin Crossroads." *Marin Independent Journal*, May 11, 2012.

——. "Lib at Large: Grateful Dead's Weir Stages Benefit for Friend with Cancer." *Marin Independent Journal*, September 7, 2012.

——. "Marin Snapshot: McCutcheon Helps Bob Weir Revolutionize Music Industry at TRI." *Marin Independent Journal*, September 16, 2012.

——. "Joan Osborne No Stranger on a Bus to Grateful Dead Family." *Marin Independent Journal*, December 28, 2012.

——. "Mill Valley Becomes Deadhead Mecca for Shows by Furthur." *Marin Independent Journal*, January 16, 2013.

——. "Lib at Large: 'Weir Here,' a Grateful Dead–Style Talk Show from TRI Studios." *Marin Independent Journal*, March 1, 2013.

——. "Grateful Dead's Bob Weir Returns to the Spotlight Two Months After Collapsing Onstage." *Marin Independent Journal*, June 12, 2013.

——. "TRI Studios Wins Digital Music Award for Live Concert Streaming." *Marin Independent Journal*, September 6, 2013.

——. "Lib at Large: Mickey Hart's Brain on Drums with 'Superorganism.'" *Marin Independent Journal*, September 12, 2013.

——. "Grateful Dead's Bob Weir Says Fare Thee Well to His Birth Father." *Marin Independent Journal*, June 27, 2015.

Lloyd, Jeffrey. "Remaining Members of the Grateful Dead Reunite to Support Obama." *Relix*, December 2008.

Malanowski, Jamie. "Levon Helm's Midnight Rambles," *New Yorker*, October 11, 2012.

Marin Independent Journal Editorial. "Phil Lesh Deserves a Fair Shake in Fairfax." September 5, 2011.

——." Lesh's Music Project a Good Fit for San Rafael." January 15, 2012.

Marks, Ed. "The Dead Kick Off a Mini Tour of Manhattan." *New York Times*, March 30, 2009.

——. "Free Dead, the Acoustic Set." *New York Times*, March 31, 2009.

Martin, Claire. "After the Grateful Dead, Phil Lesh Shows He Has a Head for Business." *New York Times,* September 19, 2015.

Mayshark, Jesse Fox. "Downloads of the Dead Are Not Dead Yet." *New York Times,* December 1, 2005.

Mnookin, Seth. "Now the Dead Will Always Be with Us." *New York Times,* April 17, 2005.

Morse, Steve. "Grateful; Dead Live on with New Releases." *Boston Globe,* October 20, 1995.

Nolte, Carl. "Artists Hear Music in Sounds of Span," *San Francisco Chronicle,* May 21, 2012.

Orlov, Piotr. "The Dead Rise Again at North Caroline Tour Kick-off." *Rolling Stone,* April 13, 2009.

Pareles, Jon. "It's Official. The Grateful Dead Are Gone." *New York Times,* December 9, 1995.

——. "The Dead Who Refuse to Die Draw 18,000." *New York Times,* July 13, 1996.

——. "The Grateful Dead's Legacy: A Firmament of Bands." *New York Times,* June 8, 1997.

——. "The Dead Resurrected and Truckin'." *New York Times,* June 6, 1998.

——. "The Living Are Grateful for the Dead's Legacy." *New York Times,* June 9, 1998.

——. "Pop Review: Life After the Dead, with Affection but Not Deference." *New York Times,* April 24, 2000.

——. "The Dead's Gamble: Free Music for Sale." *New York Times,* December 3, 2005.

——. "One Concert, Multiple Bands and a New Life for a Dead Classic." *New York Times,* January 22, 2007.

——. "Jampacked Bonnaroo, Beyond Jams." *New York Times,* June 16, 2008.

——. "Phil Lesh and Friends at the Brooklyn Academy of Music." *New York Times,* April 16, 2014.

——. "Grateful Dead 'Fare Thee Well' Tour Gets Down to the Music." *New York Times,* July 4, 2015.

——. "No Song Left Unsung; Grateful Dead Plays Its Last." *New York Times,* July 6, 2015.

Ratliff, Ben. "Phil Lesh, Still Lighting Out and Looking All Around." *New York Times,* October 21, 2000.

——. "Garcia's Shadow, but His Own Sound; Jimmy Herring, the Dead's New Member Helps Reinterpret Old Songs." *New York Times,* November 28, 2002.

——. "And the 1970s Dead Shall Arise (Sort of) and Jam with a Revolving Cast." *New York Times,* November 4, 2008.

——. "Bring out Your Dead." *New York Times,* April 10, 2009.

Rense, Rip. "Dead Ahead, Though It May Take Some Time; Q&A with Bob Weir." *Los Angeles Times,* November 23, 1995.

Robins, Cynthia. "She Never Got Off the Bus." *San Francisco Examiner,* May 25, 1997.

Rolling Stone. "Barack Obama Selects the Dead for Inaugural Ball: 'It Was Quite an Honor." February 5, 2009.

———. "Phil Lesh 'Not Completely There Yet' Processing Jerry Garcia's Death." *Rolling Stone,* April 21, 2014.

Rosman, Katherine. "Grateful Dead Fans Replace VW Vans with Jets and the Ritz-Carlton." *New York Times,* May 14, 2015.

Ross, Alex. "Critic's Notebook: A Parade of Maverick Modernists, Joined by the Dead." *New York Times,* June 19, 1996.

Sanneh, Kelefa. "Sitting in on the Night the Jammers Have Their Picnic." *New York Times,* April 28, 2005.

Schieslaug, Seth. "Jerry Garcia: The Man, the Myth, the Area Rug." *New York Times,* August 9, 2005.

Schools, Dave. "Dave Schools Interviews Phil Lesh." *Relix,* April 6, 2013.

Selvin, Joel. "The Grateful Dead Fades Away." *San Francisco Chronicle,* December 9, 1995.

———. "Garcia's Final Trip Takes Him to India / Family Angry That Widow, Bandmate Took Ashes for Ceremony." *San Francisco Chronicle,* April 9, 1996.

———. "Mickey Hart Marches to His Own Beat." *San Francisco Chronicle,* May 26, 1996.

———. "Working the Audience; Lesh, Thomas, Dead Members Lead a Sloppy Benefit Singalong." *San Francisco Chronicle,* December 8, 1997.

———. "An S.F. Shrine for Deadheads / Band Plans Huge Entertainment Center." *San Francisco Chronicle,* January 6, 1998.

———. "The Grateful Dead, Reincarnated / Lesh, Weir, Hart Reforming as the Other Ones for 'Furthur' Tour." *San Francisco Chronicle,* March 3, 1998.

———. "The Other Ones Take It Furthur / Lesh Is Out but Kreutzmann Is Back in Post-Garcia Lineup." *San Francisco Chronicle,* August 22, 2000.

———. "Mickey Hart's Drum Lesson." *San Francisco Chronicle,* October 26, 2000.

———. "Other Ones Reunite / Former Grateful Dead Mates Patch Things Up." *San Francisco Chronicle,* December 1, 2002.

———. "Dead Man Talking." *San Francisco Chronicle,* March 21, 2004.

———. "Weir Finds His Birth Father and Adopts a Vintage Guitar." *San Francisco Chronicle,* March 21, 2004.

———. "Grateful Dead Reunite for Barack Obama Benefit Show." *Rolling Stone,* February 5, 2008.

———. "Going Greene." *San Francisco Chronicle Sunday Datebook,* April 6, 2008.

———. "The Dead Resurrect Again to Show Why It Matters." *San Francisco Chronicle,* May 12, 2009.

Simon, Richard B. "Phil Lesh Goes There and Back Again." *Relix,* June–July 2002.

Sisario, Ben. "Ex-Bassist for the Grateful Dead Strikes a Deal." *New York Times,* November 3, 2013.

———. "Songs of the Dead (and Others), Alive and Kicking." *New York Times,* November 10, 2013.

Slater, Rob. "Bob Weir and John Mayer Team Up for 'Althea' and "Truckin'.'" *Relix*, February 6, 2015.

——. "Bob Weir Talks Fare Thee Well, Trey Anastasio and More." *Relix*, February 23, 2015.

Strauss, Neil. "The Pop Life: Garcia Tributes, from Books to an Avant-Garde Album." *New York Times*, October 19, 1995.

——. "The Pop Life." *New York Times*, April 25, 1996.

——. "Disneyland for Deadheads: Ultimate Nostalgia Trip; Rock Group Lives in Memory and Plan." *New York Times*, January 6, 1998.

——. "The Grateful Dead Will Tour Again (Just Don't Call It a Reunion)." *New York Times*, March 4, 1998.

——. "Playing in (What's Left of) the Band." *New York Times*, March 5, 2003.

Sullivan, James. "Doubly Grateful / Pair of Guitarists Adds Musical Heft to Other Ones' Debut." *San Francisco Chronicle*, June 6, 1998.

——. "Other Ones Looking Like Old Comrades." *San Francisco Chronicle*, July 27, 1998.

——. "Q&A with Mickey Hart." *San Francisco Chronicle*, September 27, 1998.

——. "Phil's New Zone / Grateful Dead Bassist Is Feeling Fine after Liver Transplant." *San Francisco Chronicle*, April 13, 1999.

——. "The Dead Fight over Recordings / Lesh Says They're Going Corporate with Tapes." *San Francisco Chronicle*, December 8, 1999.

Sutherland, Scott. "In the Deadheads' Footsteps." *New York Times*, June 16, 1996.

Uhelszki, Jaan. "The Dead's Phil Lesh Remains Active Despite Poor Health Rumors." *Rolling Stone*, November 11, 1998.

——. "Phil Lesh Concocts Unbroken Chain Benefit." *Rolling Stone*, February 25, 1999.

——. "Dylan May Revisit Grateful Dead Days with Tour." *Rolling Stone*, August 25, 1999.

Varga, George. "Dead Bassist Phil Lesh: Still Searching for the Sound." *San Diego Union Tribune*, May 22, 2005.

Vaziri, Aidin. "Pop Quiz: Phil Lesh/Ex-Dead Bass Player Grateful for New Life." *San Francisco Chronicle*, May 26, 2002.

——. "Pop Quiz: Bob Weir." *San Francisco Chronicle*, August 8, 2010.

——. "Pop Quiz: Mickey Hart." *San Francisco Chronicle*, July 31, 2011.

Vilanova, John. "Lesh, Weir Turn Out Short Set to Preview Grateful Dead Exhibit." *Rolling Stone*, October 22, 2009.

Waddell, Ray. "Peter Shapiro, Co-Producer of the Grateful Dead Reunion Concert, Reveals How He Got the Band Back Together." *Billboard*, June 26, 2015.

——. "'We're Off and Running': Producer of Grateful Dead Fare Thee Well Shows Addresses That Rainbow." *Billboard*, June 29, 2015.

Waddell, Ray, and Shirley Halperin. "Behind the Scenes of the Grateful Dead's Historic, Hugely Profitable Reunion." *Billboard*, April 24, 2015.

Woody, Todd. "Dead Reckoning: Jerry Garcia's Legacy Remains Suspended in the Purgatory of Probate Court, Where a Battle over the Bandleader Is Unfolding." *San Francisco Metro Reporter,* March 11, 1996.

Whiting, Sam. "Deadheads in Force as Shows Finally Arrive." *San Francisco Chronicle,* June 30, 2015.

Yeomans, Jeannine. "Deadhead Gets Wed in Mill Valley." *San Francisco Chronicle,* July 23, 1999.

Zane, J. Peder. "Who Else Would Name a Foundation for a Roadie?" *New York Times,* June 26, 1994.

Index